CHARTING THE COURSE

for

Leaders

Lessons From **Priority Schools** in a PLC at Work®

Jack **BALDERMANN** · Kimberly **RODRIGUEZ CANO** · Joe **CUDDEMI**
Michelle **MARRILLIA** · Rebecca **NICOLAS** · Robin **NOBLE** · Gerry **PETERSEN-INCORVAIA**
Karen **POWER** · Michael **ROBERTS** · Tamie **SANDERS** · Sarah **SCHUHL**

SHARON V. KRAMER | EDITOR

Solution Tree | Press a division of Solution Tree

555 North Morton Street
Bloomington, IN 47404
800.733.6786 (toll free) / 812.336.7700
FAX: 812.336.7790

email: info@SolutionTree.com
SolutionTree.com

Visit **go.SolutionTree.com/PLCbooks** to download the free reproducibles in this book.

Printed in the United States of America

Library of Congress Cataloging-in-Publication Data

Names: Kramer, Sharon V., editor.
Title: Charting the course for leaders : lessons from priority schools in a
    PLC at work / Sharon V. Kramer, editor ; Jack Baldermann, Kimberly
    Rodriguez Cano, Joe Cuddemi, Michelle Marrillia, Rebecca Nicolas, Robin
    Noble, Gerry Petersen-Incorvaia, Karen Power, Michael Roberts, Tamie
    Sanders, Sarah Schuhl.
Description: Bloomington, IN : Solution Tree Press, 2021. | Includes
    bibliographical references and index.
Identifiers: LCCN 2021006651 (print) | LCCN 2021006652 (ebook) | ISBN
    9781951075590 (paperback) | ISBN 9781951075606 (ebook)
Subjects: LCSH: Educational leadership--United States. |
    Teachers--Professional relationships--United States. | Professional
    learning communities--United States. | School environment--United
    States.
Classification: LCC LB2805 .C475 2021 (print) | LCC LB2805 (ebook) | DDC
    371.2/011--dc23
LC record available at https://lccn.loc.gov/2021006651
LC ebook record available at https://lccn.loc.gov/2021006652

Solution Tree
Jeffrey C. Jones, CEO
Edmund M. Ackerman, President

Solution Tree Press
President and Publisher: Douglas M. Rife
Associate Publisher: Sarah Payne-Mills
Art Director: Rian Anderson
Managing Production Editor: Kendra Slayton
Copy Chief: Jessi Finn
Senior Production Editor: Tonya Maddox Cupp
Content Development Specialist: Amy Rubenstein
Copy Editor: Evie Madsen
Proofreader: Sarah Ludwig
Text and Cover Designer: Abigail Bowen
Editorial Assistants: Sarah Ludwig and Elijah Oates

Acknowledgments

A simple thank-you cannot describe my gratitude and appreciation for the individuals who made this book a reality. Writing a book or chapter is one of the most difficult tasks that anyone can embark on but would be an impossible task without the support and hard work of the Solution Tree Press. The constant encouragement of Douglas Rife, president and publisher, is a gift that keeps on giving. He and the entire Press team are so appreciated for their intellect, enthusiasm, integrity, and energy that propelled this project to fruition. I began this book with a simple idea and Amy Rubenstein helped shape my thinking and focus my efforts as a first-time editor. Our work was then furthered by Tonya Maddox Cupp as she transformed our drafts into finished chapters. The entire project was coordinated under the very capable direction of Sarah Payne-Mills. And finally, I am grateful to Abby Bowen for the thoughtful and most fitting artwork that adorns the cover of this book.

Jeff Jones, the CEO of Solution Tree, is a dream maker in the true sense of the word. His ability to grow options and opportunities that directly impact districts, schools, teachers, and most importantly student learning worldwide is like none other. His vision, commitment, and integrity are evident as he approaches every task. He is a transformational influence on education.

The authors who contributed to this anthology are exceptionally busy and are sought after by schools and districts for their expertise and support. Each of them could have thought of a million reasons or excuses not to participate in this process. I extend my deepest appreciation to Robin Noble, Jack Baldermann, Karen Power, Joe Cuddemi, Tamie Sanders, Michael Roberts, Michelle Marrillia, Sarah Schuhl, Rebecca Nicolas, Gerry Petersen-Incorvaia, and Kimberly Rodriguez Cano. This is truly an amazing team of educators, consultants, authors, and PLC and priority school experts.

Finally, I am grateful for all of the educators working every day in support of the students that need us the most. These educators create breakthrough moments and opportunities that have lasting, lifelong impacts on their students. They are saving lives on a daily basis.

I also want to acknowledge the support and unending love of my family. My work and writing are a direct result of the inspiration given to me by my husband, children, and grandchildren. They are the true measure of a life well lived.

Solution Tree Press would like to thank the following reviewers:

Michael T. Adamson
Director of Board Services
Indiana School Boards Association
Indianapolis, Indiana

Craig Mah
District Principal of School Services and
Special Projects
Coquitlam School District
Coquitlam, British Columbia, Canada

Jason Williams
Assistant Principal
Country Meadows Elementary—Kildeer
Countryside Consolidated School District 96
Long Grove, Illinois

Visit **go.SolutionTree.com/PLCbooks** to download the free reproducibles in this book.

Table of Contents

Reproducible pages are in italics.

3 Employing High-Level Strategies From the District Office . . 45

Gerry Petersen-Incorvaia

4 Building Collaborative and Passionately Agreed-to SMART Goals 59

Jack Baldermann

5 Aligning the Arrows for Continuous-Improvement Planning With SMART Goals 79

Kimberly Rodriguez Cano

About the Editor

 **Sharon V. Kramer, PhD,** knows firsthand the demands and rewards of working in a professional learning community (PLC). As a leader in the field, she has done priority schools work with districts across the United States, emphasizing the importance of creating and using quality assessments and utilizing the PLC continuous-improvement process to raise student achievement. Sharon served as assistant superintendent for curriculum and instruction of Kildeer Countryside Community Consolidated School District 96 in Illinois. In this position, she ensured all students were prepared to enter Adlai E. Stevenson High School, a Model PLC started and formerly led by PLC architect Richard DuFour.

A seasoned educator, Sharon has taught in elementary and middle school classrooms, and she has served as a principal, director of elementary education, and university professor. In addition to her PLC experience, Sharon has completed assessment training by Rick Stiggins, Steve Chappuis, Larry Ainsworth, and the Center for Performance Assessment (now the Leadership and Learning Center). She has presented a variety of assessment workshops at institutes and summits and for state departments of education. Sharon has also worked with school districts across the United States to determine their power standards and develop assessments.

She has been a Comprehensive School Reform consultant to schools that have received grant funding to implement the PLC process as their schoolwide reform model, and her customized PLC coaching academies have empowered school and district leadership teams across the United States. Sharon has presented at state and national conferences sponsored by Learning Forward, the National Association for Gifted Children, the American Federation of Teachers, and California State University. She has been instrumental in facilitating professional development initiatives focused on standards-based learning and teaching, improved understanding and utilization of assessment data, interventions and differentiation that meet the needs of all learners, and strengthened efforts to ensure K–12 literacy.

Sharon is the author of *How to Leverage PLCs for School Improvement* and coauthor of *School Improvement for All: A How-to Guide for Doing the Right Work*; *Best Practices at Tier 2: Supplemental Interventions for Additional Student Support, Elementary*; and *Best Practices at Tier 2: Supplemental Interventions for Additional Student Support, Secondary*. She also contributed to the books *It's About Time: Planning Interventions and Extensions in Elementary School, The Teacher as Assessment Leader*, and *The Collaborative Teacher: Working Together as a Professional Learning Community*.

Sharon earned a doctorate in educational leadership and policy studies from Loyola University Chicago.

To learn more about Sharon's work, follow @DrKramer1 on Twitter.

To book Sharon V. Kramer for professional development, contact pd@SolutionTree.com.

Introduction

Sharon V. Kramer

Indeed, there are virtually no documented instances of troubled schools being turned around without intervention by a powerful leader. Many other factors may contribute to such turnarounds, but leadership is the catalyst.

—*Kenneth Leithwood, Karen Seashore Louis, Stephen Anderson, and Kyla Wahlstrom*

Teachers are indeed the most impactful factor contributing to student achievement. No one would argue that teachers are the defining factors in raising achievement levels in each classroom. The research is clear—they are the "single most influential component of an effective school" (Marzano, 2007, p. 9). In the same vein, the following analogy rings true: *teachers are to classrooms as leaders are to schools and districts.* The most important factor in improving a school (or entire district) is the leader. Not just any leader can improve a school and district and get results; the leader must be someone who builds the capacity of the people in the school and monitors and supports the work of the educators. In other words, a leader who harnesses the power within to ensure learning for all. In a *priority school*—an underperforming school—this often means accelerating the learning for students and staff alike.

Much has been written describing the leadership dichotomy characterized as *instructional* or *managerial*, the major difference being whether the leader spends more time on instruction or the tasks associated with managing the school or district. In reality, it is clear that any leader must do both simultaneously. This is an example of the tyranny of *or* and the genius of *and* (Collins & Porras, 1994). Learning cannot occur without a safe, orderly, and well-functioning environment, but if that is all the leader focuses on, learning will not necessarily be a priority in the school; it is highly unlikely all students will achieve the goal of learning at grade level or beyond. The most important tool in a leader's toolbox is *focus*. What the leader focuses on is exactly what the people in the school or district will focus on. It is clearly visible when a principal or superintendent operates in a managerial role because all the staff questions and comments center on these issues. In contrast, if the focus of the leader is on learning, then the staff will ask questions and make comments relative to learning. Focus, focus, focus on the things that matter most!

It is my belief that the most important role the leader assumes is the role of the *lead learner* in a school or district. Schools are learning organizations where the number-one job is learning. "Learning is required" must be the mantra because that is why schools exist. Therefore, learning is as much about the adults as it is about the students in the building and throughout the district. In the role of lead learner, the leader creates the foundations and supports necessary to accelerate learning. The foundation of the work in a professional learning community (PLC) is a mission that clearly states why it exists, a shared vision of what the school and district wants to become, and then engagement by all staff members in making commitments that actually move these beliefs forward (DuFour, DuFour, Eaker, Many, & Mattos, 2016). In other words, the mission and vision must exist beyond the wall or the piece of paper they were recorded on. *Collective commitments* are the engine that moves the learning organization. It is essential that everyone in the school and district make a commitment that describes what they are willing to do to achieve the vision (DuFour et al., 2016). The building of shared knowledge and collective capacity is how the leader creates the conditions for the continuous-improvement "magic" to happen. Individual growth does not ensure organizational growth. Organizations need more than well-developed people. Effective leaders focus on developing the culture and the organization's collective capacity.

This begs the overwhelmingly compelling questions, Does this type of leadership require superhuman powers, given all a leader must do? If the answer to this question is a resounding *no*, then, How can a leader build a system that supports learning for all? Where do leaders begin? What structures, strategies, policies, and procedures must be in place to support a culture of learning for all? How do schools and districts organize for success?

To acknowledge the barriers to reaching the goal of high levels of learning for all, in the book *How to Leverage PLCs for School Improvement* (Kramer, 2015), I outline the five greatest challenges facing underperforming schools and districts.

1. Create a culture of success.
2. Engage in the right work.
3. Shift from all to each.
4. Develop leadership for learning.
5. Engage students in owning their learning.

The book also provides strategies for turning these specific challenges into opportunities for improvement. Most of all, the book describes a journey through the challenges of the lowest-performing high school in the state of Oklahoma as the school became a model for this work. This work can be accomplished anywhere. The practices, procedures, and strategies are replicable across all schools and districts.

The Work of a Professional Learning Community in Priority Schools

To be perfectly clear, all the books and work I've referenced up to this point hinge on understanding the PLC process and culture, which is best detailed in *Learning by Doing: A Handbook for Professional Learning Communities at Work* (DuFour et al., 2016). If schools and districts are not operating as PLCs, no amount of effort or work to improve will be successful. PLCs are not about buying a new program or offering increased staff training; they are about engaging a school's or district's staff in doing the right work. To get the most out of this book, it is vital that you and your collaborative team members understand the following about PLCs (DuFour et al., 2016).

- **The three big ideas of a PLC:** (1) A focus on learning, (2) a collaborative culture and collective responsibility, and (3) a results orientation

- **The four pillars of a PLC:** (1) Mission (why we exist), (2) vision (what we must become), (3) values (how we must behave), and (4) goals (how we will mark our progress)

- **The four critical questions of a PLC:**
    1. What is it we want our students to know and be able to do?
    2. How will we know if each student has learned it?
    3. How will we respond when some students do not learn it?
    4. How will we extend the learning for students who have demonstrated proficiency? (DuFour et al., 2016, p. 59)

School Improvement for All (Kramer & Schuhl, 2017) specifically expands on and customizes these PLC concepts and processes to meet the unique needs of underperforming or priority schools. School improvement is not something different from the work of PLCs; it is doing PLCs right, not lite (García, 2015). This anthology both supports educators in implementing the PLC process deeply enough to get real results in student achievement and tailors recommendations for common challenges, barriers, and pitfalls associated with priority schools.

For this book's purposes, we define *priority schools* as those schools that a district, state, or province identifies as in need of improvement or whose data are flat, showing little or no progress over time. Individual states and provinces use a variety of labels to describe priority schools, with each designation deriving from a specific ranking and rating system. Common labels refer to schools and districts on a five-star scale, use designations like *improvement required* (IR) or *schools in need of assistance* (SINA), or rank schools on an A–F scale. When low achievement persists at such schools, state and provincial entities commonly take over and manage them. It's an unfortunate reality that these labels frame and define students and staff as deficient without highlighting the hard work, dedication, and love the educators devote to their students, families, and school community. As such, it is important to view these schools and districts through a strengths-based lens. This book is also useful for educators seeking improvement at a school that hasn't received some form of priority school designation. The practices, strategies, and protocols you will find in each chapter are essential for some and good for all.

About This Book

This anthology is a compilation of resources that add to the body of knowledge and provide specific how-to suggestions, strategies, and templates to support leaders and schools on the continuous-improvement journey. As you will see in each chapter, this anthology features research-supported resources, which is important, but always keep in mind the best, most actionable books provide both the knowledge and the means to easily apply their contents to real-world situations. Although I intend for you to read it in its entirety, this book can also serve to address specific issues or problems, as each chapter offers specific and targeted support. Each chapter is comprehensive and provides learning experiences you can share with your team or entire staff. You will also find resources to expand your team's impact and that of its leaders. The authors reference and provide high-quality resources throughout every chapter so readers can explore the specific topics in depth.

Before I address chapter specifics, consider that as educators do the work of improving schools and districts, and as educators continue to grow and learn along with the teams and administrators they work with, they commonly face a barrier to this growth in the form of poverty. Luis F. Cruz (2020), author and consultant, often characterizes educators as an elite team with the arduous task of breaking students free from the cycle of poverty. I would add that educators are an elite team with the arduous task of breaking students free from poverty *and*, in doing so, equipping them with the skills and knowledge necessary to be successful in life.

This is an essential understanding because, in this book, each chapter's author is an educator who represents this ongoing commitment to the students, teachers, schools, and districts he or she supports. I carefully selected these educators to share their knowledge and expertise because they have successfully implemented and used the strategies they write about to turn around their own underperforming schools and districts. All the authors have been in the trenches and understand the work from the inside out. They have also been successful in replicating and implementing the same strategies as coaches at other schools, helping those schools obtain the results they hope for and are working hard to achieve. The authors are an elite team dedicated to achieving high levels of learning for all students, even in the face of backbreaking student poverty and all the challenges this brings to bear. Their practical insights are invaluable in making progress toward educators' collective purpose and vision of all students learning at grade level and beyond. The schools and districts they describe in this collection are diverse in their sizes, demographics, grade spans, geographical locations, and resources available to them. The topics may not be new, but the value of each chapter lies in the practical application and examples each author presents to address the ongoing issues that plague schools and districts and get in the way of real improvement.

The following lists each chapter and explains the problem of practice it addresses, along with the focus of support.

- **Chapter 1, Leading School-Improvement Work With Intention, by Karen Power:** Priority schools are often pulled in so many directions based on the needs of the students, teachers, parents, and communities they serve that it is hard to get to the real work of improvement. The author helps leaders develop and practice strategies to prioritize time in order to get to the real and most impactful work.

- **Chapter 2, Building District Culture, by Karen Power:** This chapter focuses on the superintendent and district or central office roles in developing an improvement plan that creates the supportive environment and culture for schools essential for ensuring improvement efforts will be successful. The author includes topics such as: understanding your culture, identifying your needs, establishing vision and goal setting, keeping the work the right work, creating a shared leadership model, communicating and implementing the plan, and celebrating successes.

- **Chapter 3, Employing High-Level Strategies From the District Office, by Gerry Petersen-Incorvaia:** The district or central office's charge is to support curriculum, instruction, and a balanced assessment system so all students can learn at high levels. This multifaceted and dynamic process requires flexible, targeted, strategic yet nimble, and interdependent thinking and actions, especially in a priority or an underperforming school and district. This chapter provides specific ways to align district and school efforts to ensure equity and higher achievement levels for all students.

- **Chapter 4, Building Collaborative and Passionately Agreed-to SMART Goals, by Jack Baldermann:** Schools and districts often develop goals but never look at or review them again until the end of the school year. This chapter describes a process to ensure goals are not only collaboratively created but also collaboratively owned and an integral part of the work on a daily basis. The author outlines in detail a way to build goals that will inspire team members to ensure success for all students, lead to a more cohesive culture, support reciprocal accountability, drive results, and celebrate genuine accomplishments.

- **Chapter 5, Aligning the Arrows for Continuous-Improvement Planning With SMART Goals, by Kimberly Rodriguez Cano:** As the district and schools work together to improve, goal alignment is essential to their success. Synergy exists when district goals outline the direction, school goals support the district goals, collaborative team goals detail the specifics of improvement, and teachers operationalize these goals with students. Then, it is possible to measure student learning in an aligned effort that ensures schools and teachers are working smarter, not harder. This chapter describes a process that creates goals that establish a culture of shared responsibility for learning.

- **Chapter 6, Focusing on Collective Responsibility, by Joe Cuddemi:** This chapter moves underperforming schools from the external pressures of a fear-based (improve or we will punish you) accountability system to a healthy and safe culture through the use of protocols that engage everyone in examining their own beliefs, assumptions, expectations, and behaviors as they create collective commitments to continuous improvement.

- **Chapter 7, Leveraging Shared Leadership in the Priority School, by Robin Noble:** This chapter acknowledges the need for everyone to assume a leadership role in a priority school. The principal, no matter how knowledgeable and charismatic, is never enough to move a school or district and accelerate student learning. It requires a team effort. Shared leadership is required and crucial to the success of staff and students. The author describes in detail a rationale and model of this type of leadership, along with the benefits to staff and students of working in this collaborative manner.

- **Chapter 8, Ensuring the District Guiding Coalition and School Learning Team Have Impact, by Gerry Petersen-Incorvaia:** This chapter describes the process for identifying and clarifying the roles of a district guiding coalition and school learning team (or leadership team). Both teams are essential to building a support system for learning. The chapter builds on the mantra, *We are all in for all students*. The author includes a description of the right work of each team to ensure a positive trajectory of student achievement.

- **Chapter 9, Monitoring Productivity Instead of Activity, by Rebecca Nicolas:** The author describes a process for supporting and monitoring the work of collaborative teams. This shared leadership approach creates the conditions and structures that support the ongoing work of collaborative teams. As the instructional leadership team (ILT) monitors the work, this system provides a more effective and efficient way for it to give guidance and support to ensure all teams are high functioning.

- **Chapter 10, Providing Feedback on the Right Work, by Sarah Schuhl:** The author describes in detail the most effective ways to provide feedback to the learning team (guiding coalition or leadership team) and collaborative teacher teams to move learning forward. Feedback is tied to the learning cycle on a unit-by-unit basis to ensure that support is descriptive, targeted, and specific enough to grow the learning of all students.

- **Chapter 11, Giving All Teachers the Coach They Deserve, by Michelle Marrillia:** The author examines the four key components to implementing a successful coaching plan: (1) defining the roles and responsibilities of the instructional coach, (2) creating a leadership team that embraces a coaching mindset, (3) implementing a coaching plan that provides continuous feedback and support for every teacher, and (4) creating a meaningful and realistic coaching schedule.

- **Chapter 12, Challenging Proficient Students, by Michael Roberts:** This chapter focuses on the fourth critical question of a PLC at Work: How will we extend learning for students who have demonstrated proficiency? In every priority school and district, there are students who often demonstrate proficiency and spend an inordinate amount of time waiting to learn something new while watching others learn. The author builds the rationale and offers administrative strategies and supports a staff can easily implement to address the needs of students who demonstrate proficiency or learn quickly.

- **Chapter 13, Taking the First Five Steps in High School Improvement, by Tamie Sanders:** With all the requirements placed on them, high schools are often the most difficult places to enact change. The focus is often on meeting these requirements with the hope learning is occurring. This chapter outlines the first five steps that high school leaders should take to make an immediate impact on student achievement. The author provides actionable steps to support and lead high schools to improved results.

I hope these chapters are valuable tools for leaders at all levels who are doing the hard work of improving their schools. This collection offers specific, practical strategies for making progress toward school-improvement goals and aspirations from practitioners who have translated the research into actual practice. In doing so, each chapter creates additional pathways to higher levels of learning for all students.

It has been my privilege and honor to work side by side with each of the authors whose work appears in this collection. Their respective schools have each earned Model PLC status and three of the schools are recipients of the prestigious DuFour Award for their staff's work to improve student achievement. These authors have their own particular areas of expertise, present their ideas in their unique ways, and offer the most effective strategies for bringing about significant school improvement. But the common thread throughout this book is the deeply held belief that all students can learn at high levels and it is our responsibility to get them there. Witness this dedication in each chapter as these practitioners offer a results-driven approach to leading this work.

Finally, it is my hope all educators will use their own collective wisdom, knowledge, purposeful action, and shared commitment to make a difference in the lives of the students they serve. Real school improvement cannot come from the outside in. Instead, it must come from the inside out. It is the responsibility and commitment of the educators in a school to make this happen. In the end, the school or district leader must harness the power within to achieve the shared goal of *learning for all*—and really mean *all*. When this is the goal, substantive, continuous improvement is possible. In the absence of effective leadership, progress is often slow or impossible. The lead learner is essential and drives all improvement efforts. This is a call to action for all leaders. Leadership matters!

References and Resources

Collins, J. C., & Porras, J. I. (1994). *Built to last: Successful habits of visionary companies.* New York: HarperBusiness.

Cruz, L. F. (2020, August 26). *Welcome back and are we ready to show the world what we are capable of accomplishing?* Presentation to White River School District, Buckley, WA.

DuFour, R., DuFour, R., Eaker, R., Many, T. W., & Mattos, M. (2016). *Learning by doing: A handbook for Professional Learning Communities at Work* (3rd ed.). Bloomington, IN: Solution Tree Press.

García, H. (2015, July 1). *Avoiding the "PLC lite" scenario* [Blog post]. Accessed at www.solutiontree .com/blog/avoiding-the-plc-lite-scenario-2 on November 25, 2020.

Kramer, S. V. (2015). *How to leverage PLCs for school improvement.* Bloomington, IN: Solution Tree Press.

Kramer, S. V., & Schuhl, S. (2017). *School improvement for all: A how-to guide for doing the right work.* Bloomington, IN: Solution Tree Press.

Leithwood, K., Louis, K. S., Anderson, S., & Wahlstrom, K. (2004). *How leadership influences student learning.* Accessed at https://wallacefoundation.org/knowledge-center/Documents /How-Leadership-Influences-Student-Learning.pdf on November 10, 2020.

Marzano, R. J. (2007). *The art and science of teaching: A comprehensive framework for effective instruction.* Alexandria, VA: Association for Supervision and Curriculum Development.

 **Karen Power** is an author, consultant, and former teacher, principal, and superintendent. Karen has implemented the Professional Learning Community (PLC) at Work process both as a school and district leader and continues to support deep understanding of next steps in practices that ensure all students can learn. As principal of Lewisville Middle School, Karen and her teachers developed collaborative practices and positively impacted student learning. As a superintendent, she created expectations for school improvement and supported her thirty-eight schools in the PLC process.

Karen primarily works in priority school projects providing leadership coaching in both schools and districts in the United States and Canada. In 2020, Karen was pleased to learn that Morrilton Intermediate School, a school she coached for three years, was awarded Model PLC school status.

Karen coauthored *Leading With Intention: Eight Areas for Reflection and Planning in Your PLC at Work* and edited a Canadian edition of *Learning by Doing*. She is coauthoring a leadership book on literacy instruction and a follow-up edition to *Leading With Intention*. In 2010, 2011, and 2012, Karen was selected as one of Canada's Top 100 Most Powerful Women in the Public Sector by the Women's Executive Network.

Karen lives in New Brunswick, Canada, with her husband, Wayne.

To learn more about Karen's work, visit https://karenpower.blog or follow @power58karen on Twitter.

To book Karen Power for professional development, contact pd@SolutionTree.com.

Leading School-Improvement Work With Intention

Karen Power

> To be a leader is not a position or a title; it means
> one takes action and models behaviors. The most
> powerful and effective role the principal assumes is
> that of lead learner, not expert or "all-knowing one."
>
> —*Sharon V. Kramer and Sarah Schuhl*

At Dr. Martin Luther King Jr. Elementary School in Macon, Georgia, principal Suzan Watkins understood that to change the culture and provide opportunities for students to be successful in her priority school, she had to lead with intention. Her enthusiastic and bubbly personality was infectious, but she understood that to truly improve her school it would take strong leadership skills. When she started as principal, she carefully developed a road map for change, creating opportunities for teachers to work as a professional learning community (PLC). Watkins would be the first to admit that, many times, distractors and challenges would tempt her to change course but she knew, in a priority school, her work was urgent and required a leader's relentless focus. She was aware that creating a school motto for posters and T-shirts was not going to change the school. It would be the daily actions that would make a difference. In other words, Watkins understood that hanging a sign over her desk with a school mission, such as *All students learn here at high levels*, was not going to change her school. She knew that she had to intentionally communicate to everyone what was important. And she knew that her unwavering commitment to the school could be tested by how staff answered this question: "What is most important to your leader?"

Hanging the sign and doing the work are two different things. In priority schools and districts, lots of time is taken to have the important conversations about why we exist (the *mission*), what we want to become (the *vision*), and how we are going to act (the *collective commitments*; DuFour, DuFour, Eaker, Many, & Mattos, 2016). The problem often becomes carrying these out. What has to change in the district or school for these statements to become reality? As the leader, how do you intentionally align your daily practices to keep the focus on the right work? What has to happen so that you can keep distractors from taking you away from the mission and vision?

Watkins knew she only had twenty-four hours each day. Despite the long list of changes she wished to make, as a leader, she had to be intentional and focused on how she spent her time. She had to align her daily actions and her use of time to what was important. Watkins knew that leading with intention required a relentless commitment to staying the course and ensuring that what she did, said, and asked others to do was aligned to what was important. It isn't uncommon in a priority school for the principal to feel overwhelmed by all that is required of his or her time. Unintentionally, you may be someone who is easily distracted by emails and social media. For example, you have the very best intentions when you get to school in the morning. You know the best use of your time would be to stand near the front door, greeting staff, students, and parents as they enter. You decide it wouldn't hurt to just check your emails first. Before you know it, thirty minutes have passed, and you have missed a golden opportunity to be visible and check in with everyone as they start their day. Or, as a district leader, you have the best intentions to visit schools as often as you can. You actually start every week with a list of the schools you want to visit and principals you want to have conversations with. Before you know it, it is Thursday and you have not left the office. Board issues, a facility crisis, a bus situation, and human resources concerns take up your valuable time. You know these issues are also important but they are not as critical as being visible in your schools and aware of the needs of your school leaders. How can you change this pattern?

Aligning policies, structures, and plans is important, and as coauthors Richard DuFour and Michael Fullan (2013) remind us, *coherence* means that we are crystal clear on what is important and how to align this work. They also explain that real coherence is related to mindset (DuFour & Fullan, 2013). Recognizing the current reality and what the focus must be on to improve a district or school requires leaders to create positive synergy and mindset around the work. Changing practices requires deep commitment to the work and strong personal beliefs that the efforts will accomplish the vision of the district or school you wish to create. In priority schools, leaders need even more time to support staff's deep understanding of the purpose of the needed changes. Cultural shifts require that understanding and as the leader, intentionally developing clarity of the *why* behind your priorities through your actions, decisions, and of course, your words. Watkins successfully led her elementary school out of priority school status with a relentless focus. This chapter will support your learning of similar strategies to prioritize goals and communicate purpose through your actions.

What are your first steps in knowing and doing your priorities? What about communicating and knowing your impact and having crucial conversations?

Knowing and Doing Your Priorities

In his bestseller *Leading With Focus: Elevating the Essentials for School and District Improvement*, author Mike Schmoker (2016) reminds us there is a need for simplicity when he states, "Simplicity demands that leaders incessantly clarify and reinforce these priorities" (p. 5). As we consider intentional leadership, we must always revisit, clarify, and do everything that we can to model what is important. Focused and straightforward efforts enable leaders to communicate what they expect. DuFour and colleagues (2016) explain that it is important for leaders to get tight about the right things and then communicate "what is tight clearly, consistently, and unequivocally" (p. 14). *Tight expectations* are your non-negotiables; the few things that you expect each and every educator in the building to do on a daily basis.

Simultaneous tight/loose leadership is one way to create clear expectations and offer autonomy to staff at the same time, which helps create intrinsic motivation (Deci & Ryan, 2012). For example, in her priority school work, principal Watkins simplified a few priorities and goals to reinforce and communicate her focus over and over again. This supported deep understanding by staff of what is important. These priorities or goals are the tight expectations. Leaders do not always write their priorities as SMART goals. In a perfect world they would, but many times in coaching, we are just happy to see that they figure out their priorities and establish tight expectations around them. Many do create SMART goals, but it isn't always the case. Table 1.1 shows how tight/loose leadership can look in a school or district. Consider how defining your tights will help clarify to your staff what is important to you. How can you align your mission and vision to a few very specific expectations?

Table 1.1: Tight/Loose Leadership Expectation Examples

Examples of Tight Expectations	Examples of Loose Expectations
All teachers work in collaborative teams to respond to the four PLC questions.	How the teacher teams keep their minutes and record their student data is loose, as long as they focus on the four critical questions.
All professional learning has a focus on building common understanding and implementing the four critical questions.	Differentiate professional learning at times during the year so teachers can select which sessions to attend as needed.
All teachers create an environment of student ownership of learning.	Teachers decide how to share learning targets and proficiency expectations with students.

Source: Adapted from DuFour et al., 2016.

As important as it is to understand tight/loose leadership, in a priority school it is just as critical to lead by example through behaviors and decisions that exemplify the tight expectations. What you as the leader expect and model as your tights speaks to what you absolutely believe in and know will support your mission and vision for the school or district. For example, a principal who has a tight expectation that collaborative teams are collecting artifacts as evidence of their PLC process would ask collaborative teams to bring artifacts to faculty meetings to share with others. Each team could visit the table of another team to learn about their artifacts and learn from their work. A superintendent, with the same tight expectation, may make visits to schools, intentionally selecting collaborative team time to visit and review artifacts.

Improving schools depends greatly on clarity of expectations. In *Leading With Intention*, my coauthor and I ask readers to consider how they use their time (Spiller & Power, 2019). Keeping a log or establishing how you will spend your time around your tight expectations requires intentional decisions about where you are—your current reality—and how you spend minutes and hours during the day. Consider using a template to log your time over the course of a few days. List your intentional plans and then record how your time is actually spent. Figure 1.1 shows an example of how your completed log might look. The reproducible "Daily Time Log" (page 21) is a blank version.

Action	Day One	Day Two	Day Three
Classroom observations and feedback to teachers	48 minutes	100 minutes	100 minutes
Participation in collaborative team meetings	—	60 minutes	30 minutes
Participation in student data team meetings	10 minutes	10 minutes	20 minutes
Student discipline	100 minutes	30 minutes	40 minutes
Emails and office work	140 minutes	30 minutes	45 minutes
Duties (lunchroom, recess, bus supervision, and so on)	150 minutes	150 minutes	150 minutes

Source: Adapted from Spiller & Power, 2019.

Figure 1.1: Sample daily time log.

In this example, the leader prioritizes observing classrooms and participating in collaborative team and student data team meetings. You know where you want to spend the majority of your time, so track your time for three days and then analyze how you are actually doing modeling what is important to you.

In a priority school, it might feel that everything is urgent. As you consider where you spend your time, think about what distracts you from your priorities. For example, in the sample time log in figure 1.1, it is easy to see that the emails and office work distract from the three priorities of (1) classroom observations, (2) collaborative team meetings, and (3) student data team meetings.

You can use a reflection tool to help clarify your distractors and help you think about how you utilize your time. Figure 1.2 is an example of a completed tool. The reproducible "Reflection on Intentionality During the Day" (page 22) is a blank version.

Distractor	My Intentional Focus	What I Actually Did
Mr. Smith came to my office and asked if "I had a minute." I knew that it would not truly just be a minute. →	Visit Ms. Preston's English language arts class to observe her small-group instruction.	I told Mr. Smith that I would see him later during his preparation period. ←

Source: Adapted from Spiller & Power, 2019.

Figure 1.2: Reflecting on intention example.

During my leadership coaching in priority schools, discussions often wind up on how leaders see their work as being overwhelming and how little they sometimes feel they accomplish on any given day. Coaching involves helping leaders return to an understanding of their priorities and clarifying if leaders are or are not spending their time on the right work. It does take reflection and intentionality to honor the simplicity of a few priorities and to model what you expect. The tool in figure 1.3 (page 16) allows you to score yourself on the alignment of priorities to actions. The reproducible "Assessment Tool for Simplifying Focus and Actions in Daily Practice" (page 23) is a blank version.

Communicating and Knowing Your Impact

In his book, *HEART! Fully Forming Your Professional Life as a Teacher and Leader*, award-winning educator and consultant Timothy D. Kanold (2017) offers a multitude of insights and suggestions for pursuing a positive mindset and meaningful career as an educator. He suggests that educators have an opportunity to leave their heartprint on others. He defines *heartprint* as the distinctive impression and marked impact you have on others as the school year unfolds (Kanold, 2017). As you work to improve your school, the perception that others have of what is important to you—what you stand for—greatly influences your impact or heartprint. Leaders with influence take the time to ensure they stay focused on their mission and vision and their actions and decisions support these beliefs. What you model and communicate is noticed. You have to be intentional in all that you say and do.

How important are your communication skills in regard to the perception and impact you will have as a leader? What improvements can you make in this area of your leadership journey? Consider the following scenarios.

Directions: Use the five-point scale to assess your focus on priorities.

1. I am totally distracted from this priority and recognize I have not created a simplistic way for others to understand this focus.

2. I struggle some days with staying focused on this and believe others are not always sure this is a focus.

3. I speak about this priority often and have set up structures and systems that help others understand this work; however, my daily actions do not always align with this priority.

4. I believe most days my actions and messages represent the simplicity of what I want to accomplish at this school. However, there are times I do allow distractors to get in the way.

5. I am strongly aligning all of my actions and messages, so it is simple for others to understand this is a priority.

Priority	Score and Reflection	Actions I Can Take to Increase My Focus and Intention
Priority one: Observe classroom instruction during literacy block to understand how the implementation of small-group instruction is being done in the school.	I give myself a score of 2 because I am allowing distractors (meetings, interruptions, emails) to prevent me from being in classrooms.	I will establish a schedule for classroom observations for the next three days and manage my time more appropriately so I can visit the literacy block.
Priority two: Attend collaborative team meetings.	I give myself a score of 4 because I have attended seven of nine collaborative team meetings in the past ten days. I have prioritized my time to do this.	I will prioritize my time to ensure that I attend the two meetings that I missed in the past two weeks so that I attend those meetings this week.
Priority three: Meet one-to-one with teachers to discuss student data.	I give myself a score of 1 because I have not started a schedule of meetings with individual teachers despite stating this as a priority for this school year.	I will establish a schedule for the next thirty days to ensure that I meet with one teacher each day to discuss student data.
	Total: 7	

Source: Adapted from Spiller & Power, 2019.

Figure 1.3: Score alignment of priorities to actions.

Here is scenario one.

Principal Taylor is struggling with health and safety protocols during COVID-19. She is finding it difficult to implement the district's requirement for masks being worn at all times in the building, and she is also unsure how to ensure people are staying six feet apart as requested. Her high school students are refusing to do either, and the longer she has let it go the worse it has become. One day, the superintendent visits the school and asks principal Taylor to revisit this with her school community. The superintendent suggests that Taylor meet with students by grade level and talk to them about the seriousness of spread, effects of COVID-19, and how important it is that everyone work together to keep the school open for learning. The superintendent helps Taylor write out the key points that she should make and emphasizes how crucial it is to engage the students in understanding why this is so important.

After the superintendent leaves, Taylor decides that it would take too much time to meet with the students by grade level and that she doesn't feel that it will matter if she explains to or engages with the students. So, she decides to go on the intercom system and announce to the entire population that she will now be passing out suspensions immediately to all students who refuse to wear their masks and that the suspensions will impact their graduation. A group of students decide to lead a protest and begin a march to the cafeteria without masks. The school is soon in chaos.

Here is scenario two.

A few blocks away, the superintendent visits another high school. Principal Brown has requested help dealing with students who are refusing to wear masks in the building. The superintendent engages the principal in the same activity as he had done in the previous school with principal Taylor. He helps Brown plan student meetings and the key messages that need to be conveyed to build common understanding of why masks must be worn in the school. Brown decides to start with a small group of students who have influence with other students in his school. He holds this student focus group, explains his concerns, and asks them to help him determine the best way to change what is happening in his school. The students review his key messages and develop some with him that they think will support a stronger understanding. The students agree to help lead the student assemblies and will also speak at each assembly. They create a schedule of grade-level meetings and a plan. They also develop a plan for some positive school activities once they will be able to meet in larger groups in the school and announce these to the students at the same time. Prior to the assemblies, Brown meets with the faculty and ensures that they understand his plan and support the work of the student leadership group. He asks the faculty for their support in the grade-level assemblies and in their classrooms. The assemblies also include some examples of the positive behaviors and successes the school was having despite the COVID-19 pandemic. The assemblies go very well and the high school no longer has to address a lot of students not wearing masks.

Use the reproducible "Reflection on Communicating the *Why*" (page 24) to reflect on the difference between these two practices.

As a leader, principal Brown understands the importance of building collective capacity with staff and students, including ensuring a common understanding of how communication will be managed with students on the mask issue. In her school, principal Taylor leads from a position of authority because she announces the changes rather than engaging staff or students in discussion. She assumes the students will follow her lead rather than consider the impact of the changes and the need to communicate this effectively. When we lead with intention, we pay attention to clarifying what is important and what behaviors are expected. Leaders intentionally create plans for communication and, prior to taking action, consider the consequences of what will be said and done. Intentionally involving others when we think and plan builds common understanding of the why.

In their book, *Time for Change: Four Essential Skills for Transformational School and District Leaders*, coauthors Anthony Muhammad and Luis F. Cruz (2019) name four skills leaders need—skills that focus on the *why*, the *who*, and the *how* of the change, which lead to being able to *do* what is needed to make change. The authors summarize these skills this way:

- **Leaders must effectively communicate the rationale—the why of the work:** People tend to resist change to practice and lack motivation to improve when leaders have not skillfully communicated the rationale or case for improvement. To embrace a vision, people have to clearly understand the vision and feel personally compelled to contribute to the vision.

- **Leaders must effectively establish trust—the who of the work:** A transformational leader needs the very essential ability to connect with others' emotions. Facts and objective evidence alone do not inspire people; people need to connect with their leader on a personal level and know that their leader has not just an intellectual connection but also an ethical connection to their purpose.

- **Leaders must effectively build capacity—the how of the work:** People will more willingly take a risk and try a new idea if leaders have prepared them professionally. Leaders must invest in training, resources, and time if they want educators to enthusiastically embrace new ideas and practices.

- **Leaders must get results—the do of the work:** Ultimately, improvement cannot be optional. A transformational leader must skillfully assess and meet the needs of those he or she leads, but eventually, he or she has to demand full participation in the change and improvement process. (Muhammad & Cruz, 2019, p. 6)

Consider Muhammad and Cruz's (2019) descriptions of transformational leaders and the two principals in the earlier scenarios. Principal Brown was demonstrating an understanding of these practices. He focused on the *why*, *who*, and *how* before expecting the *do*. He knew he had to make a change and get results, but he didn't jump into this first. He intentionally took the time to build capacity and understanding. Principal Taylor, on the other hand, went straight to the *do* and expected change would happen. Unfortunately, she took the long way to getting results and improving her school even though she likely saw this as the fastest way to make a change. In your priority school, can you think of a time when a more intentional message—from you or someone else—about the purpose or the *why* would have created a more positive change?

Having Crucial Conversations

In addition to being very intentional when they consider how and what to communicate, leaders who want to improve their schools and districts also must face the task of having effective and productive crucial conversations. A *crucial conversation* is a "discussion between two or more people where (1) stakes are high, (2) opinions vary, and (3) emotions run strong" (Patterson, Grenny, McMillan, & Switzler, 2012, p. 3). Patterson and colleagues (2012) write when we face crucial conversations, we can do one of three things: (1) we can avoid them, (2) we can face them and handle them poorly, or (3) we can face them and handle them well. As leaders of both adults and students, it is very important to develop the skills to face and handle these conversations well. Pretending not to notice relationship issues in your school or district and not taking care of the culture can be a disaster.

Three of Stephen R. Covey's (2013) seven habits of highly effective people illustrate some leadership habits that intentionally create opportunities for positive conversations.

1. Put first things first.

2. Think win-win.

3. Seek first to understand and then to be understood.

Consider these habits as you prepare for crucial conversations. Consider how each habit might help you have a more successful conversation with someone on your staff. For example, you are meeting after school today with a teacher who has consistently come to school late or not at all. When she does come, she is not well prepared. Her coworkers have been trying to help her, and it is becoming difficult for them as well. You know this teacher is dealing with a very ill family member and struggling financially. You are not looking forward to this conversation. How can thinking about putting first things first or thinking win-win help you? What should you first focus the conversation on? What would be a win-win outcome for you and your teacher? How can you successfully seek first to understand and then to be understood?

Because you urgently want to make changes in your priority school, you owe it to your students and other staff members to deal with this situation. However, you want to be fair and provide an opportunity to truly understand and have a positive outcome. Intentionally considering these three habits prior to your meeting and keeping the focus on what is important (first things first) will help you be more successful.

Coauthor Jeanne Spiller and I (Spiller & Power, 2019) state:

> You are the architect. You are the designer. You are the motivator. You are the planner. You fix things. You truly are the builder, the creator of futures, and the keeper of dreams. You are responsible. You have impact. *You are a school leader*. (p. 171)

Conclusion

You are ultimately responsible for leading your school or district, and you greatly impact overall school improvement and student success by how intentional you are with all your daily decisions and practices. With the enormous responsibility of leading change in a priority school, leadership skills truly matter. You do not have to be an expert at everything, but you do need to be aware of how you spend your time and what you consider your priorities. You do need to understand the perception of what is important to you and how valuable it is to lead through example, rather than because of your title. And this includes bringing clarity on why decisions are made and how actions must be taken to focus on what is needed.

In the continuous cycle of school improvement, leaders develop intentional actions, adults change their behaviors, and students succeed because of these actions. Schools cannot improve without intentionality.

Daily Time Log

Category	Day One	Day Two	Day Three
Daily Focus	**Spending most of my time in classrooms and with collaborative teams**	**Increasing time in classrooms and with collaborative teams**	**Increasing time in classrooms and with collaborative teams**
Classroom observations			
Student discipline			
Duties (hall, lunchroom, bus yard supervision, and so on)			
District meetings			
Emails and office work			
Collaborative team meetings			
Community engagement			
Human resources			
Other			

Source: Spiller, J., & Power, K. (2019). Leading with intention: Eight areas for reflection and planning in your PLC at Work. *Bloomington, IN: Solution Tree Press.*

Reflection on Intentionality During the Day

Reflect on the difference between the two example practices given in chapter 1.

Distractor	My Intentional Focus	What I Actually Did
→		←

Distractor	My Intentional Focus	What I Actually Did
→		←

Source: Spiller, J., & Power, K. (2019). Leading with intention: Eight areas for reflection and planning in your PLC at Work. *Bloomington, IN: Solution Tree Press.*

Assessment Tool for Simplifying Focus and Actions in Daily Practice

Directions: Use the following five-point scale to self-assess your focus on priorities.

1. I am totally distracted from this priority and recognize I have not created a simplistic way for others to understand this focus.

2. I struggle some days with staying focused on this and believe others are not always sure this is a focus.

3. I speak about this priority often and have set up structures and systems that help others understand this work; however, my daily actions are not always aligned with this priority.

4. I believe most days my actions and messages represent the simplicity of what I want to accomplish at this school. However, there are times I do allow distractors to get in the way.

5. I am strongly aligning all of my actions and messages so it is simple for others to understand this is a priority.

Priorities	Score and reflection	What actions can I take to increase my focus and simplify the direction if necessary?
Priority one	I give myself a score of _____ because	
Priority two	I give myself a score of _____ because	
Priority three	I give myself a score of _____ because	

Source: Spiller, J., & Power, K. (2019). Leading with intention: Eight areas for reflection and planning in your PLC at Work. *Bloomington, IN: Solution Tree Press.*

Reflection on Communicating the *Why*

Reflect on the difference between the two example practices given in chapter 1.

The Difference in Practice	Communicating the Why First (Scenario One)	Communicating the Why First (Scenario Two)
How did the principal ensure staff fully understood and were on board with the decision? What happens when this does or does not happen?		
Why is the students' response in each situation almost predictable?		
In what ways can you relate a personal situation to either or both of these scenarios?		
What support do you need to increase your leadership capacity in this area?		

References and Resources

Covey, S. R. (2013). *The seven habits of highly effective people: Powerful lessons in personal change* (25th anniversary ed.). New York: Simon & Schuster.

Deci, E. L., & Ryan, R. M. (2012). Self-determination theory. In P. A. M. Van Lange, A. W. Kruglanski, & E. T. Higgins (Eds.), *Handbook of theories of social psychology* (pp. 416–436). Thousand Oaks, CA: SAGE.

DuFour, R., DuFour, R., Eaker, R., Many, T. W., & Mattos, M. (2016). *Learning by doing: A handbook for Professional Learning Communities at Work.* (3rd ed.). Bloomington, IN: Solution Tree Press.

DuFour, R., & Fullan, M. (2013). *Cultures built to last: Systemic PLCs at Work.* Bloomington, IN: Solution Tree Press.

Kanold, T. D. (2017). *HEART! Fully forming your professional life as a teacher and leader.* Bloomington, IN: Solution Tree Press.

Kramer, S. V., & Schuhl, S. (2017). *School improvement for all: A how-to guide for doing the right work.* Bloomington, IN: Solution Tree Press.

Muhammad, A., & Cruz, L. F. (2019). *Time for change: Four essential skills for transformational school and district leaders.* Bloomington, IN: Solution Tree Press.

Patterson, K., Grenny, J., McMillan, R., & Switzler, A. (2012). *Crucial conversations: Tools for talking when stakes are high* (2nd ed.). New York: McGraw-Hill.

Schmoker, M. (2016). *Leading with focus: Elevating the essentials for school and district improvement.* Alexandria, VA: Association for Supervision and Curriculum Development.

Spiller, J., & Power, K. (2019). *Leading with intention: Eight areas for reflection and planning in your PLC at Work.* Bloomington, IN: Solution Tree Press.

 **Karen Power** is an author, consultant, and former teacher, principal, and superintendent. Karen has implemented the Professional Learning Community (PLC) at Work process both as a school and district leader and continues to support deep understanding of next steps in practices that ensure all students can learn. As principal of Lewisville Middle School, Karen and her teachers developed collaborative practices and positively impacted student learning. As a superintendent, she created expectations for school improvement and supported her thirty-eight schools in the PLC process.

Karen primarily works in priority school projects providing leadership coaching in both schools and districts in the United States and Canada. In 2020, Karen was pleased to learn that Morrilton Intermediate School, a school she coached for three years, was awarded Model PLC school status.

Karen coauthored *Leading With Intention: Eight Areas for Reflection and Planning in Your PLC at Work* and edited a Canadian edition of *Learning by Doing*. She is coauthoring a leadership book on literacy instruction and a follow-up edition to *Leading With Intention*. In 2010, 2011, and 2012, Karen was selected as one of Canada's Top 100 Most Powerful Women in the Public Sector by the Women's Executive Network.

Karen lives in New Brunswick, Canada, with her husband, Wayne.

To learn more about Karen's work, visit https://karenpower.blog or follow @power58karen on Twitter.

To book Karen Power for professional development, contact pd@SolutionTree.com.

Building District Culture

Karen Power

> Leadership consists of both pressure and support.
> A leader must create more pressure for change than
> there is resistance to change or nothing will change.
>
> —*Sharon V. Kramer and Sarah Schuhl*

You are a new superintendent. You sit at your desk for the first time and reflect on your career journey. How did it happen that you are leading a district? How overwhelming is it to feel this much responsibility? Where will you spend your time? What will you focus on? How will you decide where to start? Author Patrick Lencioni (2012) thinks his research might have some of those answers, asserting that *smart* means you focus on strategy, marketing, finance, and technology; *health* means you intentionally minimize politics and confusion, have high morale and productivity, and experience low turnover. Despite well-intended plans, leaders seem more comfortable with spending their time discussing the tangible and perhaps tweaking, rather than courageously having the difficult conversations and facing the brutal reality of situations in order to improve their learning organization's health.

Leaders often prefer to look for answers where the light is better and where they are more comfortable, even when where they are looking doesn't make sense. And, the light is certainly better in the measurable, objective, and data-driven world of organizational intelligence (the smart side of the equation) than it is on the messier, more unpredictable world of organizational health.

Not for one minute as district leaders can we ignore the smart side of Lencioni's (2012) thinking. We must function on evidence and take care of the systems, resources, and policies that create alignment and success in our schools. This cannot be done in isolation without understanding and defining our purpose for the work and how we are going to work together.

In this chapter, district leaders explore a road map for where to start with an overall improvement plan that creates a supportive, healthy culture for schools. The following four stops occur along the way.

1. Understanding your culture

2. Keeping the work the work

3. Creating a shared leadership model

4. Communicating, implementing, monitoring, and celebrating

The entire improvement plan must focus on the students. Educational consultants Jeanne Spiller and Karen Power (2019) share a district decision-making protocol (figure 2.1) that provides leaders an opportunity to ensure students are the focus of every step along the way to improvement. The reproducible "Student-Centered Decision-Making Protocol" (page 37) is a blank version.

As you consider the four stops on the journey this chapter describes, it is most critical that the *students* be at the forefront of all action plans. Any decisions must consider the question, How does this impact the students in my district?

Using this template, complete each square, beginning with the first priority—the students. This is the first criteria in this decision-making protocol, the second priority being safety, the third policy compliance, and the last, how these impact resources.

What issue requires me to make a decision?	
1. Students *Describe how this decision will impact students.*	2. Safety *Describe how this decision will impact the safety of students and staff.*
3. Policies *Will this decision go against any school, district, school board, federal, or state or provincial policies?*	4. Resources *Consider the resources (human and otherwise) necessary to address this issue. Are they available? What will be required?*

Source: Adapted from Spiller & Power, 2019.

Figure 2.1: Student-centered decision-making protocol.

Understanding Your Culture

For leaders to move from *positional leadership* (having leadership authority based on the position) to leadership based on *permission* (gaining the respect and confidence of others by gaining their permission to lead), it requires the ability to build relationships with people (Maxwell, 2011). Leaders who lead by position place more importance on tasks, purchases, and paperwork, and work from a position of "I directed you to do this because I am the boss" versus a position of trust and respect. To lead your district from a position of permission (supportive) rather than position (telling), you should start by understanding the culture of your organization. That means understanding the needs of your people—staff and students.

When I met with the leadership team at Huntsville Independent School District in Huntsville, Texas, I soon recognized the district's need and willingness to talk about school culture. As we reviewed the comprehensive needs assessments for each of their schools, we looked at the similarities and differences and established expectations for school improvement. The district had identified four "big rocks": (1) quality instructional leadership, (2) quality first-time instruction, (3) social-emotional learning (including culturally responsive practices), and (4) effective classroom management (including restorative practices). These were the curricular and instruction priorities, and the leaders knew that to improve in these four areas, there had to be a focus on culture. Initially, the conversations were about each school's culture and diversified needs. During our discussions, the team circled back to what culture truly means and what work might be done first as a district to establish a student-centered culture of learning.

Districts often redirect this area in discussions; in other words, district leaders unintentionally shift the focus to schools (not the district) when figuring out cultural needs and issues, expecting district-level improvement without supporting the discussions and changes that must take place. In fact, organizational decisions might work against the cultural changes schools need. For example, a high school team might identify increasing attendance as a necessary cultural shift and put a plan in place to do this work. At the same time, a board or district office decision might be made to suspend students who are tardy more than five days. This decision is done without consulting the high school team and certainly feels counterintuitive to their hard work on improving student attendance.

Unpacking the Meaning of *Culture*

Technical change occurs to the tools or mechanism professionals use to do their jobs effectively; *cultural change* is a much more difficult form of change to accomplish (Muhammad, 2018). Cultural change cannot occur through force or coercion. Culture expert and consultant Anthony Muhammad (2018) explains that it takes a leader's ability to be aware of where a school has been and agreement with all staff about where the school will go.

This important work helped the leaders in Huntsville understand the district's and schools' needs. They were able to have challenging conversations about the poverty and inequities preventing a districtwide belief in all students' capacity to learn. They uncovered some truths about conditions they needed to address systemwide. For example, there was a need to help all teachers and school leaders understand how student engagement is linked to poverty and that some schools needed more conversations with staff about what inequity means in a school system. The team discussed unconscious bias—"prejudice or unsupported judgments in favor of or against one thing, person, or group as compared to another, in a way that is usually considered unfair"—and agreed there needed to be more awareness of how, as educators and leaders, this bias (whether intentional or unintentional) was impacting decisions and actions (Vanderbilt University, n.d.). The team agreed that the more teachers worked in collaboration, the more likely they would be to keep bias in check. They also saw a need to build empathy in their district.

The Huntsville team also learned some of their schools' leaders had not talked with staff about clarifying their mission or vision (or had only briefly started these discussions) and had not addressed collective commitments (page 104) to meet their goals. It was an important time for the district leaders and the school leaders to think about the four pillars that create a healthy culture in a professional learning community (PLC): (1) mission, (2) vision, (3) collective commitments or values, and (4) goals (DuFour, DuFour, Eaker, Many, & Mattos, 2016; see page 3). Each of these pillars asks a different question of the educators and leaders and requires conversations focused on honest discourse and reflection. In many districts and schools, this work is seen as "fluffy" or not necessary, especially when leaders focus more on Lencioni's (2012) smart side of the equation. Or, the work is done on paper only and the actual needed implementation, monitoring, adjusting, and celebrating just don't happen. Figure 2.2 outlines what each pillar means and what and how each pillar will support and provide clarity for all who do this culturally important work in the system.

In the Huntsville district, although the schools had all set goals through their school-improvement plans, not all had the discussions that lead to deep understanding of the *why*—the purpose of these goals or how adults would work together to reach them. As a district, there was also a need to start here and to ensure that as a system, there was clarity on the beliefs and values that would create consistent expectations for how adults would work together to meet the needs of each student. Lastly, the leadership team and school leaders reflected on the questions in the reproducible "District Culture Activity" (page 38) to truly understand their culture.

Figure 2.3 (page 32) is the Huntsville district's authentic examination of their culture. Instead of telling schools what the vision and expectations are, the district leaders embraced an opportunity to work shoulder to shoulder with school leaders to identify needs and have challenging conversations. They could now move forward to focus on collaboration, learning, and results to build a student-centered culture for learning. The reproducible "District Culture Examination" (page 39) is available for your school.

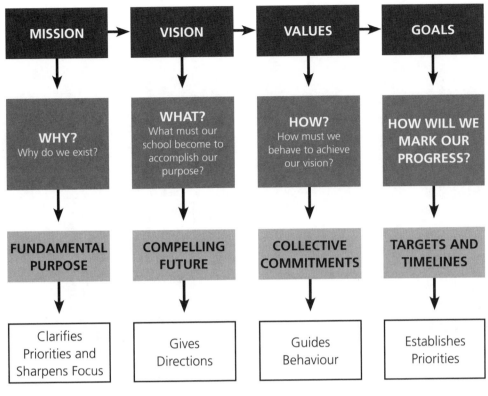

Source: DuFour et al., 2016, p. 39.

Figure 2.2: The four pillars of a PLC.

*Visit **go.SolutionTree.com/PLCbooks** for a free reproducible version of this figure.*

Taking the Next Steps

The next steps for the Huntsville district will include establishing districtwide *tights* (non-negotiables) based on knowing that to achieve their four "big rocks," the district must remove barriers (see the right column in figure 2.3, page 32) that cause inequities. They must first identify a few areas to focus on and establish an action plan that includes professional learning, implementing expectations, monitoring, and adjusting as the culture changes. And of course, the district will need to authentically use their goals to celebrate the work. It will be important for the district to remember to deeply ensure understanding of *why* and *what* the work is.

Many times, there are assumptions made that "a one and done" is all that is needed; in other words, carefully planning professional development that aligns coaching, modeling, monitoring, feedback, revising, and celebrating will be important. It will also be important for the curriculum and instruction leaders to ensure the board or cabinet members are well informed of the purpose of this work. Figure 2.4 (page 34) shows what this action plan might begin to look like for the Huntsville district. The reproducible "District Action Plan" (page 41) is available for your school and district.

Priorities	Ideally, what does this look and sound like in your district and school?	What is the current reality? What evidence do you currently have?
Quality instructional leadership	• School leaders are students of instruction: professional development on common understanding of effective classroom practices, quality lesson planning, and leading and supporting this work are ongoing priorities of the school leaders. • Principals and assistant principals lead through a shared leadership team that holds meetings focused on instructional discussions. For example, the leadership team analyzes data from collaborative team common formative assessments and then discusses what is needed instructionally and for interventions for students. • School leaders ask guiding questions of collaborative teams to ensure members focus on improving instruction and intervention practices. • Administrators and instructional coaches conduct classroom observations together, with well-established look-fors based on quality instructional practices teachers understand and have seen modeled. Feedback includes coaching, modeling, practice, and revision.	• The leadership team inconsistently holds meetings that mostly deal with administrative trivia. Members' conversations are not instructionally based. • School leaders, who attend collaborative team meetings, often take notes and listen to the instructional coaches who facilitate the discussions. They are not all comfortable asking instructional questions yet. • School leaders visit classrooms and give feedback mostly for evaluation purposes. They find it challenging to be in classrooms to provide guidance and coaching for instruction for two reasons: (1) time and (2) lack of instructional knowledge. • School leaders primarily rely on the instructional coaches to be the instructional leaders in their schools.
Quality first-time instruction	• In all classrooms, teachers plan lessons based on grade-level expectations in all curricula. • All teachers receive support to deeply understand what strategies and practices they will engage students in, including student ownership of their learning. • A district tight expectation is for teachers to provide first-time well planned, engaging, and differentiated instruction to meet the needs of all students. • Classroom observations and feedback are based on expectations teachers understand for effective classroom practices. • Teachers struggling with first-time instruction receive coaching, modeling, observations, feedback, and an expectation for improvement.	• Consistent highly engaging classroom practices are not the norm yet. • Instructional coaches are working diligently to improve instruction, but as a school or district, we have not clearly defined the expectations. • Many teachers just want the students removed who are misbehaving and there is not a high level of differentiation in lessons, which leads to some of the misbehaviors. • Teachers need more support in understanding how to teach at grade level and to engage the students in their lessons. • Many students are still passive about their learning, and teachers do not expect them to be responsible for their own learning goals.

	• As a district, our professional learning plan includes a great emphasis on instructional practices including differentiation, Tier 1 and 2 of interventions, engaging practices, small-group instruction, hands-on learning, and so on.	• Teachers often feel administrators only evaluate them when they need more support through professional learning and coaching for instruction.
Social-emotional learning (including culturally responsive practices)	• We model equitable decisions and practices in all aspects of this work. For example, the district's mission includes a statement that it will not matter who the child's teacher is, the experience will be the same. • Teachers and leaders have a common understanding of what it means to be culturally responsive and inclusive in all practices both in the school and district. • This common understanding has led to more successful and engaging practices in the classroom that honor student differences and celebrate uniqueness. • The school or district acknowledges and eliminates inequities including race, gender, bias, orientation, and more. • Our school or district encourages and supports students to understand global citizenship and how to give back to their community.	• In the comprehensive needs assessment reports, several student interviews include comments of students believing there are inequities in how teachers perceive them. • The comprehensive needs assessment reports also include reports of classroom observations that confirm there are inequitable practices in schools. • Leaders admit they are not confident they know what or how to support culturally responsive practices in the district or schools. There is work to be done in learning more about this. • As a district and in most schools, there have not been authentic discussions around gender, bias, race, and so on or about how this is impacting student learning.
Effective classroom management (including restorative practices)	• All teachers receive training on how to effectively manage their classrooms, including restorative justice practices. • District leaders define tights to include what an effective classroom looks like and how to use restorative justice practices. • All teachers apply the above learning to their classroom planning. • Leaders immediately identify teachers who need support in this area, and school administrators and instructional coaches support them. • Leaders' classroom observations intentionally provide feedback and support to improve expected effective classroom practices. • Teachers keep parents and students well informed of the use of restorative justice practices.	• Ineffective classroom management practices heighten discipline issues, and many teachers hyper-focus on discipline versus effective practices. • School leaders, in some schools, spend much time focusing on discipline issues rather than proactive restorative justice practices and effective management strategies. • There has not been any attempts to deepen understanding of restorative practices and overall effective classroom management yet. • Students' discipline issues overwhelm teachers, who express they are not sure what to do.

Source: © 2020 by Huntsville Independent School District. Used with permission.

Figure 2.3: Example of completed template.

The Journey	Priority One: Quality Instructional Leadership	Priority Two: Quality First-Time Instruction	Priority Three: Social-Emotional Learning	Priority Four: Effective Classroom Management
Problems of practice along the journey to improvement	Problem of practice one: School leaders need professional development and collaborative efforts to understand what quality instruction looks like and how to build tights around this work.	Problem of practice two: All teachers need to understand the importance of grade-level planning and implementation of effective lessons and have coaching support in classrooms.	Problem of practice three: Because students feel inequities in the way teachers teach classes and treat them, teachers and leaders need to develop common understanding of what equitable practices look like in schools and districts and apply these to everyday decisions.	Problem of practice four: Teachers need more support and guidance in building a toolbox of effective classroom management strategies so they can engage students in lessons and so students want to be in school.
Understanding your culture *What first step can we take?*	The district leadership team (district and school leaders and coaches) will support this work by first working with both the school leaders and the instructional coaches to create look-fors for quality instruction and to prepare an observation tool. The district leadership team will practice observing and debriefing classrooms to learn together and calibrate our findings.	The district leadership team will support this work by first ensuring all collaborative teams understand how to select essential grade-level standards, unpack the standards, and write learning targets that align with the standards. Teachers should be visible in their planning and in their classroom practices. The instructional coaches will gradually release the responsibility to collaborative teams so that they can spend more time in classrooms focusing on instructional coaching.	The district leadership team will support this work by first being transparent in the concerns and awareness of inequitable expectations in the district and addressing bias that may be intentional or unintentional and supporting teacher awareness of what it looks like to make student-centered decisions that are equitable for all students.	The district leadership team will support this work by first identifying effective classroom strategies, including small-group and differentiated strategies, that will be tight expectations and form the basis of an instructional professional development plan for all teachers.
Keeping the work, the work *What first step can we take?*	• District leaders will visit classrooms with school administrators and coaches to align look-fors, debrief together, and offer feedback to teachers based on district expectations. • District leaders will keep this focus and develop district professional learning plans based on the observations.	• District and school leaders will communicate tight expectations for the work of collaborative teams (answering the four critical questions of a PLC). • District and school leaders will observe collaborative teams and offer coaching and support through questions that support grade-level expectations.	• District leaders will lead awareness of the need for equitable practices in our district. • District leaders will define tights that include a focus on bias (intentional or unintentional) the district will not tolerate and develop a district belief that all students will learn at high levels.	• District and school leaders will support teacher learning of effective classroom management through professional learning. • District and school leaders will intentionally observe classrooms looking for effective classroom management practices and then providing feedback, coaching, and support to improve.

	• District leaders will protect school leaders' time from interrupting classroom support.	• District and school leaders will communicate overall expectations for grade-level planning and that they expect collaborative teams to be visible in classroom practice.	• District leaders will develop and implement a communication plan to help all teachers, parents, and students understand our focus on equitable practices.	• The district leadership team will focus professional development on supporting teachers in understanding what engaging strategies look like in a classroom.
Creating a shared leadership model *What first step can we take?*	• The district leadership team will determine instructional tights together, monitor classroom practices together, and determine district next steps for professional development based on observations.	• The district leadership team will identify the tight expectations for instructional practices and create a plan, together, for coaching, modeling, implementing, and providing ongoing support to teachers.	• The district and school leadership teams will own the cultural shift of moving from a district with inequitable practices to a district where there is common understanding that each student will learn at high levels.	• The goal of the district leadership team is to move the instructional coaches from leaders of the PLC to leaders of instruction in classrooms. A goal of this team is to share leadership of classroom instruction practices, including classroom management strategies.
Communicating, implementing, monitoring, and celebrating *What first step can we take?*	• The district leadership team will ensure training for all teachers in effective practices and know what the district expectations are. This team will also monitor its successes and challenges. • The district leadership team will communicate with the board, cabinet, parents, and students, as well as all staff. • District and school leaders will continue to meet regularly to share celebrations and honor the work of schools.	• The district leadership team will communicate why effective classroom practices are important and how it will support this work. • The district professional learning plan will model what district leaders expect in classrooms, and district leaders will monitor and align feedback to support deep understanding of the work. • As a district leadership team, we will use data from our classroom observations to celebrate the growth we see in teacher practices.	• The district leadership team will develop common messages that model equitable expectations and practices in schools. • The district leadership team will monitor implementation of any policies, practices, and so on, that will create equitable opportunities for all students. • When district and school leaders see inequitable practices, they will reflect on why and what needs to be done to correct them. • District and school leaders will celebrate cultural changes as they unfold.	• The district leadership team will create tights of effective classroom management practices and build a communication plan for professional learning. • The district leadership team will develop a professional development plan that supports deep understanding of effective classroom management plans. • The district leadership team will implement this professional development plan. • The district leadership team will monitor the effectiveness of the plan through classroom observations and student learning. • The district leadership team will celebrate improvements in classroom management practices.

Figure 2.4: A sample work plan.

As figure 2.4 (page 34) illustrates, the next steps for the Huntsville district are to focus on a plan of action that will ensure that it keeps at the work, shares leadership of the work, and continuously communicates, progress monitors, and celebrates its successes. Richard DuFour and Michael Fullan (2013) remind us, "sustaining an improvement process demands that leaders do more than *hope* for short-term wins. They must *plan* for short-term wins" (p. 76).

Conclusion

Think of the work that the Huntsville district has done and continues to do to begin understanding and changing the culture of its system. By embracing opportunities for all district and school leaders to have challenging conversations and plan from the needs, they are fostering a system of one. When the purpose of the work is understood and collective commitments are developed that align to what we want to improve, districts are in a much better place to support schools, rather than tell schools what to do.

The ultimate test, for you as a leader, is when you leave the system. Did you leave a healthy, sustainable district culture because it is embedded and understood by staff? Did you support and encourage the people in your system to grow? School improvement requires a relentless ability to build capacity and explain the purpose over and over again to school boards, cabinets, parents, guardians, teachers, students, and anyone who is part of your circle of influence.

Student-Centered Decision-Making Protocol

Using this template, complete each square, beginning with the first priority—the students. This is the first criteria in this decision-making protocol, the second priority being safety, the third policy compliance, and the last, how these impact resources.

What issue requires me to make a decision?	
1. Students *Describe how this decision will impact students.*	2. Safety *Describe how this decision will impact the safety of students and staff.*
3. Policies *Will this decision go against any school, district, school board, federal, or state or provincial policies?*	4. Resources *Consider the resources (human and otherwise) necessary to address this issue. Are they available? What will be required?*

Source: Adapted from Spiller, J., & Power, K. (2019). Leading with intention: Eight areas for reflection and planning in your PLC at Work. *Bloomington, IN: Solution Tree Press.*

District Culture Activity

Using ten-point increments from 10 to 100, how strongly do you believe this question?

Question	Points
1. Do we believe all students can learn?	
2. Do we believe educators are the key contributors to student learning?	
3. Do we believe education is critical to the future of our students?	
4. Do we believe we can make a difference in the lives of our students?	
Total	

Source: Adapted from DuFour, R., DuFour, R., Eaker, R., & Karhanek, G. (2010). Raising the bar and closing the gap: Whatever it takes. *Bloomington, IN: Solution Tree Press.*

District Culture Examination

Priorities	Ideally, what does this look and sound like in your district and school?	What is the current reality? What evidence do you currently have?

page 1 of 2

Priorities	Ideally, what does this look and sound like in your district and school?	What is the current reality? What evidence do you currently have?

Source: © 2020 by Huntsville Independent School District. Used with permission.

District Action Plan

The Journey	Priority One:	Priority Two:	Priority Three:	Priority Four:
Problems of practice along the journey to improvement				
Understanding your culture *What first step can we take?*				

Keeping the work, the work *What first step can we take?*		
Creating a shared leadership model *What first step can we take?*		
Communicating, implementing, monitoring, and celebrating *What first step can we take?*		

References and Resources

DuFour, R., DuFour, R., Eaker, R., & Karhanek, G. (2010). *Raising the bar and closing the gap: Whatever it takes*. Bloomington, IN: Solution Tree Press.

DuFour, R., DuFour, R., Eaker, R., Many, T. W., & Mattos, M. (2016). *Learning by doing: A handbook for Professional Learning Communities at Work* (3rd ed.). Bloomington: IN: Solution Tree Press.

DuFour, R., & Fullan, M. (2013). *Cultures built to last: Systemic PLCs at Work*. Bloomington, IN: Solution Tree Press.

Eaker, R., & Keating, J. (2012). *Every school, every team, every classroom: District leadership for growing Professional Learning Communities at Work*. Bloomington, IN: Solution Tree Press.

Kramer, S. V., & Schuhl, S. (2017). *School improvement for all: A how-to guide for doing the right work*. Bloomington, IN: Solution Tree Press.

Lencioni, P. (2012). *The advantage: Why organizational health trumps everything else in business*. San Francisco: Jossey-Bass.

Maxwell, J. C. (2011). *The five levels of leadership: Proven steps to maximize your potential*. New York: Center Street.

Muhammad, A. (2018). *Transforming school culture: How to overcome staff division* (2nd ed.). Bloomington, IN: Solution Tree Press.

Spiller, J., & Power, K. (2019). *Leading with intention: Eight areas for reflection and planning in your PLC at Work*. Bloomington, IN: Solution Tree Press.

Vanderbilt University. (n.d.). *Unconscious bias*. Accessed at www.vanderbilt.edu/diversity/unconscious-bias on February 10, 2021.

Gerry Petersen-Incorvaia, PhD, has worked at both school sites and district offices while implementing professional learning communities (PLCs). Gerry is an assistant superintendent for educational services for the Glendale Elementary School District in Glendale, Arizona. He has served as a teacher, principal, university professor, and curriculum and instruction director. While director for curriculum and instruction and assistant superintendent, Glendale Elementary School District became a Model PLC district.

Gerry has trained and presented with Rick Stiggins and Jan Chappuis on assessment, presented with the State Collaborative on Assessment and Student Standards, and written curriculum and presented with Jay and Daisy McTighe on Understanding by Design. Gerry's diverse experiences in schools and districts have invigorated his philosophy that all students have equity of access to a rigorous education.

Gerry earned a bachelor's degree from Luther College and master's and doctoral degrees from the University of Arizona.

To learn more about Gerry's work, follow @DrGerryPI on Twitter.

To book Gerry Petersen-Incorvaia for professional development, contact pd@Solution Tree.com.

Employing High-Level Strategies From the District Office

Gerry Petersen-Incorvaia

> Establishing a guaranteed and viable curriculum as
> a school or district provides a critical framework for
> collaborative teams as they work to do what is tight
> (team actions and commitments everyone will do) and
> use that information to move student learning forward
> in a way that is loose (teacher actions that can differ).
>
> —Sharon V. Kramer and Sarah Schuhl

As a principal, a curriculum director, and an assistant superintendent, I lived this work to create and put in place the structures and support systems to help my district (Glendale Elementary School District in Glendale, Arizona) become a Model professional learning community (PLC) district. However, before working in a PLC, the staff and I had a hard time deciding where to begin when there was so much to do. Nonexplicit pacing guides, a lack of a balanced assessment system aligned with instruction and the state assessment, nonalignment of professional development to promote student learning, and a misunderstanding of PLCs was the reality of our district. Asking these questions is extremely important to start the work.

- "How do you create a guaranteed and viable curriculum that ensures all students have equal access?"

- "How do you ensure a collaborative and inclusive process instead of a top-down approach to the right work?"

- "How do you balance what is identified as tight versus loose as a district versus school, collaborative team, or individual teacher?"

A school district office's duty is to ensure that a guaranteed and viable curriculum, rigorous instruction, and a balanced assessment system are all in place so all students can learn at high levels. This duty is multifaceted and dynamic in that it is flexible yet targeted, strategic yet nimble, and interdependent yet intradependent. Triangulating the right work of developing, implementing, and evaluating curriculum; implementing, supporting, and monitoring Tier 1 instruction, Tier 2 intervention, and Tier 3 remediation; and developing, implementing, and evaluating assessment supports the creation of the district standard for all schools in the learning organization—the school district. The questions to answer follow.

- "How does this occur in a continuous-improvement model?"
- "How does school district leadership lead the work of continuous improvement when schools are underperforming?"
- "What are the strategies for the work where support precedes accountability?"

In a priority school district, moving student achievement student by student, teacher by teacher, collaborative team by collaborative team, or as a whole school may not be accelerated enough to ensure a positive trajectory for an entire school district. When the school district has pockets of achievement or growth, but that growth is not prevalent throughout the district, implementing high-leverage strategies districtwide will help advance student achievement. High-leverage strategies help ensure equity of access for all students to learning that yields student growth and achievement. Priority school district work lends itself to the following four high-leverage district strategies.

1. Leading a cultural shift
2. Identifying the tight and loose of the right work
3. Implementing a support and monitoring system
4. Enacting a communication loop

In priority school districts, you should implement all four strategies at the same time and in a balanced manner due to the need to accelerate the work.

Leading a Cultural Shift

In a priority school district, to ensure the school district is using the PLC process and working as a collaborative team is a high-leverage strategy in that it moves the district to not only success, but leveraged, more sustainable success. As a district PLC, making sure to address the cultural shift needed to ensure the right work is implemented with the least amount of resistance is important and cannot be overlooked. When the cultural shift is lead with aplomb, there is less resistance. Sharon V. Kramer (2015) states that the "cultural shift begins by adopting specific core principles that guide the work and set the tone for school improvement.

1. Do not blame the students.
2. Learning is required.
3. Hope is not a strategy." (p. 10)

This is the same cultural shift that a district may need as well. Having discussions and commitments with the district office staff, site administrators, and the district guiding coalition about the foundation of a PLC is important in this process to ensure all staff are on the same page. The four pillars of a PLC (see page 3) are important to this work.

Leading this work from the district office needs a balance of acceleration with support and monitoring with celebration. District office and site leaders must keep in mind what consultant Laurie Sudbrink (2015) states: "while [we are] relentlessly going toward that vision, we must balance it with respect and appreciation for people. Believe in your people. Your ability to visualize them as successful will accelerate their success and yours" (p. 195). Like our students, adults respond similarly to high expectations, belief they can do it, and feedback along the way (Donohoo, 2017). Leaders must also balance the work by investing "a reasonable amount of time attending to fears and feelings, or squander an unreasonable amount of time trying to manage ineffective and unproductive behavior" (Brown, 2018, p. 70). Hence, to be highly effective while leading PLC work, it takes balancing the right work (Erkens & Twadell, 2012).

Another important philosophy to remember is that as a leader, whether at the school or district level, "you can't get to courage without rumbling with vulnerability" (Brown, 2018, p. 2). You do not have all the answers or know all the specifics about every element of the continuous school- and district-improvement process. Asking teams of leaders, including the district guiding coalition and other colleagues, is important to not only build capacity in the organization but also allow others to see there is no knight in shining armor riding in on a white horse. It takes *collective* efficacy, which supports collaborative teacher teams (Donohoo & Velasco, 2016) and school learning teams, the district guiding coalition, and site administration teams. Similar to a guiding coalition, a school learning team is made up of a diverse group of teacher leaders at a school site whose sole focus is on increasing student achievement. Site administration teams are the principal and assistant principals. Moving from "I can do it" to "We can do it" is important; it helps leaders foster collective teacher efficacy by "creating opportunities for meaningful collaboration, empowering teachers, establishing goals and high expectations, and helping interpret results and provide feedback" (Donohoo, 2017, p. 35).

In essence, one of the most important aspects of the work is what school culture experts Anthony Muhammad and Luis F. Cruz (2019) state, "An effective leader focuses on improving organizational performance, but at the same time, he or she realizes that all the organization's members must possess a personal passion to improve organizational performance" (p. 47). This focus is something that a priority school district needs to move all schools forward.

Identifying the Tight and Loose of the Right Work

The district office's educational services department is responsible for aligning a guaranteed and viable curriculum, rigorous instruction, a balanced and coherent assessment system, a balanced response to intervention (RTI) pyramid, and the professional learning to support the alignment (Bambrick-Santoyo, 2018; Van Clay, Soldwedel, & Many,

2011). Supporting the school sites in a manner that allows collaborative teams to be the catalysts for continuous school improvement is important (DuFour & Marzano, 2011).

As you and your team develop simultaneously tight and loose work, educator and consultant J. Richard Dewey (2018) asks, "On which priorities are you going to be tight?" You and your team should also ask the following.

- "What are the specific conditions we expect to see in every collaborative team?"

- "What must we do to build the capacity of people throughout the school or district to create these conditions?" Remember, support precedes monitoring.

- "What indicators of progress will we monitor?"

- "Are we aligning leadership behaviors with the articulated purpose and priorities (and likewise paying attention to things we need to stop doing)?"

These questions are important to answer during the process. In a priority district, identifying evidence-based strategies and systems that will accelerate the work is imperative to ensure a positive trajectory. Figure 3.1 is an example of a one-page document that showcases the tights of a learning organization.

Commitment: We recognize that the fundamental purpose of our school and the reason we come to work each day is to ensure all students learn at high levels. We understand that helping all students learn requires a collective collaborative effort rather than a series of isolated efforts. Therefore we work in teams and constantly gather evidence of student learning to inform our individual and collective practice and to better meet the needs of individual students for intervention and extension.

Professional Learning Community Tights:

1. The fundamental structure of the school becomes the collaborative team.

2. The team establishes a guaranteed curriculum.

3. The team develops common formative assessments to hold tight to pacing and guaranteed curriculum for all students.

4. The school creates systems of intervention and extension.

5. The team uses evidence of student learning to inform and improve practices.

School District Tights:

1. Fidelity to the balanced literacy framework and comprehensive mathematics framework as part of a guaranteed curriculum
   a. Essential standards deconstructed into learning targets and Staircase of Complexity
   b. Learning targets mapped out for the quarter in a proficiency map or long-range plan

c. Guided reading for every student every day

d. Cold reads implemented on a regular basis, scaffolded to paired texts

e. Small-group instruction for students needing targeted skill support

f. Number talks implemented to develop flexible fluency and persistence

g. Mathematics variety practice (MVPs): six questions or items that deal with the same content in multiple ways (for example, an array, base ten blocks, naked numbers, and so on; for one mathematical concept; more or less, a variety of ways a student may see a mathematical concept on an assessment)

2. Common formative and summative assessments in the cycle of learning

a. Common formative assessments collaboratively created and analyzed using item specifications from the state assessments

b. Common formative assessments mapped for the quarter to ensure pacing is on track and spiraled-in previously learned standards

c. Rolling assessments mapped and "rolled" throughout the quarter

3. Data analysis that supports all three tiers of intervention

a. Tier 1: within first best instruction using informal checks for understanding or exit tickets to create pulled small groups

b. Tier 2: within a flexible time of the day for one to two days (flex days or buffer days) to intervene for students by learning target; the results of the common formative assessment kicks in Tier 2 intervention

c. Tier 3: a flexible time that occurs daily for instruction through a specific program; a universal screener is used to identify students needing grade-level remediation

4. Students as partners in their learning

a. Student data trackers created from learning targets, Staircase of Complexity, rolling assessment expectations, or both

b. Students participate in Test Talks with released state assessment items.

c. Students utilize schoolwide, agreed-upon student strategies such as annotation frames as a form of developing student self-efficacy in thinking and assessment-taking strategies

Figure 3.1: Example of learning organization tights.

If these are the learning organization tights outlining the work of the superintendent, the district educational services, or curriculum and instruction department, a principal and the collaborative teams support and monitor the work (see figure 3.2, page 50). Each of these teams must work collaboratively to address the implementation of the right work. The reproducible "The Right Work for the Learning Organization Tights" (page 55) is available for your planning.

Aligning the work to each role is necessary to ensure acceleration of the improvement process. A priority school district must decide how to tackle each of the bulleted items in figure 3.2 in a thoughtful, meaningful timeline.

Purpose of the Work	The Work
Superintendent	

To ensure equity and access to a comprehensive, safe, supportive learning environment districtwide	• Create district master plan with goals.
	• Create and support structures that maximize time in schools, like the following.
	    ➤ Provide time for site administration to focus on learning.
	    ➤ Provide time for students to learn essential content to mastery.
	    ➤ Provide time for site administration to be on campus as the instructional leader.
	• Support data-informed instructional systems that utilize effective, evidence-based practices.
	• Identify and support flexible models of turnaround and collaborative shifts for the schools.
	• Lead school principals through support and monitoring.
	• Consistently communicate celebrations of progress toward goals and lessons learned.
	• Monitor the work of site administration.

Educational Services and Curriculum and Instruction	
To ensure equity and access to a guaranteed and viable curriculum, rigorous instruction, and a balanced and coherent assessment system	• Ensure school master schedules adhere to district standards. • Identify district essential standards. • Map out essential standards for the school year. • Align benchmark assessments to state assessment and sequenced standards mapped out for the school year. • Provide curriculum support resources that align with essential standards. • Identify district tights with content areas. • Create and implement professional learning that aligns with district tights. • Align the district-improvement plan with the academic needs of the district. • Develop site support and monitoring plans that focus on the tights. • Support the creation of school site master schedules that optimize time for student learning and teacher collaboration. • Monitor data analysis and assessment alignment. • Monitor districtwide instructional coaching and mentoring through the work of instructional coaches. • Ensure time is available for meaningful collaboration. • Implement professional learning on evidence-based instructional strategies.
Principal	
To ensure equity and access to a comprehensive, safe, supportive learning environment schoolwide	• Increase shared leadership. • Support and monitor professional learning around the learning organization tights. • Support and monitor collaborative team work around a learning cycle and the learning organization tights. • Develop partnerships with community and businesses. • Increase parent and guardian involvement.

	• Create and protect time for collaboration. • Develop school site master schedule that optimizes time for student learning and teacher collaboration. • Monitor assessment data at a student, teacher, collaborative team, and school level.
Collaborative Teams	

To ensure equity of access for all students to grow in their learning and achievement	• Unwrap essential standards.
	• Create proficiency map of the standards unit by unit.
	• Create, schedule, implement, and evaluate common formative assessments.
	• Explore evidence-based and effective instructional strategies.
	• Implement tiered RTI.
	• Look at student work.
	• Analyze summative assessment data.
	• Revise the process as needed.
	• Monitor student assessment data by student and teacher.
	• Some items, like the following, may not explicitly live in the learning cycle of instruction unit by unit.
	   ➤ Inter-rater reliability for common formative assessments, progress monitoring tools (such as running records), and summative assessments
	   ➤ Implementation of cold reads in reading instruction to ensure students are able to access grade-level text without instruction
	   ➤ How guided reading is set up and implemented in elementary grades
	   ➤ Grading equity throughout the grade level and content area
	   ➤ Test Talks or bell work that simulates the task of state assessments
	• Support diverse-population (gifted, special education, English learner) achievement and strategies to impact learning.
	• Develop countdown plans for the state assessment, which practices the spiraled standards from previous units of study.
	   ➤ Progress monitoring system implementation

Figure 3.2: The right work for the example learning organization tights in figure 3.1 (page 48).

Implementing a Support and Monitoring System

For a school district and a school to achieve greater coherence, the *right work* is to ensure building of capacity, clarity, precision of practice, transparency, monitoring of progress, and continuous correction (Fullan & Quinn, 2016). This aligns with a continuous school-improvement framework.

Ensuring all collaborative teams are working effectively and focusing on the right work is part of the work of a site administration team in collaboration with the school learning team and district guiding coalition. The superintendent, educational services department, and site administration can either consult, collaborate, or coach with clarity, support, and feedback (Many, Maffoni, Sparks, & Thomas, 2018).

Monitoring the work can be and should be done in a professional manner. One way to do this is through *checkups* (a leader in authority initiates when someone is struggling to accomplish something) and *checkbacks* (productive experts initiate; Muhammad & Cruz, 2019; Patterson, Grenny, McMillan, & Switzler, 2005). Whoever names a monitoring system, the important thing to remember is that *support must precede monitoring*. Students, teachers, collaborative teams, and site administrators must have the support to ensure success prior to being held accountable to something they may not understand or know how to implement.

DuFour and Marzano (2011) ask those in charge of professional learning at a school and district level to remember:

> A commitment to building collective capacity requires school environments in which the professional learning of educators is:
>
> - Ongoing and sustained rather than episodic
> - Job-embedded rather than separate from the work and external to the school
> - Specifically aligned with school and district goals rather than the random pursuit of trendy topics
> - Focused on improved results rather than projects and activities
> - Viewed as a collective and collaborative endeavor rather than an individual activity (p. 20)

The attributes of professional learning are examples of supporting professional learning and monitoring that professional learning for impact.

Implementing a support and monitoring system helps move the right work forward. Since support precedes monitoring, identifying the entire support structure comes first. The support centers around the tights. Here are a few reflective questions to ask at the district and site levels that inform a support and monitoring cycle.

- "What are the district tights to support?"
- "What professional learning structures are in place to support new and continuous learning?"
- "How will professional learning reflect the different levels of implementation of the tights? In essence, how will we differentiate professional learning?"
- "Who will we train in a trainer-of-teacher model to ensure content capacity is built into the organization? Who will do the training? What will ongoing training look like?"
- "How will site administrator training compare with teacher leader training?"
- "What part of the implementation will we monitor and how often?"
- "What will happen after the monitoring?"

Enacting a Communication Loop

Seemingly simple in concept, communicating process and products is imperative in any continuous-improvement process. Enacting a communication loop throughout this process is important not only for getting people the information they need but also for building trust throughout the organization. Communicating the foundational aspects, expectations, support and monitoring system, and celebrations mirrors the process at the school site as well. Communicate, communicate, and communicate again.

Depending on the school district, the superintendent's or educational services division's communication plan in place will help all stakeholders understand the purpose, process, and products of the work. Here are reflective questions to ask while creating or revising a comprehensive communication plan.

- "Who needs to receive the information?"
- "What information do we need to transparently communicate?"
- "How will we share the process in a clear and concise manner?"
- "How will we share the information?" The following are ways to communicate the information.
    ‣ Social media
    ‣ Phone apps
    ‣ Newsletters
    ‣ Email
    ‣ Presentations
    ‣ Meetings
- "How will the organization ensure all stakeholders have access to the information?"
- "Will feedback be part of the communication loop? How will feedback impact implementation?"
- "How will we communicate celebrations of progress and lessons learned?"

Conclusion

Shifting an entire school district's culture is important work. This shift ensures equity of access for all students in the district to a guaranteed and viable curriculum, rigorous instruction, and a balanced assessment system which lends itself to higher levels of student achievement. Implementing systems requires an accountability plan to ensure alignment. System-level alignment and accountability are integral to continuous improvement at both the school and district levels. Moving from a district of isolated schools to a school district moving in a positive trajectory is important in the process. The school district is the PLC. School districts can do this work by starting with the simple and moving to the more complex. Communicating the process throughout is key to a successful change process.

Continuous improvement means constantly looking at your current reality and problem solving to do better. Figuring out which staff need what type of professional learning and support changes the people given new positions, addresses new complexities to requirements from state and federal levels, and initiates new collaborative teams. When the district office puts a system of high-leverage strategies in place, the path of progress is clearer and accelerates student achievement at school sites; hence, moving the entire school district forward.

The Right Work for the Learning Organization Tights

Purpose of the Work	The Work
Superintendent	
Educational Services and Curriculum and Instruction	
Principal	
Collaborative Teams	

References and Resources

Bambrick-Santoyo, P. (2018). *A principal manager's guide to leverage leadership 2.0: How to build exceptional schools across your district.* San Francisco: Jossey-Bass.

Brown, B. (2018). *Dare to lead: Brave work, tough conversations, whole hearts.* New York: Random House.

Dewey, J. R. (2018, June 27). *Do the right work: Develop your PLC roadmap* [Blog post]. Accessed at https://allthingsplc.info/blog/view/371/do-the-right-work-develop-your-plc -road-map on September 23, 2020.

Donohoo, J. (2017). *Collective efficacy: How educators' beliefs impact student learning.* Thousand Oaks, CA: Corwin Press.

Donohoo, J., & Velasco, M. (2016). *The transformative power of collaborative inquiry: Realizing change in schools and classrooms.* Thousand Oaks, CA: Corwin Press.

DuFour, R., DuFour, R., Eaker, R., Many, T. W., & Mattos, M. (2016). *Learning by doing: A handbook for Professional Learning Communities at Work* (3rd ed.). Bloomington, IN: Solution Tree Press.

DuFour, R., & Marzano, R. J. (2011). *Leaders of learning: How district, school, and classroom leaders improve student achievement.* Bloomington, IN: Solution Tree Press.

Erkens, C., & Twadell, E. (2012). *Leading by design: An action framework for PLC at Work leaders.* Bloomington, IN: Solution Tree Press.

Fullan, M., & Quinn, J. (2016). *Coherence: The right drivers in action for schools, districts, and systems.* Thousand Oaks, CA: Corwin Press.

Goble, T. (2012, September 4). *Leadership and the PLC* [Blog post]. Accessed at https:// allthingsplc.info/blog/view/193/leadership-and-the-plc on September 23, 2020.

Kramer, S. V. (2015). *How to leverage PLCs for school improvement.* Bloomington, IN: Solution Tree Press.

Kramer, S. V., & Schuhl, S. (2017). *School improvement for all: A how-to guide for doing the right work.* Bloomington, IN: Solution Tree Press.

Kullar, J. K. (2020). *Connecting through leadership: The promise of precise and effective communication in schools.* Bloomington, IN: Solution Tree Press.

Many, T. W., Maffoni, M. J., Sparks, S. K., & Thomas, T. F. (2018). *Amplify your impact: Coaching collaborative teams in PLCs at Work.* Bloomington, IN: Solution Tree Press.

Muhammad, A., & Cruz, L. F. (2019). *Time for change: Four essential skills for transformational school and district leaders.* Bloomington, IN: Solution Tree Press.

Patterson, K., Grenny, J., McMillan, R., & Switzler, A. (2005). *Crucial confrontations: Tools for resolving broken promises, violated expectations, and bad behavior.* New York: McGraw-Hill.

Reeves, D. (2020). *Achieving equity and excellence: Immediate results from the lessons of high-poverty, high-success schools*. Bloomington, IN: Solution Tree Press.

Sudbrink, L. (2015). *Leading with grit: Inspiring action and accountability with generosity, respect, integrity, and truth*. Hoboken, NJ: Wiley.

Van Clay, M., Soldwedel, P., & Many, T. W. (2011). *Aligning school districts as PLCs*. Bloomington, IN: Solution Tree Press.

 **Jack Baldermann** has been a passionate educational leader for over thirty years. In 2017, Jack was named the Illinois Principal of the Year. In 2018, he was one of three finalists for National Principal of the Year. In 2020, Jack led his team—as principal of Westmont High School in Westmont, Illinois—to win the DuFour Award as the best professional learning community (PLC) in the United States.

Jack's experience includes leading several high-poverty urban schools to significant success. He has also worked as a consultant to support five priority or high-poverty schools from across the United States to become Model PLCs.

He led Westmont High School to become one of the most improved and top-performing schools in the United States, with a 99 percent graduation rate, double-digit increases in state test scores, exceptional culture and climate results, one of the most improved Advanced Placement programs in the United States, the highest rating (Exemplary) from the Illinois State Board of Education, and the greatest improvement of any regular high school in three different U.S. rankings.

Jack has worked with school districts in forty-six U.S. states and Canada while continuing his duties as a full-time administrator. He also helped lead Riverside Brookfield High School to excellent student-achievement success and Model PLC school status, and was one of the first principals to implement PLC concepts at Carl Sandburg High School in 1996.

To book Jack Baldermann for professional development, contact pd@SolutionTree.com.

Building Collaborative and Passionately Agreed-to SMART Goals

Jack Baldermann

> All too often the challenges facing a school in urgent need of improvement are numerous and varied. Determining where to start can be overwhelming; yet changes are critical to achieving student success. It takes a focused and intentional leader to create the effective leadership structures necessary to move teachers, students, parents, and community members toward a collective vision of teaching and learning.
>
> —*Sharon V. Kramer and Sarah Schuhl*

On my desk sits a clock given to me as a gift from colleagues in Hartford, Connecticut, where over 85 percent of our students live in economic poverty (Quick, 2016). The clock serves as a constant reminder of the sacred work that educators in high-poverty schools engage in each day. All schoolwork is important, but the additional challenges that high-poverty or priority schools staff face demand a special admiration and respect.

One of the most powerful things we, as leaders, can do to increase learning and achievement for our students is to implement collaboratively built and passionately agreed-to SMART goals—those that are strategic and specific, measurable, attainable, results oriented, tracked and time bound (Conzemius & O'Neill, 2014). SMART goals done well, as outlined in this chapter, bring a team's mission and vision to life. A team can create a mission statement and collective commitments, but how will members measure whether they are accomplishing their ideals? The words and beliefs are valuable, but the SMART goal results give evidence that the school or district is following through and making a difference. These goals provide focus, a sense of accomplishment for teachers and students, and an opportunity to celebrate, and should be the fuel to energize us and maintain continuous improvement. When done well, they bring joy to our work because they are the tangible evidence that our efforts have had a powerful, positive impact for the school communities we serve.

I love building meaningful SMART goals with the teams I work with as a principal and consultant, and I am obsessed with the process because of the joy and satisfaction it brings to students, teachers, and their schools. I will share a collaborative process that will lead your team to being passionately committed to your SMART goals with a focus on increasing learning and achievement. Having SMART goals and using a collaborative process to develop and sustain these goals is essential. The process I will outline is *a* process, not *the* process. What is non-negotiable is that the goals are built collaboratively and eventually passionately agreed on. Take the process offered and make improvements based on the knowledge you have of your own school and community.

The process I will outline has produced results that far exceeded expectations and led to tremendous school success and growth. This is a process I have utilized during my thirty years as an educational leader in my own schools and in schools across the United States. This process was crucial to Westmont High School earning the 2020 DuFour Award as the best professional learning community (PLC) in the United States. Prior to using this process, Westmont's graduation rate stood at 88 percent. Since implementation in 2013, the average graduation rate has been 99 percent for six years, including 100 percent of African American and Latino students graduating with no one dropping out eight years in a row (Illinois Report Card, 2013, 2020). Our SMART goals process was central to developing the most improved Advanced Placement (AP) program in Illinois, including increases in the number of passed exams (from 29 to 304), AP Scholars (from 3 to 67), and exams passed by underrepresented students (from 2 to 71). Student performance on state-mandated exams increased by double digits and outpaced achievement and growth by all schools with similar demographics. These significant achievement gains were made with the same financial resources, same enrollment, and same demographics in our student body. What did change was our intense commitment to our collaboratively built SMART goals. As coauthors Jan O'Neill and Anne Conzemius (2006) advise, "Great opportunities for improvement are being lost if teams of teachers are not using specific goals on a regular basis" (p. 4).

Our SMART goals influenced everyone's behavior in the school, and they helped inspire and drive actions on a daily basis. To gain this level of passionate commitment from all team members, it was essential that administrators, teachers, students, and parents continuously work together to sustain ongoing implementation. At Westmont from the outset, everyone worked together, and at every step, we agreed to build, affirm, implement, monitor, improve, celebrate, and learn from our SMART goals. There were mistakes and minor setbacks, but in the end, we achieved powerful results because we were a cohesive team that stayed committed to our process. I will outline in detail how we were able to accomplish this. First, a few important guidelines and explanations.

SMART Goals

Many professionals engaged in schoolwork may already be familiar with the *SMART acronym*: strategic and specific, measurable, attainable, results oriented, and time bound (Conzemius & O'Neill, 2014). I would like to add some practical insights that will hopefully make implementation less stressful and more successful. The ideal is to have districtwide goals that are aligned to school goals that are aligned to department goals and then to grade-level, subject, or teacher team goals. However, the absence of goals at any stage of the process should not restrict serious leaders or teams from implementing goals at whatever level they work at.

Strategic and Specific

The goals should be strategic in the sense that you are clear about exactly what the promised land looks like and the goals align with your mission, vision, and values. Where you want to go in the future is clearly linked to what you are doing right now and every day. The goals provide short- and long-term feedback about your progress to accomplishing what you set out to do. The more specific the target, the more likely it is to achieve. Be as precise as possible in constructing the goals. Figure 4.1 is an example of specificity.

By <u>May 30, 2021</u>, the percentage of students attaining <u>proficiency</u>
      Date   **Achievement**

<u>(a score of 540 or higher)</u> on the <u>state-mandated mathematics</u> exam will
      Numeric score   **Targeted assessment**

increase from <u>47 percent (September 2019)</u> to <u>60 percent or higher</u>, and
                  Current data and date   **Achievement percentage**

the students who <u>do not meet proficiency</u> will increase their score (from
                    Contingency

the preassessment of September 2020) by at least <u>fifty or more points</u>.
                                                  Growth by numeric score

Figure 4.1: Sample SMART goal showing specifics.

This goal is specific, and it includes the achievement of all students While there is a realistic concession that not all students will meet state proficiency targets this year, with this goal you are still accountable for all students achieving growth. This is especially important in high-poverty schools where a disproportionate number of students may be facing significant learning deficits. In its *The Condition of Education 2016* report, the National Center for Education Statistics (Kena et al., 2016) attributed living in poverty during early childhood, in part, to lower levels of academic performance "beginning in kindergarten and extending through elementary and high school."

Your focus should be the growth, not the gap. We certainly should be aware of and close learning gaps, but we have to eat these elephants one bite at a time. Teachers and students facing significant deficits are better served by charting the progress they are making than focusing on what they have not yet accomplished. While some students may fall short of the state's target, celebrate the real gains these students and their teachers make. Celebrations that can move a team forward are most powerful when they are genuine and specific (Gostick & Elton, 2007).

Measurable

Making a goal *measurable* means having a quantifiable or qualitative way of knowing that progress has been made. We have to have some way of knowing whether we have had some success. Specific measurements provide the feedback to drive your school and chart your progress. Do not beat yourself up trying to create the perfect measurement. It does not exist. Instead, focus on the things your team and students are held most accountable for (and ideally that all are passionate about) and design the most reasonable measurement possible. By targeting growth and not gaps, you can track and celebrate learning and achievement gains.

Often, measuring what people do repels them because they fear unfair judgment or having what they do reduced to a number. These are reasonable concerns you must address. We need to listen to concerns and make certain that fair, collaboratively built goals will be set with expectations for growth. As an example, if a student or group of students is three or more years below grade level, it is unreasonable to set a goal of making up the deficit in one year. Setting unrealistic goals will discourage people and lead to disengagement. However, do not rob your team, school, and students from the genuine satisfaction that comes from having a measurable goal and achieving it. There is power in short-term wins. Goal attainment provides fuel for your journey. If you come up short, then adopt the growth mindset (Dweck, 2016) and learn from the data's feedback so you can make gains on your next attempt.

Attainable

No one wants to engage in a hopeless struggle. People benefit from regular and genuine boosts of recognition to sustain them on the long journey of continuous improvement. If people rarely or never attain goals, the team is deprived of the occasional "shot in the arm" essential for ongoing dedication. Setting unrealistic goals will undermine passion and commitment. The team must believe they are on a journey where they can be successful.

Researchers Edward L. Deci and Richard M. Ryan (2012), Daniel H. Pink (2009), and Susan Fowler (2014) all argue that to remain motivated, people need to experience a sense of competence or mastery in the work they are doing. People are more likely to stay focused, work harder, and sacrifice if they receive feedback that they are making progress.

Finally, in addition to making goals attainable, I would add it's important to make them *ambitious*. Developing stretch goals in conjunction with SMART goals is another opportunity. I urge teams to set goals just one step below crazy. Not unattainable, but certainly something that will stretch people and be worthy of their best efforts. I take inspiration from the race car driver Mario Andretti (as cited in McLeod, 2015), who said, "If everything seems under control, you're not going fast enough." Pushing ourselves ignites passion. When we are a part of something special, it can be easier to dig a little deeper and remain committed.

The SMART goals are attainable, ambitious, and should be celebrated when achieved. The stretch goals represent what is attainable under a best-case scenario or if everything goes right. For schools facing deep challenges, the focus perhaps should not be on attaining the "best" scores but rather on being the most improved. This is both attainable and ambitious. Again, the focus is on growth.

Results Oriented

I constantly ask myself and the teams I work with, "How do we know we are making a difference?" Have you attended a meeting or engaged in efforts and left wondering, "Did that really make a difference?" SMART goals can provide evidence—the results—that you are making real impact in your sacred work.

With results-oriented SMART goals, you move from intentions to real signs you are making progress and your efforts have led to tangible gains. One of the major themes from *Results: The Key to Continuous School Improvement* author Mike Schmoker (1999) notes is that teachers and schools work too hard; they engage in such important work they should not be left guessing whether they are realizing success. I will readily admit you cannot measure some of the most beautiful efforts and achievements of teachers and students. However, feedback from the results gained from SMART goals give us the real sense that we are making a difference and accomplishing the success we intended.

Some see SMART goals as a tool to hold people accountable, and you should hold one another mutually accountable for the goals the team agreed are important. However, the primary purpose of SMART goals is to celebrate the hard work of your team and to see that your accomplishments are getting you closer to the envisioned promised land. The feedback can also provide guidance as you make your way through your important work.

Tracked and Time Bound

It is important to set clear goal deadlines so you can mark your achievements or take the feedback and chart an improved course of action. You can always try again, but without tracking and time-bound parameters, you will be unable to mark progress and act on relevant feedback.

Tracking is also essential. If the team is serious about its goals, then members should be relentless in tracking the data that will eventually lead to goal attainment. By *relentless* I mean *obsessed*. This tracking becomes manageable when you commit to no more than three goals at a time, you believe passionately that these are the right goals, and you are relentless in their pursuit. To be clear, we commit to no more than three schoolwide goals. Each grade level, department, or teacher team adopts three macro goals for the year. These goals and the progress made toward them should be monitored on a continuous basis and should drive the team's actions.

Here is a summary of how the staff at Westmont High School track and monitor student progress toward graduation on a continuous basis. Before students even enter our school, we have articulation meetings with our eighth-grade sender school to identify students most likely to encounter academic struggles when they enter high school. We expect these students to take part in a bridge program over the summer so they start day one with several advantages instead coming in cold.

My school's team places students who need academic support in a class and monitors their progress daily. Teachers know the minute a student starts digging a hole by not completing work that the team needs to act. Teachers use formative assessments and collaboratively analyze data to strategize how best to support struggling students. Every week, the entire team receives a report that shows every student who is receiving a below-average grade. The data team meets weekly to provide support for failing students. There is a weekly mandatory intervention period to support those students.

Our most valuable work takes place between teachers who interact with students on a daily basis. These teachers, who are committed to seeing all students successful, provide timely interventions in an attempt to alleviate failures in their classes. In addition to the teachers, administrators and counselors build relationships and meet regularly with struggling students (at least once a week and sometimes more) to problem solve and provide supports. Students and their parents are well aware that if the time during the regular school year is not enough, the school has a standards-based additional summer session where all staff recognize students for the work they master and give them an opportunity to complete unfinished work. As soon as students start deviating from the path toward graduation, our entire schoolwide cohesive team with a system of interventions takes action because the SMART goal–focus on graduation (the result) is constantly driving our work.

The SMART Goals Process

As you begin, keep in mind schools should "replace the voluminous strategic planning process with a few very specific goals" (DuFour, DuFour, Eaker, & Many, 2006, p. 120). In addition to focusing on a limited number of SMART goals, the authors lay out the importance of having the staff dedicate itself to the goals. They write, "there is *nothing* more important in determining the effectiveness of a team than each member's understanding of and commitment to the achievement of results-orientated goals to which the group holds itself mutually accountable" (DuFour, DuFour, Eaker, Many, & Mattos, 2016, p. 103). This should come as welcome news to school teams that often feel overwhelmed. The call is to remain focused on a few collaboratively built goals they passionately agree on and pursue with relentless follow-through.

What you are building here is more than just schoolwide SMART goals. You are setting the foundation and practices of your PLC and establishing the beliefs and culture that will sustain the successful implementation of those goals. This process serves as a model for how you will work with one another and what you will focus on as a school community.

Often educators will cite that people do not buy into the PLC process or concepts or that they are not following through with a sense of true commitment. The explanation and steps of this process is to proactively prevent and directly remediate these types of challenges. The reproducible "SMART Goals Process Checklist" (page 76) can help you plan. The process assumes you are starting from the very beginning. I encourage leaders to adapt and improve these steps according to where they are and create revisions that will better serve their school and team.

Encourage People to Dream Big While You Listen and Learn

This step may take between two and four weeks depending on the size of your staff.

The guiding coalition or leadership team should meet with every professional in the school (either individually or in small groups of no more than four). These meetings should be set for about thirty minutes each. With each professional, share the goals, guidelines, and questions for the meeting at least a few days prior.

The goals for these meetings include establishing or sustaining the following.

- Stronger relationships among all team members
- A culture where we listen and learn from one another
- A workplace where we practice collaboration and shared leadership
- A place where we see the best in one another and our school yet are also dedicated to being honest about where we can grow and commit to continuous improvement
- A shared commitment to learning for all students
- A focus on what we can do versus discussing things beyond our control
- A recognition that every minute spent complaining is a minute we should have used to problem solve
- A shared vision we are excited about (big dreams) following through to make come alive with a results orientation
- An approach to our work people are passionately committed to instead of just compliant
- A dedication to celebrating one another and our genuine successes
- A process where we begin to develop, collaboratively build, and passionately agree on three or four schoolwide SMART goals that will lead to significant gains in student learning and achievement

Consider the following guidelines for the meetings.

- We are attempting to develop collaboratively built goals our team can passionately agree on.
- Please be honest and know what you share will be kept in confidence. If there is something you offer we wish to share, we will only do so with your explicit permission.

- We welcome positive comments about colleagues, but please do not make any negative comments about individuals.

- Please share your dreams and aspirations for your own work and for our school. What will bring you joy and fulfillment in the work you do as a professional here? We want to collect these shared dreams in the attempt to bring them to life for our school.

Ask attendees to bring answers to the following questions.

- What are our school community's greatest strengths?

- Where do we most need to improve?

- What will it look like when we are the most improved school in our state? Please be specific.

As your guiding coalition or leadership team members listen, learn, and take notes, make sure to encourage your colleagues to dream big. You are attempting to create SMART goals that will inspire your entire school community.

Draft Three or Four SMART Goals Based on Meetings and What Your School Wants to Achieve

This step may take two or three meetings of the guiding coalition or leadership team.

There will be many benefits from listening and learning from your colleagues and getting them to reflect on their dreams for your school. Not only will you gain valuable insights as a leader from your teammates, you will strengthen your relationships and model excellent listening and learning skills that are crucial in your collaborative teams. Your job now is to take what they share and integrate these thoughts into meaningful SMART goals. It is imperative that as leaders we align the goals with learning for all students. Remember, collaboration should include the guiding coalition's or leadership team's ideas and passions too.

The best goals focus on student achievement and learning gains. Make sure the goals follow the SMART format, and as much as possible, link the rough drafts to the thoughts from *dream big* staff meetings. There may not be perfect alignment, but these goals will be a tangible way to mark progress in areas of most importance to the staff and the students.

Often, schoolwide goals will focus on the following.

- Improving student-achievement performance the local, district, state, and national assessments measure at each grade level

- Increasing the graduation rate

- Reducing the failure rate

- Increasing student involvement in rigorous classes (including AP or International Baccalaureate [IB] courses)

- Increasing student success on AP or IB exams

- Decreasing the number of disciplinary referrals

- Improving social-emotional well-being as measured by pre- and post-student surveys

- Increasing the number of student service and volunteer hours

Your team has some autonomy and latitude in creating the goals. However, it makes sense to align them with district, state, or province expectations. The team's desire to see students have opportunities and to demonstrate gains in learning could be present in goals connected to gatekeeping exams. We are not reducing everything to standardized tests scores, but acknowledging that students and educators are often held accountable for results on these assessments. Therefore, I suggest having one of the three or four goals target the district, state, or province expectations. Pay attention to growth instead of simply bottom-line scores; you can pursue other passions with the remaining goals.

When a schoolwide SMART goal includes standardized test performance, the teams and students I have worked with find relevance and purpose in breaking down the test into the meaningful skills and knowledge being evaluated. Here, students and teachers can find learning and growth in specific, relevant learning targets being assessed.

If your school's goals are predetermined for you, or the state mandates goals you must follow, do your best to integrate what your colleagues believe in to match the required goals. This is not ideal, but under the circumstances, it is the next best thing. Once again, do not look for the perfect measurement. Instead, find connections between what you believe in, what you want to accomplish, and a measurable way to mark real progress.

Develop Research and Real Evidence to Support the First Draft

This may take two to three hours per goal.

Once you have your first draft and before you present these SMART goals to your entire team, marshal the evidence to demonstrate your goals are worth your school's time and energy. There is a mountain of research to support your team's efforts to increasing reading and mathematics proficiency, including more students in rigorous courses, increasing graduation rates, reducing failure rates, attending to students' social-emotional welfare, and boosting service hours. Make a rock-solid case that research supports what you are doing to move the school in the right direction.

Gather the supporting research, prepare to make a presentation to your staff, and be creative in finding ways to present your case and why it is so important everyone follow through with the SMART goals. Provide a small packet of evidence for each goal. In each packet, cite and present the evidence in the form of literature, white papers, and research articles. Make the purpose clear to all team members.

In addition to the supporting research packet for each goal, offer other forms of evidence that may move your team. For example, when we set out to increase our graduation rate, we presented significant data to show the devastating impact dropping out has on individual students and the United States at large. We also made it personal. We showed photographs of our former students as freshmen who eventually dropped out. The percentages and statistics were compelling, but seeing the photos of the students who dropped out made it personal and had an impact. Behind the numbers and goals are real students, and by showing the faces of these students, it brought the data to life.

We also gathered all incoming ninth graders in the auditorium with our entire staff. For years, 10 percent or more of our students did not graduate. As a visual for students, we separated 10 percent of the incoming class to one side of the auditorium and announced that if the trends of the last ten years continued, these students represented the number who would drop out and never graduate. Seeing that 10 percent brought the statistic to life. It was also made clear to the students that they are part of the solution.

Present the Draft of the SMART Goals, Supporting Research, and Evidence at an All-Staff Meeting

This step may take about one hour or one all-staff meeting.

During this meeting, thank the staff for taking the time to share their ideas and dreams with you. Let them know that you attempted to integrate what they shared as your team created these SMART goals. Remind staff that the plan is to develop goals that will provide direction and a sense of accomplishment for your entire school team. Reiterate the aim to collaboratively build goals everyone can pursue with passion.

Remind everyone of the purpose of the *dream big* meetings that produced the goals, and make it clear these are a first draft, you will present accompanying research, and goals may be revised based on feedback from the team. Clarify that you will discuss the goals, concerns, and questions with them in upcoming meetings and create a plan and take action to support the pursuit of these goals. (This action should include meeting the needs the team identifies, including staff development and training and interventions to ensure successful implementation.)

It may be beneficial to present the research on why a team needs SMART goals. Visit **go.SolutionTree.com/PLCbooks** for the reproducible "Why Do We Need SMART Goals?" for a list of research references and quotes.

Present the first draft of the goals to the entire staff, along with the research and evidence. Make connections between what was shared in the individual or small-group meetings as often as possible. Give the entire staff time to read and digest the materials, and ask them to prepare questions, concerns, suggestions, and needs based on what you presented for the next time you meet.

Facilitate All-Staff Discussions About the SMART Goals, Possible Revisions, and How to Pursue Their Meaningful Implementation

This step may take three or four all-staff meetings that last between forty-five minutes to an hour.

The leadership team must perform a real balancing act at this point in the process. We cannot rush, but at the same time, there is a need to move forward and utilize others' steps to make progress. It is essential to elicit the staff's true thoughts. I cannot overemphasize the need for the most honest of communication. As leaders, we must make ourselves vulnerable to ideas that may be critical of the SMART goals we present. In the beginning of this process, respect and answer all concerns and questions. If we disallow authentic concerns and questions, the result will be team members not sharing their concerns and doing this work with lingering doubts, and our being unable to establish a culture of peak performance and true collaboration.

We want real collaboration and passionate commitment. At this stage, we are also modeling the type of listening and collaboration we want to see in our teacher-led data team meetings. It is better for the concerns to be out in the open than kept shut away until the next meeting. Collaboration and compromise are part of the process. There will be obstacles, but if we do not identify them, we will not be able to start to remove them, and we must be certain to not only listen but take action when possible to alleviate genuine constraints toward progress.

If we rush the process, we will not gain genuine commitment. Our team members deserve to have a deep understanding of the *why* (mission) and *what* (vision) we are trying to accomplish. Ask for feedback, but do not get bogged down by team members who may be what Luis F. Cruz (2020) calls *C.A.V.E.* people (Colleagues Against Virtually Everything). My experience is that most team members are honorable and dedicated to doing what is right. A few people are habitual contrarians. While we should take all concerns and questions seriously, the leadership team is wise enough to sort out authentic concerns from those that may be less than reasonable. Reasonable people may also have legitimate concerns about the SMART goals and the direction we are set to take as a school. It is better to have a chance to address these concerns, clear up misperceptions, or make fair concessions before asking the staff to proceed with passion.

The days between the three or four meetings allow ideas to percolate. Encourage questions, and answer them on an individual basis. Small-group conversations should take place. Follow up on concerns voiced in the large-group setting with very supportive and positive individual or small-group meetings between members of the leadership team and staff members. Conduct a fourth meeting to address remaining concerns.

If the consensus of the group points toward revising the goals, it is wise to incorporate thoughtful adjustments the majority of the team recommends or endorses. This is our initial implementation that we will monitor over time (hopefully several years). We can make adjustments going forward based on what we learn and the student-performance information we collect. As part of building consensus and as a cohesive team, making minor, reasonable adjustments that lead to greater support from team members is fair and a wise way to proceed.

The next steps will also be useful in addressing concerns and building consensus.

Ask Every Staff Member to Anonymously Respond in Writing to *Why I Passionately Support Our SMART Goals* or *This Is What I Need to Passionately Support Our SMART Goals*

For this step, give staff members advance notice and thirty minutes to complete a response. If people ask for more time or the chance to do the work outside the meeting, allow it.

Think of this part of the process as a formative assessment. In PLC work, we ask teachers to review data, adjust, reteach, and not blame students when the desired outcome is unmet. As leaders, we should model what we expect from our teachers. If the majority of the staff is supportive, how can we build an even more cohesive team and more support for the SMART goals? If serious concerns exist and the majority of the staff is not passionate, what adjustments might you need to make to bring about the desired results?

The question is also important because it asks staff members with concerns not just to reject the proposed SMART goals, but to lay out a plan of action and to problem solve. They cannot just reject the proposed goals. They must be clear about specifically what they need to be passionate. In a sense, they may be helping to create a pathway to agreement and commitment.

The focus here is to do some progress monitoring and have another opportunity to learn about and address concerns all in the service of building a cohesive team with mutually agreed-on goals. There will also be staff members who appreciate the process and what has been created. They are eager to move forward. Hear and recognize these voices. Some team members may both be passionate and have lingering concerns. Honor this sentiment as well.

While attempting to create a community of trust and openness, you want to remove any barriers to the staff communicating their most authentic ideas. It is better to have little doubt that staff are communicating their true thoughts than people holding back and telling leaders what they think they want to hear. That is why we ask for typed (not handwritten), anonymous answers to our questions.

Formulate Written Responses to Staff Affirmations of and Concerns About SMART Goals

This step may take three or four hours, and the leadership team or guiding coalition should share the work with the entire staff.

As the leadership team or guiding coalition reads the responses from the staff, look for and separate them by theme. It is also important to note staff members who express real passion for the work that has been done and excitement for the work ahead. Recognize opportunities to take action that will support staff needs and successful pursuit of the goals.

Create a document that authentically expresses the team's hopes and needs. Admit that some of the challenges you face still need some time and more work. The purposes of writing your responses include clearing up misconceptions, addressing legitimate concerns, sharing positive responses to encourage fellow team members, and demonstrating that some consensus is emerging for the SMART goals. Your answers will not be comprehensive or address every single concern in detail. The goal is not to solve every problem. It is to demonstrate that you are building a cohesive team whose members listen to one another and engage in problem solving. Make copies of this document (your leadership team responses to concerns and needed supports) for each staff member and distribute at the next meeting.

Share Responses to Affirmations and Concerns About the SMART Goals With Staff and Discuss What Was Written

This step may take one meeting but no more than two.

Share the document with all staff members, and ask everyone to read it silently and independently. Keep the goal of this process at the forefront. Facilitating a collaborative discussion honors staff concerns but moves toward passionate consensus. While reading the staff responses and during continued conversations, recognize opportunities to take action that will support staff needs and successful pursuit of the SMART goals.

Your entire team has listened, gathered, and presented data and ideas; engaged in genuine discussion; shared ideas in writing; and expressed ideas in a whole-team setting. There is value in these exchanges, but now identify a few actionable items to put in place to support your efforts. Doing this will also demonstrate that you will follow through on ideas to support the efforts and goals of the team. People need to realize that you are serious about follow-through. Taking action will show that we will make things happen.

Respond to Concerns With Specific Actions and by Implementing Programs to Support Team and SMART Goals

By this time, teachers will most likely have identified specific staff development or training necessary to successfully implement the SMART goals. They might also have requested programs, resources, and supports that will aid them in accomplishing the goals. As much as possible, honor these requests. Taking action and following through on needs staff articulate shows you are serious and willing to stand shoulder to shoulder in implementation. People feel valued when they get this kind of support. Principal support is one of the most significant indicators of job satisfaction (Olsen & Huang, 2019). When leaders address concerns with actions that support staff, educators are more likely to be passionate about their commitment to the work.

During our process, teachers voiced the following concerns.

- They needed training on how to develop learning targets and better common formative assessments in order to reach our goals. We provided staff development.

- They needed protected time to work collaboratively as teacher-led data teams. We built weekly time into the teacher workday so they could collaborate.

- They worried about students who would not complete meaningful work outside class or who needed additional time and practice to be successful. We built a pyramid of interventions to support these students and their teachers.

Conduct an Anonymous Survey to Gauge Support for Chosen SMART Goals

It is imperative to get authentic feedback about the team members' commitment to the goals you processed together. Conduct an anonymous staff survey that asks for this information. You should *want* to know exactly where the team stands in regard to its level of commitment. Once again, you are modeling how you expect teachers to respond to student-performance information and data. Teachers may feel intimidated to examine and share student-performance results. We ask teachers to engage in this work and learn from the feedback. Leaders can show the way.

Our team asked our teacher union leaders to administer the survey anonymously so we could elicit the most honest feedback possible. You don't want teachers to fear possible retribution from administration and not give real answers. If you do not have a teachers' union, find an informal leader from your faculty who is mutually trusted and respected to administer the survey. Ask teachers to respond to statements like those you see in figure 4.2.

	Strongly agree	Agree	Disagree	Strongly disagree
I am passionately committed to a graduation rate of 99 percent or higher for every class.				
I am passionately committed to our SMART goal that claims by the state exam in May 2021, the percentage of fifth-grade students meeting or exceeding grade-level proficiency on the state reading assessment will increase from 40 percent to at least 60 percent, with any student not meeting proficiency demonstrating at least one year of growth.				
What will it take to get behind the SMART goals if you are not committed at this time?				

Figure 4.2: Anonymous survey gauging SMART goals support.

Because of the level of engagement and collaboration in this process, there should be consensus. However, leave room in the survey for staff to explain specifically what it will take to get behind the SMART goals if they are not committed at this time. That said, do not expect a unanimous response. Some people need to see the work in action before they will commit. Some team members may be C.A.V.E. people (Cruz, 2020). No matter what the survey outcome, share the results with the entire staff. If 67 percent or more of the team in an anonymous survey a fellow teacher administers answer that they agree or strongly agree with a SMART goal, it is a strong consensus. Present the survey results to the entire staff, and let them know the team has generally agreed, but that you will continue looking for ways to provide support. Explain that you ask for commitment from those staff who have continued concerns so you can operate as a cohesive team for the benefit of your students and school.

If slightly less than two-thirds of the staff cannot commit, then there may be need for some further adjustments or clarification. After more discussion and some revision, take another survey. If less than half of the team is not committed, your leadership team or guiding coalition may not be listening carefully to concerns, or perhaps you need significant revisions and different SMART goals. There may be situations where a significant portion of a staff is unreasonable. However, if it is more than half the staff, either there is a real culture problem, or you and your guiding coalition did not follow the SMART goals process with fidelity.

Most often, this process results in more than two-thirds of the team expressing a real commitment to the goals. This sends a clear message to those still dissenting—they are in the small minority and need to get on board. The tail cannot wag the dog. Send the message that you are moving forward and the fair thing to do is to support the will of the team.

Monitor Progress

This part of the process is ongoing.

Your intensity to monitor progress toward these SMART goals demonstrates your commitment to them. You should collectively look at data on a weekly, if not daily, basis. The data come from intermittent progress monitoring of your SMART goal measurements. Share that data with the team. Your leaders and team must be thinking strategically. Break long-term SMART goals into much smaller components. Ask yourself, "What are the specific interim actions I must take, and what are the specific short-term measurements that will make course corrections and interventions feasible for reaching our long-term goal?" While you are monitoring progress, you are always keeping the ultimate goal in mind.

Real-world examples of this kind of progress monitoring are abundant. Medical staff constantly monitor patients in the intensive care unit. If you are preparing a special meal, you stay at the stove. If you are playing a competitive game, the minute you lose focus is likely when you will lose points. Teams must pay careful, constant attention to student-performance information directly related to SMART goals.

Westmont High School did not attain a true 99 percent graduation rate for six years in a row by only beginning to track progress when students were juniors or seniors. We knew we wanted to be four years into the future—with every student graduating—so we *backward designed* (Wiggins & McTighe, 2005) every step before those students even attended our school. We used backward design by starting with their graduation and figuring out, step by step, what it would take to get students there. If we waited until the end of their first year (or even their first semester or first quarter), it might be too late. We were proactive, anticipating where students might start struggling, and took proactive measures to prevent those struggles. The minute students started falling off the path, we knew because we were monitoring their progress in their classes at least weekly. We created immediate interventions driven by weekly progress checks.

If you fall short, then learn from the feedback, adjust, and recommit.

Celebrate Short- and Long-Term SMART Goal Successes

This part of the process is ongoing.

You must celebrate every genuine instance of growth and progress. The purpose of creating the SMART goals is to provide direction and give people a sense of accomplishment. The celebrations and positive encouragement are the fuel that keep your team going through the challenging work.

Find every opportunity to celebrate authentic success. Post SMART goal success on placards in your classrooms. Print it on the backs of T-shirts and on banners hanging in your hallways. Announce it at every student assembly and faculty, parent, and board of education meeting. Psychologist and mindsets expert Carol S. Dweck (2016) encourages it, and at Westmont, we agree it is worth recognizing and celebrating effort and learning and not just accomplishments. Include recognitions and celebrations of teams and people who took risks and maybe came up short but learned something valuable in the process.

Just about every other Friday, we hold a twenty-minute all-school assembly to celebrate our culture, have fun together, inspire one another, and give a short update on SMART goal progress. Sometimes the goal update takes only a minute, and sometimes it is the assembly's major focus (like when we won a national award or move up substantially in a national or state ranking). The point is that we all come together to reinforce the focus, celebrate accomplishments, and take joy in our collective endeavor. Having fun celebrations is crucial to achieving and sustaining long-term success.

Conclusion

The process I offer requires a little less than a semester to implement. However, the work of continuous improvement is never finished. A semester may seem a little long to some, but if the foundation is built well, it can set you on the right course and serve your team for years to come. I offer specifics because I want to be as clear as possible on a way to proceed. My hope is that you will take these ideas, use the creative genius of your team, and make improvements to this process so that it will best serve the needs of your school, students, and staff.

Our team at Westmont High School in Illinois was honored to be selected as the 2020 DuFour Award winner as the top PLC in the United States, primarily because of our student learning gains and achieved results. The process I share was essential in achieving these results. Our team knows we have much more work to do. However, it was their humility, willingness to learn, and commitment to seeing the best in one another that also drove the change and improvement process.

It inspires me to know that fellow educators from everywhere engage in this noble struggle and that together, we will make a powerful difference in the lives of our students. My hope is that these ideas can benefit what you are doing to fight poverty and support your students, and if they do help, then I will be honored to have made a small contribution to your most noble work. Be tenacious and passionate in your sacred work, and I wish you the very best on your most important journey.

SMART Goals Process Checklist

Step	Accomplished
1. Encourage people to dream big while you listen and learn.	
2. Draft three or four SMART goals based on meetings and what your school wants to achieve.	
3. Develop research and real evidence to support the first draft.	
4. Present the draft of the SMART goals, supporting research, and evidence at an all-staff meeting.	
5. Facilitate all-staff discussions about the SMART goals, possible revisions, and how to pursue their meaningful implementation.	
6. Ask every staff member to anonymously respond in writing to *Why I passionately support our SMART goals* or *This is what I need to passionately support our SMART goals*.	
7. Formulate written responses to staff affirmations of and concerns about SMART goals.	
8. Share responses to affirmations and concerns about the SMART goals with staff and discuss what was written.	
9. Respond to concerns with specific actions and by implementing programs to support team and SMART goals.	
10. Conduct an anonymous survey to gauge support for chosen SMART goals.	
11. Monitor progress.	
12. Celebrate short- and long-term SMART goal successes.	

References and Resources

Buffum, A., Mattos, M., & Malone, J. (2018). *Taking action: A handbook for RTI at Work.* Bloomington, IN: Solution Tree Press.

Conzemius, A. E., & O'Neill, J. (2014). *The handbook for SMART school teams: Revitalizing best practices for collaboration* (2nd ed.). Bloomington, IN: Solution Tree Press.

Cruz, L. F. (2020, January). *Time for change: What do we do when colleagues at our site refuse to participate in the RTI at Work process?* [Conference presentation]. RTI at Work Institute, Houston, TX.

Deci, E. L., & Ryan, R. M. (2012). Self-determination theory. In P. A. M. Van Lange, A. W. Kruglanski, & E. T. Higgins (Eds.), *Handbook of theories of social psychology* (pp. 416–436). Thousand Oaks, CA: SAGE.

DuFour, R., DuFour, R., Eaker, R., & Many, T. (2006). *Learning by doing: A handbook for Professional Learning Communities at Work.* Bloomington, IN: Solution Tree Press.

DuFour, R., DuFour, R., Eaker, R., Many, T. W., & Mattos, M. (2016). *Learning by doing: A handbook for Professional Learning Communities at Work* (3rd ed.). Bloomington, IN: Solution Tree Press.

Dweck, C. S. (2016). *Mindset: The new psychology of success* (Updated ed.). New York: Ballantine Books.

Fowler, S. (2014). *Why motivating people doesn't work . . . and what does: The new science of leading, energizing, and engaging.* San Francisco: Berrett-Koehler.

Gostick, A., & Elton, C. (2007). *The carrot principle: How the best managers use recognition to engage their people, retain talent, and accelerate performance.* New York: Free Press.

Illinois Report Card. (2013). *Westmont High School, CUSD 201, Westmont, Illinois.* Accessed at http://webprod.isbe.net/ereportcard/publicsite/getReport.aspx?year=2013&code=190222 0100001_e.pdf on March 10, 2021.

Illinois Report Card. (2020). *Westmont High School (9–12).* Accessed at www.illinoisreportcard.com/school .aspx?source=trends&source2=graduationrate&Schoolid=190222010260001 on March 9, 2021.

Kena, G., Hussar, W., McFarland, J., de Brey, C., Musu-Gillette, L., Wang, X., et al. (2016). *The condition of education 2016.* Accessed at https://files.eric.ed.gov/fulltext/ED565888.pdf on March 22, 2021.

Kramer, S. V., & Schuhl, S. (2017). *School improvement for all: A how-to guide for doing the right work.* Bloomington, IN: Solution Tree Press.

McLeod, L. E. (2015). *Everything is not under control: That's a good thing.* Accessed at www.huffpost.com /entry/everything-is-not-under-control-thats-a-good-thing_b_8332204 on November 16, 2020.

O'Neill, J., & Conzemius, A. (2006). *The power of SMART goals: Using goals to improve student learning.* Bloomington, IN: Solution Tree Press.

Olsen, A. A., & Huang, F. L. (2019). Teacher job satisfaction by principal support and teacher cooperation: Results from the schools and staffing survey. *Education Policy Analysis Archives, 27*(11), 1–31.

Pink, D. H. (2009). *Drive: The surprising truth about what motivates us.* New York: Riverhead Books.

Quick, K. (2016). *Hartford Public Schools: Striving for equity through interdistrict programs.* Accessed at https://tcf.org/content/report/hartford-public-schools/?agreed=1 on March 8, 2021.

Schmoker, M. (1999). *Results: The key to continuous school improvement* (2nd ed.). Alexandria, VA: Association for Supervision and Curriculum Development.

Wiggins, G., & McTighe, J. (2005). *Understanding by design* (Expanded 2nd ed.). Alexandria, VA: Association for Supervision and Curriculum Development.

 **Kimberly Rodriguez Cano,** a consultant with over thirty years' experience, is a former transition specialist, special education coordinator, professional development director, and school improvement specialist for the Florida Department of Education, supporting educators in that state and across the United States.

She served as a leader for the revision of state-improvement plans, the development of a multi-tiered system of supports framework, and the advancement of professional development workshops focusing on impactful outcomes. She has presented nationally to unite improvement efforts and school culture with a focus on professional learning communities (PLCs), response to intervention (RTI), student engagement, and special student groups.

She was also a high school special education teacher and transition specialist in Virginia before returning to her home state of Florida in 2007.

Kimberly is an innovative leader in educational improvement and organization restructuring. Her collaborative approach to school improvement, professional development, and educator quality maximizes learning opportunities for all students. Kimberly works to improve outcomes by facilitating the effective use of data-driven instruction planning through a collective problem-solving approach. She continues to generate evidence of increased achievement results for aspiring schools, especially those that serve diverse populations.

She earned a bachelor's degree in psychology from Saint Leo University as class valedictorian and holds a master of science in special education leadership from Old Dominion University.

To book Kimberly Rodriguez Cano for professional development, contact pd@ SolutionTree.com.

Aligning the Arrows for Continuous-Improvement Planning With SMART Goals

Kimberly Rodriguez Cano

School improvement should never depend on who
will do the work, but rather on how educators work
together to achieve success for all students.

—*Sharon V. Kramer and Sarah Schuhl*

It was October 11, 2016, when I was completing the final revisions of a needs-assessment summary for a middle school in Georgia. It was identified as a *focus school*, indicating that it needed to significantly improve student-achievement results the following spring. Along with reviewing multiple data sources and classroom environments, I met with administrators, teachers, parents, and students to further gather information to assist me in developing an effective action plan for the year. Christopher Ridley, the principal at the time, was enthusiastic about the support and communicated his vision to me almost immediately: "to provide a community-based school that continues to move from good to great by striving for excellence in everything that they do" (personal communication, October 11, 2016).

We reviewed the SMART goals (Conzemius & O'Neill, 2014) from the school's current improvement plan and how he and the leadership team were ready and willing to make the necessary changes to improve the outcomes for all students. As I met with the other groups, it was clear they wanted improved outcomes. It was evident there were many improvement efforts going on. There were substantial supports from the district staff, a structure for teacher collaboration, and a genuine belief in student learning. I recall thinking at the time, "How can we coordinate and align all these efforts? How can we get these arrows pointing and eventually flying in the same direction?"

I had completed many of these reports at different schools, and it became clear this work would mirror the others. Sure, each school has unique characteristics, but creating an environment where educators align their efforts has always been a challenge. Many times this work is conducted in isolation. Luckily, Ridley was ready, willing, and able to take on this challenge.

Various industries use the term *continuous improvement* to describe a process or approach to problem solving that represents an ongoing effort to improve outcomes (American Society for Quality, n.d.). In continuously improving systems, change occurs both quickly and incrementally, as organizations learn from experience while testing and refining strategies to produce better results. In schools that require improvement, *continuous improvement* refers to a school, district, or other academic institution's ongoing commitment to quality, evidence-based improvement efforts that are integrated into the daily work of individuals, contextualized within a system, and iterative (Park, Hironaka, Carver, & Nordstrum, 2013). At a school or district level, continuous improvement may refer to ongoing efforts to improve operational practices and processes related to efficiency, effectiveness, and student outcomes.

Even though it is considered at all levels of the school, at the classroom level, continuous improvement may refer to using timely, accurate data to regularly inform and improve teaching practices. Collaborative teacher teams engage in the learning cycle to ensure that they are using common formative assessment data to drive quality instruction practices. Leaders at priority schools can sustain the school-improvement process if they align SMART goals using a common focus from their teachers, teams, and school. The guiding coalition or leadership team should develop and monitor goals on a frequent basis, and modify them according to student-achievement data. In many instances, the guiding coalition collaboratively develops a school-improvement plan's SMART goals, but rarely provides them to teacher teams to develop their team goals, and they are seldom given to teachers to support development of individual growth goals.

If leaders facilitate a coordinated set of activities in their school that transcend the improvement plan itself, they can exponentially enhance school-improvement efforts. I furthered Jan O'Neill and Anne Conzemius's (2006) SMART goals by developing SMARTer and SMARTest goals to calibrate, expand, and align school-improvement efforts beyond the guiding coalition. Collaborative teams design and align these *SMARTer goals* to maximize their efforts to support the schoolwide SMART goals. Collaborative teams should focus on classroom-level data as it impacts schoolwide goals, breaking the SMARTer goals further. Individual teachers then develop *SMARTest goals* to support student learning and professional growth.

This chapter will explore how schools can maximize improvement results by taking a deeper dive into already established SMART goals and aligning these goals to all levels of school functioning.

Goal Establishment

A school accountability system can vary from location to location, but most concentrate on summative assessment results in reading, writing, mathematics, and student groups and growth, with additional factors such as graduation rate, attendance, parent involvement, and community engagement. For those schools identified as in urgent need of improvement or deemed as a priority school, these goals become additionally significant.

A diverse team should collaboratively develop SMART goals to include in a well-designed school-improvement plan that guides schools to annually sustain improved results. These goals are typically grounded in an established accountability system intended to be a road map to guide each school's activities annually. According to Richard DuFour, Rebecca DuFour, Robert Eaker, Thomas W. Many, and Mike Mattos (2016), "A critical step in moving an organization from rhetoric to reality is to establish the indicators of progress to be monitored, the process and timeline for monitoring them, and the means of sharing results and getting input from people throughout the organization" (p. 35). The annual state summative assessments are driven by mastery of grade-level standards. However, schools will maximize improvement opportunities by refining implementation endeavors.

I would insist teachers hold the most vital role in ensuring student learning and they are the catalysts that pilot the school's outcomes. Goals that align with the individual teacher level and are based on student performance and growth are the SMARTest goals of all. A continuous-improvement culture, where leaders reinforce teachers to reflect on their practice as it relates to student-learning data, is most advantageous.

Using the professional learning community (PLC) process to drive monitoring of formative assessment data will ensure individual teachers and collaborative teams also monitor these goals to improve the overall school-performance level. School-improvement plans will truly be a working document that will better support guiding coalitions to engage in an authentic continuous-improvement model. Student-achievement data that reflect the goals will drive student-centered learning. This focus and aligned efforts on improving student learning assures positive outcomes for priority schools.

Educators often perceive improvement planning as a daunting task, but most schools can maximize results by designing an aligned action and monitoring plan. Leaders can follow these steps to design a plan.

1. Establish SMART school-level goals (page 59).
2. Establish SMARTer collaborative team-level goals.
3. Establish SMARTest individual teacher-level goals.

Establishing School-Level Goals

The guiding coalition collaboratively develops schoolwide (or SMART) goals. In priority schools, teams must carefully consider the accountability measures the state's department of education establishes and the district's improvement goals. When considering the attainable portion of the SMART goal, primary consideration to reflect on these accountability measures is the focal point. The guiding coalition should be composed of a diverse group of leaders, teachers, and staff who have a collective responsibility and expertise to effectively review current data and determine the overall strategic plan for the school. This team has a solid understanding of the established accountability parameters and not only models collaborative practices but also establishes these structures for teams. The school-level guiding coalitions also have defined roles and expectations for teams that clearly delineate the school-level SMART goals.

Leaders and the guiding coalition critically identify SMART goals from the school's improvement plan. They should consider a review of the prior year's goals and most recently developed goals. After reviewing the goals, along with pertinent and current data, the goals should emphasize and focus on student achievement and growth. Some state, provincial, and district offices set growth targets while others may not; instead, these groups rely on the schools themselves to determine their own targets. A goal example is: *By June 2023, ABC School will improve outcomes in English language arts (ELA) and mathematics by increasing the proficiency rate to meet the school's annual target rates, as set by the state, of 47.35 percent (ELA) and 33.42 percent (mathematics) by the 2022–2023 state summative assessment.*

Your guiding coalition should consider these questions during schoolwide SMART goal development.

- What are the expected accountability requirements?
- Which student groups need the most support?
- What will be the monitoring plan?
- What will we modify if progress is not being met?
- Which roles will we need to consider?
- How will we communicate the expectations to collaborative teams?

Establishing Collaborative Team-Level Goals

The unique structures of the school can help develop and determine collaborative team-level goals, depending on how leaders establish the collaborative teams. For example, secondary schools may have content-specific collaborative teams while elementary schools may have grade-specific collaborative teams. Some smaller schools may have unique team configurations. In any case or situation, the collaborative teams should determine their goals after careful consideration of the school-level goals. Leaders should emphasize the importance of how the team goals will support the school-level goals, not the task of goal completion. Depending on the dynamics of each collaborative team, the guiding coalition may need to facilitate this process.

Depending on common practice, the teams should identify SMARTer goals for their collaborative or grade-level teams. These collaboratively team-developed goals should align with the school-improvement plan goals. For example, *By June 2022, the eighth-grade team will improve the overall student proficiency rate in reading by 10 percent and in mathematics by 13 percent, each quarter, as measured by common formative assessment data and diagnostic benchmark assessments.*

Your collaborative teams should consider these questions while developing SMARTer goals.

- Do our goals align and support the school-level goals?
- How do we prioritize classroom instruction and the development of formative assessments to support achieving improved performance?
- Are there student groups we need to more closely monitor?

- What evidence will we use and review to determine progress?

- What resources and support do we need as a collaborative team to support us reaching and exceeding our goals?

- How will we communicate progress to the guiding coalition, families, and students?

Establishing Individual Teacher-Level Goals

When considering individual teacher goals, leaders should be especially encouraging of this mission. Teachers not only are responsible for planning for daily instruction, but are at the heart of student learning. By aligning these efforts, teachers can be the key to schools' improved performance each year. Supporting the use of common formative assessment data to drive their individual results, along with frequent monitoring of individual student growth and standard mastery, must be at the epicenter of these SMARTest goals. Leaders can further boost these efforts by providing effective and descriptive feedback in a timely manner when conducting classroom observations (page 163).

After collaborative teams establish their SMARTer goals, teachers can develop the SMARTest goals for individual growth and reflection. These goals should align with the collaborative team goals and may also be considered for professional-growth plans. Leadership and administrators can review each teacher evaluation system to ensure buy-in from teachers. Developing evaluative growth-plan goals that also align with the school-level and collaborative team goals are certainly a win-win for all.

Since teachers are at the forefront of student learning in all schools, leaders must ensure that not only are the goals teachers develop for sustained student growth focused on viable student groups but also are strategically designed for enhanced student achievement and improvement results. For example, *By June 2022, Mr. Smith will improve classroom student performance by increasing Lexile scores for students who are receiving special education services by at least 200 points as measured and monitored monthly by progress monitoring data (accelerated reader).*

When developing these goals, the guiding coalition, collaborative teams, and individual teachers should consider the impact of how these goals align to drive the overall improvement efforts. Keep in mind that simply developing goals in a collaborative manner will support a unified approach to improvement efforts. However, real improvement is achieved by aligning the efforts of all staff members instead of random acts of improvement. Figure 5.1 (page 84) shows the alignment of SMART and SMARTer goals to SMARTest goals.

Leaders should support each set or level of goal development by reconsidering the following questions.

- Is the goal written in SMART format? Is each of the goals interdependent?

- Are the data for each set of goals aligned to the overall schoolwide SMART goals? How can we use the same set of data to monitor each goal level? What are the data sources that provide evidence for the goals?

SMART Goal	By June 2023, ABC School will improve outcomes in English language arts (ELA) and mathematics by increasing the proficiency rate to meet the school's annual target rates, as set by the state, of 47.35 percent (ELA) and 33.42 percent (mathematics) by the 2022–2023 state summative assessment.
SMARTer Goal	By June 2022, the eighth-grade team will improve the overall student proficiency rate in reading by 10 percent and in mathematics by 13 percent, each quarter, as measured by common formative assessment data and diagnostic benchmark assessments.
SMARTest Goal	By June 2022, Mr. Smith will improve classroom student performance by increasing Lexile scores for students who are receiving special education services by at least 200 points as measured and monitored monthly by progress monitoring data (accelerated reader).

Figure 5.1: Alignment of SMART and SMARTER goals to SMARTEST goals.

- Does each goal set have a monitoring schedule? How often will we monitor the schoolwide (SMART) goals? How often will we monitor the collaborative team (SMARTer) goals? How often will we monitor the individual teacher (SMARTest) goals?
- Who will be responsible for reporting on each goal?
- How will we monitor if we are on track to reach our goals?
- What evidence will we collect to show progress on each goal?
- How can the data we collect support other schoolwide initiatives?

Table 5.1 can guide leaders in supporting staff with each set of goals at each level of alignment.

Through this process, leaders designing and supporting the SMARTest goals collaboratively with individual teachers can support the alignment of school-improvement efforts. As teachers gain a better understanding of their role in improvement efforts, leader can begin to identify areas of critical need for student learning.

Table 5.1: Developing Aligned Goals

Staff	Outcomes
SMART Goals	
Guiding Coalition	• Understanding and documenting strategies that support the school-improvement plan • Customizing the school-improvement plan to fit the needs of the district and school • Determining assumptions, constraints, and expectations for teams to include when calibrating vocabulary • Establishing structures for collaborative teaming and facilitating collaborative team practices and data review protocols • Defining standards of higher learning for all students and student groups • Utilizing summative and formative data to drive modification of action planning • Defining the roles of all stakeholders • Developing understanding of the data and how they impact student learning • Establishing leadership teams and strategies that integrate all stakeholders (including communities and families) into the process • Structuring communications that support a collaborative mindset • Implementing guidelines for data-based instructional practices
SMARTer Goals	
Collaborative Teacher Teams	• Establishing communications structure within teaming structures • Understanding data protocols to focus on student learning and results • Understanding individual teacher strengths • Developing lesson plans that drive learning improvement • Allocating resource requests by aligning district- and school-based initiatives to student learning
SMARTest Goals	
Individual Teachers	• Establishing systematic sharing events to report, evaluate, and adjust strategies • Understanding best practices to meet the needs of all students • Using communication to support growth plan goals and promote student progress • Aligning resources to student needs • Using common formative data to guide progress • Planning actions by aligning them with collaborative teams' efforts • Streamlining classroom action plans and concentration of efforts • Supporting student groups and individual student learning

School-Improvement Goal Monitoring

Now that staff have goals at each level, how do school leaders ensure monitoring takes place? As with any improvement plan, staff should develop a monitoring schedule (if not immediately after establishing the SMART, SMARTer, and SMARTest goals). Depending on the availability of data sources, school leaders should consider how to effectively utilize data inside the current sources. For example, if collaborative teacher teams are frequently looking at common formative assessment data, how can the school as a whole successfully review and apply these data to determine progress toward each level of the goals? Figure 5.2 shows how to monitor established goals with common data. The reproducible "Goal Monitoring With Common Data" (page 90) can help you plan.

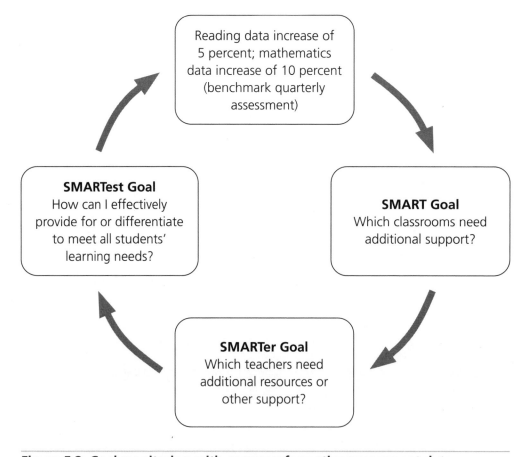

Figure 5.2: Goal monitoring with common formative assessment data.

In an effort to create an efficiency of practice, staff should utilize current common formative data readily available as the primary source to monitor progress toward all established goals. When collecting and reviewing data, the data should be applicable and inform goal progress at each level. Evaluate SMART, SMARTer, and SMARTest goals accordingly, and modify them to ensure positive progress. The annual state summative assessments are driven by mastery of grade-level standards. You should guide your work through a thorough data review based on progress of standard mastery for each grade level.

Most schools, especially schools deemed in need of urgent improvement, have multiple measures of data at their disposal: state summative, benchmark, and common formative assessments. Harnessing and making these data meaningful to reflect on student learning is of primary importance. Leaders can effectively drive improvement efforts by streamlining how staff use data in their schools. A strategic data set can apply to many levels of goal monitoring. Teachers can critically evaluate observational data to support how leaders look for instruction practices conducive to enhancing the SMARTest goal monitoring.

Purposeful Continuous-Improvement Activities

The purpose of all schools is to improve student learning and ensure all students learn at high levels. An aligned effort is best practice when designing improvement efforts. Supporting these efforts can be not only challenging but also purposeful. The work of school improvement should not be seen as just another effort. Sharon V. Kramer and Sarah Schuhl (2017) assert that a schoolwide focus is necessary with able and willing adults ready to implement any needed changes in order for students to reach proficiency. In order to assess the effectiveness of our work and the student progress, there must be evidence of student learning continuously. A school must be prepared to respond immediately to students who need intervention or extensions.

When developing each set of goals and activities for sustained improvement, staff should implement best practices for improvement as shown in table 5.2 (page 88) at all levels to ensure they engage in the right work. These practices are crucial to ensure all students learn at high levels, as evidenced in improvement outcome measures (like annual state summative assessments).

Table 5.2: Critical Practices and Guiding Principles for Continuous School Improvement

Culture of Success	A culture of success supports a safe, orderly, and equitable learning environment. There is an expectation of high levels of learning for all and culture of doing whatever it takes for each student to succeed. Creating collective commitments is a first step in establishing a culture of success.
Engaging in the Right Work	Engaging in the right work involves the implementation of an ongoing process in which educators work collaboratively in recurring cycles (unit by unit) of collective inquiry and action research to achieve better results for the students they serve. Collaboration is the engine that drives the school-improvement process. Teams focus on answering the four critical questions of a PLC to guide the process and ensure everyone is engaged in the right work (DuFour et al., 2016).
Four Critical Questions of a PLC	
1. What is it we want our students to know and be able to do?	A guaranteed and viable curriculum (1) gives students access to the same essential learning regardless of who is teaching the class and (2) allows teachers to teach the essential learning in the time allotted. Teachers must work collaboratively to determine the guaranteed and viable curriculum for each course and grade level. The essential learnings are derived from the state standards, and teams break them down into learning targets.
2. How will we know when each student has learned it?	Teachers collaboratively create common formative and summative assessments to help students acquire agreed-upon knowledge and skills. Formative assessments for learning are part of an ongoing process to monitor each student's progress on a continuous basis, to inform the teachers of the effectiveness of their practices, and to provide scaffolding to students. Schools establish SMART goals to monitor progress.
3. How will we respond when some students do not learn it?	A multitiered system of interventions in a schoolwide plan ensures every student in every course or grade level will receive additional time and support for learning as soon as they experience difficulty in acquiring essential knowledge and skills. The intervention occurs during the school day, and students are required to devote the extra time they need to secure the skills. This is a collective schoolwide responsibility.
4. How will we extend the learning for students who have demonstrated proficiency?	Teams create extension opportunities for students who have reached proficiency with the guaranteed and viable curriculum. These students engage in extensions of learning connected to the essential learning.

Shifting From All to Each	School schedules, operational systems, grouping of students, and any activities impacting student learning focus on providing each student with the necessary skills and knowledge to become proficient with the guaranteed and viable curriculum. All decisions are made with this purpose as the most crucial goal.
Leadership for Learning	A guiding coalition composed of teachers and administrators is established to lead and monitor the school-improvement processes to ensure learning for all. The building principal is responsible for implementing the PLC at Work process with fidelity. This includes, but is not limited to, weekly data review, scheduling, protecting instruction time, and supporting teachers with embedded professional development and time to do the work.
Engaging Students in Owning Their Learning	Teachers adopt and ensure a growth mindset to improve achievement for each student. Students set their own learning goals in the form of SMART goals and track their own growth. Teachers create learning opportunities that personalize and engage students in owning their learning, bringing meaning to the process.

Source: Adapted from DuFour et al., 2016; Kramer & Schuhl, 2017.

Conclusion

As schools, collaborative teams, and individual teachers monitor goals, their efforts should keenly focus on the preceding areas. The activities at schools should align and focus on best practices that ensure student learning and sustain achievement. In working with schools in urgent need of improvement and that have unique needs, many can become derailed and overwhelmed with daily activities not in alignment with the outcomes they desire. Maintaining an unwavering focus on the purposeful activities and aligning how schools impact successful improvement on SMART, SMARTer, and SMARTest goals can only improve the results and learning outcomes for all students. Creating a culture of success where collaboratively established goals align and unified improvement efforts ground all staff is certainly the smart system in which schools should function. Aiming all of the arrows in the same direction will establish a culture of collective responsibility that calibrates the data-driven decision making for leaders.

Goal Monitoring With Common Data

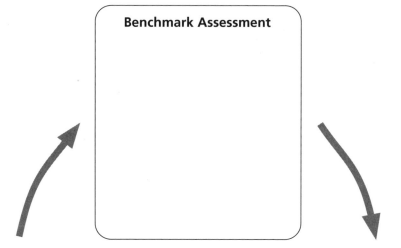

Benchmark Assessment

SMARTest Goal
How I can provide or
differentiate to meet all
students' needs:

SMART Goal
Classrooms that need
additional support:

SMARTer Goal
Teachers who need additional
resources and support:

References and Resources

American Society for Quality. (n.d.). *Continuous improvement.* Accessed at https://asq.org/quality-resources/continuous-improvement on September 23, 2020.

Buffum, A., Mattos, M., & Weber, C. (2009). *Pyramid response to intervention: RTI, professional learning communities, and how to respond when kids don't learn.* Bloomington, IN: Solution Tree Press.

Conzemius, A. E., & O'Neill, J. (2014). *Handbook for SMART school teams: Revitalizing best practices for collaboration* (2nd ed.). Bloomington, IN: Solution Tree Press.

DuFour, R., DuFour, R., Eaker, R., Many, T. W., & Mattos, M. (2016). *Learning by doing: A handbook for Professional Learning Communities at Work* (3rd ed.). Bloomington, IN: Solution Tree Press.

Hattie, J. (2012). *Visible learning for teachers: Maximizing impact on learning.* New York: Routledge.

Kramer, S. V., & Schuhl, S. (2017). *School improvement for all: A how-to guide for doing the right work.* Bloomington, IN: Solution Tree Press.

O'Neill, J., & Conzemius, A. (2006). *The power of SMART goals: Using goals to improve student learning.* Bloomington, IN: Solution Tree Press.

Park, S., Hironaka, S., Carver, P., & Nordstrum, L. (2013, May). *Continuous improvement in education.* Accessed at www.carnegiefoundation.org/resources/publications/continuous-improvement-education on September 23, 2020.

Joe Cuddemi has over thirty-five years of experience in education serving as a teacher, counselor, and principal in a wide variety of educational settings, including adjunct professor at Colorado State University.

Since 2015, Joe has been an educational consultant serving hundreds of districts and schools across the United States. Joe delivers keynotes, facilitates workshops, and coaches educators in the Professional Learning Community (PLC) at Work process, Transforming School Culture, Response to Intervention (RTI) at Work™, Priority Schools in a PLC at Work, and Social-Emotional Learning.

Joe taught at schools on the Fort Belknap Reservation in Montana, and in Jamaica and Colorado. As a counselor, Joe created an award-winning experiential educational program that includes horsemanship for students facing high levels of adversity.

As principal, Joe opened Kinard Core Knowledge Middle School and received several national recognitions, including the 2015 National Blue Ribbon School award and 2013 Green Ribbon School award. In 2012, Kinard was named a Model PLC.

Joe earned a bachelor's degree in biology from Boston College, a master's degree in teaching mathematics from Northern Arizona University, and a principal licensure at Colorado State University.

To book Joe Cuddemi for professional development, contact pd@SolutionTree.com.

Focusing on Collective Responsibility

Joe Cuddemi

No amount of outside pressure will make schools
improve; they only do so when the adults who work
directly with the students decide it is their job to
ensure all students learn at high levels.

—*Sharon V. Kramer and Sarah Schuhl*

Just recently, the principal of a struggling school introduced me like this: "Our state is one of the lowest-performing states in the country [United States], our district is the lowest-performing district in the state, and our school is the lowest-performing school in our district. The district got a grant to improve our school, and that's why Joe is here. Joe, the staff is all yours." As you might imagine, I didn't receive a standing ovation. I stood in front of the staff for five very long, uncomfortably silent seconds, and then asked, "Which of you contacted me to improve your school?" After a few giggles and grins, I said, "In my work with schools across the United States, I operate under two fundamental assumptions: educators care deeply for the students they serve, and educators work very hard for the students they serve." The dilemma in priority schools is that those schools must improve or face sanctions such as replacing staff or closing the school. Unfortunately, accountability is then viewed as something that happens when something goes wrong. The improvement process, however, occurs when the educators focus on their sphere of influence and the things that they can control, like their mindset (thinking) and professional practices (actions). No one educator has the skills and talents to meet the individual and varied needs of every student. Instead, educators must work together to improve learning outcomes for students and consider the question, How can we work collectively to meet the learning needs for each of our students?

Throughout this chapter, I will help you reframe accountability, learn how to establish a cohesive guiding coalition, and use protocols to create a culture of collective responsibility. This leadership work is difficult, but it is doable. Most importantly, it's an essential component to ensuring learning for all students.

I want to honor the hard work, deep concern, and contextual expertise you have for your students, your community, and your school. My hope is to join you in your efforts to meet the learning needs of your students by offering a process that will help you to reclaim your school and your students by focusing on what you can control and influence. I have created a five-step process to help guide the leadership team to lead the staff in creating and sustaining a culture of collective responsibility.

1. Examine the research and evidence of effectiveness in high-performing schools.

2. Distinguish between cultural change and technical change.

3. Understand and use a framework for the change process.

4. Learn how to establish and purpose a cohesive guiding coalition.

5. Use protocols to create a culture of collective responsibility.

There is a high level of urgency to improve the learning results for students in our most struggling schools. Underperforming schools are required to improve student achievement or suffer consequences such as closing the schools, turning the schools over to the state, or dismissing staff members (DuFour, 2015). Too often, the accountability strategies leaders try to use to motivate educators to improve student learning have an external point of control, are fear based, and result in learning environments filled with distrust and low morale (Muhammad, 2018). Embracing accountability with an internal locus of control will help provide our students and educators with safe environments to improve learning.

If we blame students who are struggling to learn on factors that we have no control over (like a lack of parental involvement, a poor home environment, or a low socio-economic level), then we render ourselves powerless to make change. Our traditional public school system was never designed to ensure high levels of learning for all students (Muhammad & Cruz, 2019). We know that no one teacher has all of the skills and talents to meet the individual and varied needs of every student. Improving our schools is not about tweaking the traditional school system. Sustainable school improvement requires *collective responsibility*: a shared belief that the primary responsibility of each member of the organization is to ensure high levels of learning for every child (Buffum, Mattos, & Malone, 2018). Professional educators make hundreds of decisions every day that impact student learning; we need to make those decisions based on the evidence and research that support and demonstrate the best results for the students we serve (DuFour, DuFour, Eaker, Many, & Mattos, 2016).

Examine the Research and Evidence of Effectiveness in High-Performing Schools

As professionals engaged in building a culture of collective responsibility, it is critical that we examine our experiences, our thinking, and our actions in light of their impact on student learning outcomes. Educators make hundreds of decisions each day that impact student learning. What are those professional decisions based on—tradition or the way we've always done things? Are those decisions based on personal preference and our comfort zone? Are those decisions based on complying to top-down mandates? Our professional decisions need to be based on the evidence and research for best practice.

When we examine the research in our profession, we notice that there are four levels of research, which increase in sample size, reliability, and validity. The first level of research is the individual educator's limited personal and professional experiences and intuition. The second level of research is from a group of educators who collaborate and bring together all of their individual experiences and intuition. The third level of research derives from statistically valid and reliable research studies, such as Lawrence W. Lezotte's (1991) thirty-five-year study on the correlates of effective schools. Lezotte's (1991) longitudinal research study shows that effective schools produce results that mitigate, almost completely, the effects of a student's history if it hasn't been conducive to learning, proving that it's not what happens to us, it's what we do with what happens to us.

The fourth level of research combines data from multiple studies and is referred to as *meta-analysis*. Researcher and author John Hattie's (2012) *Visible Learning for Teachers: Maximizing Impact on Learning* identifies over two hundred factors that impact student learning. Hattie's (2012) meta-analysis demonstrates over thirty high-impact strategies that are more powerful than the effects of poverty! Three of the top-five ranking factors require a collective effort: (1) collective teacher efficacy, (2) collective expectations of student achievement, and (3) response to intervention, which is how we collectively respond when, despite our best efforts, a student is not learning (Hattie, 2012). In *School Improvement for All*, coauthors Sharon V. Kramer and Sarah Schuhl (2017) encapsulate Hattie's meta-analysis findings by stating, "response to learning or interventions and remediation are more powerful than the negative effects of poverty" (p. 47).

In addition to research that supports the correlation between effective schools and collective responsibility, hundreds of schools demonstrate evidence of effectiveness. At AllThingsPLC (www.allthingsplc.info), you can locate these schools (large, small, urban, rural, or suburban) and examine their practices, stories, achievements, and resources. These learning-focused schools embrace a culture of collective responsibility and demonstrate significant increases in student achievement. The educators in these schools believe all their students, regardless of their backgrounds, can learn, and that student learning depends on the actions of educators.

Distinguish Between Cultural Change and Technical Change

Collective responsibility requires a common understanding of the terms that we use. As educational consultant and professor Kent D. Peterson states, *school culture* is defined as a school's "norms, values and beliefs, rituals and ceremonies, symbols and stories that make up the 'persona' of the school" (as cited in Muhammad, 2018, p. 20). A *healthy school culture* is when:

- Educators have an unwavering belief in the ability of all of their students to achieve success, and they pass the belief on to others in overt and covert ways.

- Educators create policies and procedures and adopt practices that support their belief in every student's ability. (Muhammad, 2018, p. 20)

In such a culture, the staff commit to working collaboratively in recurring cycles of collective inquiry and action experimentation in order to seek the promising practices for the students they serve (DuFour et al., 2016).

In an unhealthy or toxic school culture, the staff might believe students can learn, but that belief is conditional. For example, the students could learn *if* their parents were more involved; *if* the students just did what we said; *if* the students were not on an individualized education program; *if* the students weren't a poor White, poor Hispanic, or poor Black; or *if* the central office would just leave us alone (Muhammad & Cruz, 2019). In toxic school cultures, there is gossip among the adults, students are kept at a distance using humiliation and ridicule, the staff are divided into cliques, and the staff use negative language when describing the students and the school (Gruenert & Whitaker, 2015).

In toxic school cultures, where the trust level is low, I often start the relationship-building process with a powerful activity called the School History Map (Williams & Hierck, 2015). This activity engages the entire staff in telling the story of the school's history, deepening everyone's understanding and appreciation for the context of the school's journey. It also validates the hard work, dedication, and resilience of the veteran staff, while at the same time giving voice and providing a safe environment for the newest staff members to share their first-year perceptions.

Following are the steps for the School History Map activity.

1. Make a timeline of the decades since the school opened on butcher paper, shelf paper, or wallpaper.

   ‣ Leave ample space between decades for stories.

   ‣ Mark the paper with prompts to help staff recall stories, such as events, key people, building changes, and so on.

2. Divide the staff into random groups or by the era in which they began working in the school.

3. The staff write significant stories or memories that contribute to the school's history on sticky notes.

4. Place the sticky notes in the appropriate eras on the timeline.

5. Staff walk along the wall, writing notes about events, processing what happened, why it's important, and how the group can use the information.

6. The facilitator guides the staff debrief, including questions such as, What observations did you have during this activity? and What feelings or thoughts did this activity conjure up for you?

In addition to culture health (or lack of it), there are two other kinds of change that are both important and necessary: technical change and cultural change (Muhammad, 2018). *Technical change* refers to changing the structures, like changing the master schedule or implementing a new curriculum or instructional strategy. On the other hand, *cultural change* refers to "addressing the beliefs, values, motivations, habits, and behaviors of the people who work within the organization" (Muhammad & Cruz, 2019, p. 4). Changing the culture of a school is more difficult than changing the structures. If a low-performing school does not address its culture, then changing the structures is like moving furniture around on the *Titanic*. Renowned culture expert Anthony Muhammad (2018) frames the dilemma this way: "Substantial cultural change must precede technical change" (p. 25). While technical changes are necessary to improve our schools, they produce few positive results when the people using them do not believe in the intended outcome or the change.

Muhammad (n.d.) ingeniously uses an agricultural metaphor to explain the dynamic between the structures (seed) and the culture (soil): If you plant good seed in fertile soil, then the seed will grow; conversely, if you plant good seed in toxic soil, then the seed will not grow. If you implement the best structures like collaborative teams, intervention time, and common formative assessments in a toxic culture, then the strategies will not produce the expected results. The soil needs to be nurtured with proper light, nutrients, and water in order for the seed to grow (Muhammad, n.d.). Similarly, the school's culture needs to be healthy in order for the high-impact strategies and structures like collaboration and intervention to work and produce positive results. Building a culture of collective responsibility requires that leaders take the initiative. Sustaining a culture of collective responsibility requires ownership from *everyone*.

Understand and Use a Framework for the Change Process

Change is not an event; it's a process. Individual change is difficult, and organizational change is monumental; however, both are possible. One of the key changes for priority schools is to create and sustain a shift from a culture of complaint to a culture of commitment. This is not a linear shift; it's not about checking off boxes on a new list of school improvement to-dos. Instead, the shift occurs when the staff take ownership for the hundreds of decisions they make each day and are willing to examine those decisions together in light of their impact on student learning.

The change process requires a framework. The framework that Anthony Muhammad and Luis F. Cruz (2019) use in *Time for Change: Four Essential Skills for Transformational School and District Leaders* includes the following four essential behaviors.

1. Communicating the rationale
2. Establishing trust
3. Building capacity
4. Getting results

The change process requires that systems of support need to precede systems of accountability. When educators have clarity on why they need to change, trust the leadership initiating the change, and have the capacity to make the change, the structural changes are more likely to create positive outcomes for adult and student learning. To sustain change, all staff need to know and understand the process.

Learn How to Establish and Purpose a Cohesive Guiding Coalition

Leading change, especially in schools entrenched in a cycle of failure, requires a guiding coalition (DuFour et al., 2016). Leadership in this context is not defined by position, title, or years of experience but instead by influence. Leadership thought leader and professor emeritus John P. Kotter (2007) states:

> No one person, no matter how competent, is capable of single-handedly developing the right vision, communicating it to vast numbers of people, eliminating all the key obstacles, generating short-term wins, leading and managing dozens of change projects, and anchoring new approaches deep in an organization's culture. Putting together the right coalition of people to lead a change initiative is critical to its success.

This is where the guiding coalition is needed. The following sections explain the guiding coalition's purpose and the selection process.

The Guiding Coalition's Purpose

The first step in developing collective responsibility among the entire education staff is to create a guiding coalition. A guiding coalition is an "alliance of key members of an organization who are specifically charged with leading a change process through predictable turmoil" (DuFour, DuFour, & Eaker, 2008, p. 467). In other words, the guiding coalition are staff who work with the principal to lead the process of examining all the school's practices, procedures, policies, and mindsets in light of their impact on student learning. The team is not an inner circle of the principal's favorite staff members who are a pipeline to the administrators, nor is it focused on operations like dress code, phones, or schedules. From a macro-level perspective, the guiding coalition honestly assesses the school's current reality based on data, learns deeply about best practices, determines next steps to improve the school, identifies possible obstacles and points of leverage, and plans the best way to create staff consensus and commitment. Members of the guiding coalition are charged with facilitating conversations between and among the collaborative teams that they represent.

The following six questions can help the guiding coalition lead their teams, and ultimately the staff, through the change process (Buffum, Mattos, & Weber, 2012).

1. How will we provide a compelling case for change?
2. What must we do differently?
3. How do we know these changes will work?
4. What concerns do we expect, especially from staff members traditionally against change?

5. What is the best setting or structure for the conversations needed to create consensus?

6. How will we know if we have reached consensus?

The Selection Process

It is critical that principals select members for the guiding coalition based on the following criteria: (1) a transparent selection process, (2) a balance of essential leadership competencies, and (3) a team that represents the entire staff (Williams & Hierck, 2015). A principal can use several strategies to create a fair selection process, including principals soliciting nominations for the application process. The total number of educators on a guiding coalition will vary from school to school depending on the school's size; the key is to ensure that the entire staff is represented and that all voices are heard when making decisions that impact everyone.

When selecting members for the guiding coalition, principals need to seek a balance of the competencies listed in figure 6.1. Principals can use the figure to ensure that each member of the guiding coalition possesses at least one of these essential competencies.

Competency	What That Competency Might Look or Sound Like
Systems thinker	Ability to see the big picture of how the entire school functions and interconnects (not limited to advocating only for their grade-level or content department)
Critical thinker	Ability to identify, anticipate, and articulate possible obstacles and opportunities when examining a proposal
Influencer	Ability to positively influence colleagues while championing the professional learning community (PLC) process
Facilitator	Ability to facilitate conversations among team members while ensuring that all voices are heard

Figure 6.1: Different guiding coalition competencies.

Building trust among team members, which can be made or broken each day, is an essential component for developing a high-performing guiding coalition. To help begin building trust among the new guiding coalition members, principals can use the Personal Histories activity in Patrick Lencioni's (2012) *The Advantage: Why Organizational Health Trumps Everything Else in Business*. The principal would ask members of the guiding coalition to respond to each of these four questions.

1. Where were you born?

2. How many siblings are in your family?

3. Where do you fall in the order of children?

4. What was the most interesting or difficult challenge when you were a kid? (Lencioni, 2012)

I have helped principals facilitate and debrief this activity dozens of times. During the debrief, team members often express appreciation for the commonalities they have with each other and empathy for the differences that make each person unique.

Use Protocols to Create a Culture of Collective Responsibility

Change occurs through conversations, not presentations. Have you ever attended a meeting where some team members did most or all of the talking and some team members didn't talk at all? Or a meeting where the group veered off topic? Members of the guiding coalition don't need to burden themselves with becoming experts in every aspect of the PLC process. However, they do need to either have or develop the skills necessary to lead conversations with their team members. Guiding coalition members can use protocols to help support the facilitation of these conversations. Protocols guide and structure conversations among professionals and assist teams in building consensus through the communication loop and laying the foundation.

Building Consensus Through the Communication Loop

When does a team reach consensus? "When all points of view have been heard and the will of the group is evident even to those most opposed" (Cuddemi, 2017a). To reach consensus with the entire staff for a proposed change, the guiding coalition members need to facilitate conversations about that proposed change with each of their respective teams and then share the outcomes of those conversations with the guiding coalition. As the principal of Kinard Middle School in Fort Collins, Colorado, from 2003 to 2015, I developed a communication loop that helped ensure that all voices on the staff were heard and that we reached consensus on decisions that impacted the entire staff. We used the fist-to-five strategy as a simple way to determine each group's will:

> **Five fingers:** I love this proposal. I will champion it.
>
> **Four fingers:** I strongly agree with the proposal.
>
> **Three fingers:** The proposal is okay with me. I am willing to go along.
>
> **Two fingers:** I have reservations and am not yet ready to support this proposal.
>
> **One finger:** I am opposed to this proposal.
>
> **Fist:** If I had the authority, I would veto this proposal, regardless of the will of the group. (DuFour et al., 2016, p. 33)

Then we used the communication loop to ensure that we reached consensus with the entire staff.

1. Before proposing a new or different idea to the entire staff, you need to first reach consensus with the guiding coalition. If you can't reach consensus with them, it is unlikely that you will reach consensus with the entire staff.

2. If the guiding coalition reaches consensus for an initiative, then members facilitate a conversation about that initiative with their respective teams.

3. The guiding coalition reconvenes and collectively shares the input and feedback from their team meetings.

4. If there is consensus among the teams for the initiative, then the guiding coalition presents the proposal to the entire staff to finalize the consensus process. (For more about this process, see chapter 3, page 45.)

5. If consensus among the entire staff is *not* reached, then you do not move forward with the change. However, an individual team or teams can engage their own action research to bring more evidence to the staff.

Laying the Foundation

Every high-performing Model PLC school has a shared foundation. The shared foundation drives the daily work of the school and helps to create a culture of collective responsibility. The guiding coalition members use protocols to facilitate conversations with their respective teams in order to establish this shared foundation. The four essential pillars of the PLC foundation are (1) mission, (2) vision, (3) collective commitments, and (4) goals (DuFour et al., 2016). Each of the four pillars asks a different question that the faculty must converse about and ultimately reach consensus on for a shared foundation. In the next section, I will address the mission, vision, and collective commitment pillars. See chapters 2 and 5 in this book for more about creating and aligning school and team goals, and *School Improvement for All* (Kramer & Schuhl, 2017, pp. 141–143) for an in-depth process. Visit **go.SolutionTree.com/PLCbooks** for free reproducible versions of example foundations.

In priority schools, leadership teams collect student demographic data and qualitative data from focus-group interviews to create a comprehensive needs assessment. This needs assessment provides schools with the data to create a compelling case for change anchored in a shared foundation.

Protocols

Protocols are tools that structure our conversations to ensure all voices are heard and there is a balance between advocacy and inquiry. They turn data into information, as well as help us establish a mission, vision, and collective commitments. A great resource that includes several protocols to address a variety of purposes can be found in *How to Cultivate Collaboration in a PLC* (Sparks & Many, 2015). As you read, consider what protocols might work for your school and use the reproducible "Planning on Protocols" (page 107) to plan.

Protocols for Turning Data Into Information

One of the first steps the guiding coalition should take is examining three-year data trends in the areas of academic achievement, student behavior, and attendance. Visit **go.SolutionTree.com/PLCbooks** for access to free reproducibles that help organize the data.

The Here's What. So What? Now What? data-analysis protocol can help make sense of the data.

1. Look at the data, and use factual statements to say Here's what.

2. Move to So what? and discuss the implications.

3. Move to Now what? and determine what to do about it and create a plan of action.

Protocols for Mission

The mission asks, *What is our fundamental purpose?* Without a shared purpose, it would be very difficult for faculties to work collectively toward a common goal. In my work with schools across the country, I have found that most schools have a mission statement of some sort. However, I have also noticed that when engaged in conversations about their mission statement, not all staff members are clear about the meaning of the words in their mission statement, nor are they clear about when it was developed or by whom. Consider the following guiding questions as you examine your school's mission.

- Does our mission statement reflect a commitment to high levels of learning for all students?

- How do we know if all staff members know and understand our mission statement?

- How can we use our mission statement to drive our daily work?

- What current practices in our school align with our mission statement, and which practices do not?

I have used the following two protocols to help faculty address these questions.

- **Gallery Walk Protocol:** The purpose of this protocol is to help the staff members share their current understanding and alignment for the school's mission. At a faculty meeting, the guiding coalition facilitates this protocol. Each staff member independently writes on a sticky note his or her response to the questions, *What mission are we on?* and *What is our mission statement?* Place the notes around the room, and have the faculty do a silent gallery walk. During the walk, ask staff to consider the following questions: *Where are we aligned?* and *Where are we not aligned?* Then, in small groups, the staff discuss their observations and interpretations. Each group then shares their common themes and trends. The duration for this protocol is typically twenty or thirty minutes.

- **Final Word Protocol:** The purpose of this protocol is to develop a deeper understanding for key terms and concepts that are written in a school's mission statement. A good starting point is to discuss the words and concepts typically found in high-performing PLC schools such as, "We exist to ensure high levels of learning for all students." In the book *Concise Answers to Frequently Asked Questions About Professional Learning Communities at Work* (Mattos, DuFour, DuFour, Eaker, & Many, 2016), the authors clarify several terms and concepts, including what is meant by *high levels of learning* and *all students*:

What does *high levels of learning* mean? We define *high levels of learning* as "high school plus," meaning every child is on a trajectory to graduate from high school with the academic skills, knowledge, and dispositions needed to continue to learn. A high school diploma will not be enough to compete in the global marketplace and make a living. Postsecondary education can include attending a university, community college, trade school, internship, apprenticeship, or some other type of specialized training. To achieve this, all students must learn at grade level or better every year. For example, a first grader who ends the year unprepared for second grade is at risk of ultimately not graduating from high school, let alone successfully transitioning to postsecondary levels of education. A school focused on high levels of learning would not allow students to be tracked in below-grade-level learning. (Mattos et al., 2016, pp. 13–14)

Does *all* really mean all? Without question, committing to a mission of high levels of learning for all students is a daunting task. But if a school settles for less—that *most* students will learn at high levels— then how does the school determine which students deserve a substandard education and diminished opportunities in life? How many failing students would such a school deem acceptable? Once a school falters on its commitment to high levels of learning for every student, it starts down a slippery slope of lowering expectations for some students. (Mattos et al., 2016, p. 14)

Organize the staff into groups of three. (If some groups need to include four, then the facilitator creates a variation of the roles.) This protocol occurs in three rounds, and each round lasts three minutes. The first step is for each person to read the preceding excerpts and highlight three to five words, phrases, or sentences that resonate most with them. Round one begins with person A sharing an ah-ha, but not elaborating. Then, for two minutes, persons B and C discuss person A's ah-ha. Then, person A has the final word, building on the discussion. During rounds two and three, rotate roles. The duration for this protocol is ten minutes.

Protocols for Vision

The vision pillar asks, *What must we become in order to accomplish our fundamental purpose?* Most schools that I have worked with have not collectively created a description of the kind of school they hope to become in order to help all students learn. How do you know if your school is heading in the right direction if your staff hasn't clearly and collectively articulated this? Consider the following guiding questions as you examine the vision of your school.

- Do we have a shared vision for the school that we hope to become?
- Did the faculty have a voice or a role in developing our vision?

- How do we know if our faculty has a common understanding for our vision?

- Does our vision statement focus on what we, the faculty, can do? On what the parents and guardians, students, central office, or board of education can do?

The following protocols help staff to examine and develop a vision for the kind of school they hope to become.

- **Jigsaw Protocol:** The purpose of this protocol is to help facilitate conversations among the staff regarding research-based PLC practices. Divide the staff into groups of four or five. Each group is assigned a specific Model PLC school (from www.allthingsplc.info/evidence-of-effectiveness) and reads, discusses, and records answers to the questions, *What is the staff's thinking?* (see PLC Story tab on the AllThingsPLC website) and *What are they doing?* (see PLC Practices tab on the AllThingsPLC website). Small groups share their findings for the kind of thinking and behavior that Model PLC schools demonstrate. The duration of this protocol is between thirty and forty-five minutes.

- **Carousel Brainstorm:** The purpose of the carousel brainstorm is to share perspectives and build on each other's ideas and successful experiences. Imagine an entire staff with "an unwavering belief in the ability of all their students" (Muhammad, 2018, p. 20)! Ask everyone to imagine it's five years from now and you've fulfilled your mission to ensure high levels of learning for all. Break the staff into groups of four to five, and post chart paper around the room with one of the following questions on each sheet: *What are we doing differently in our classrooms?*, *What are we doing differently on our collaborative teams?*, *What are we doing differently in our relationships?*, and *What are we doing differently when students have not learned the behavioral skills that are expected?* For two to three minutes at each piece of paper, groups brainstorm and write the professional practices that describe what they are doing differently; then everyone rotates. A small group of staff members draft a vision statement based on this brainstorm in order to reach consensus. The carousel brainstorm takes about thirty to forty-five minutes.

Protocols for Collective Commitments

The mission is philosophical and the vision is aspirational; both are important pillars in a shared foundation. The third pillar, collective commitments, asks, *How must we behave toward one another, our students, and our parents and guardians in order to accomplish our mission and become the school we aspire toward?* Collective commitments consist of two types of behaviors: collaborative tasks and interpersonal dynamics. Figure 6.2 is an example of the collective commitments that we created at Kinard Middle School. The first five collective commitments describe the collaborative tasks of a high-performing PLC (DuFour et al., 2016); collective commitments 6, 7, and 8 address the behaviors needed for effective interpersonal dynamics.

As of a result of our shared mission to ensure high levels of learning for each student . . .

1. We commit to ensuring all staff members are organized into meaningful (share common student outcomes) collaborative teams and have time, during the contract day, to meet as a team at least once a week (sixty minutes) to effectively engage in the teaching-assessing cycle for teams (DuFour, DuFour, Eaker, & Many, 2010).

2. We commit to ensuring all our students learn the essential content standards and skills in mathematics, English language arts, history, science, art, music, gym, technology, and world language (DuFour et al., 2010).

3. We commit to ensuring all our students learn the essential academic skills and behavioral expectations (prompt, prepared, polite, participation, positive mental attitude, and productive; Cuddemi, 2017b; DuFour et al., 2010).

4. We commit to providing at least sixty minutes per week for students who need additional time and support to learn the essential content standards, academic skills, and behavioral expectations (DuFour et al., 2010).

5. We commit to continuously seeking the most promising practices, procedures, and processes for the students we serve; therefore, we commit to making professional decisions based on evidence that students are learning at grade level or above (DuFour et al., 2010).

6. We commit to treating our students, parents, guardians, and one another with dignity and respect (versus focusing on power, control, shame, and blame).

7. We commit to using a solution-focused mindset and solution-focused language when confronting problems and frustrations (versus complaining).

8. We commit to holding ourselves and one another accountable to these commitments. If we have a concern, we must take our concern directly to the person with whom we have the concern and then use the healthy goals of dialogue (seek the truth, learn from one another, strengthen the relationship, and create results) when resolving conflict (Patterson, Grenny, McMillan, & Switzler, 2005).

Figure 6.2: Collective commitments examples.

If you are new to the PLC at Work process and would like a more detailed description of the research supporting collective commitments, it can be found on pages 39–43 in *Learning by Doing* (DuFour et al., 2016). Also, in *School Improvement for All*, Kramer and Schuhl (2017) provide excellent tools for implementing the collaborative tasks described in the first five collective commitments in figure 6.2.

In my experience with priority schools, I've learned that creating collective commitments that address the interpersonal dynamics among the adults—commitments 6–8 in figure 6.2—is critical to achieving the student learning results.

Consider the following guiding questions as you examine and develop collective commitments.

- Has our faculty clarified the collective commitments we need to make in order to advance our school's vision?

- Are these collective commitments stated as actions, not as beliefs?

- Do these collective commitments focus on what we can control or on what others must do?

- Do our collective commitments include a commitment for how we will hold each other accountable?

Here are a few protocols to help facilitate collective commitments.

- **Groups of Increasing Larger Size (GOILS):** The purpose of the GOILS protocol in this case is to help the staff reach consensus on the collective commitments for the interpersonal dynamics. First, each staff member independently writes three interpersonal behaviors. They then consider questions like, *How do we want to treat each other?*, *What does healthy communication look like and sound like?*, *How will we resolve conflict?*, and *How do we make decisions?* Staff members pair up, and each partner shares the three interpersonal behaviors (six total). Then, each pair reaches consensus on the three behaviors they resonate with the most. Once consensus is reached, each pair finds another pair and repeats the process. The process continues as the groups increase in size and three interpersonal dynamics emerge and the entire staff reaches consensus. This protocol takes about thirty minutes.

- **Keep, Drop, and Create:** The purpose of this protocol is to improve on either an exemplar of collective commitments or the school's current list of collective commitments. In groups of four or five, staff members examine a list of collective commitments and engage in a conversation to determine what they would like to keep, drop, or create anew. All small groups then submit their input to a subcommittee of wordsmiths who consider all input and create an improved list of collective commitments. This protocol can take thirty minutes.

Conclusion

Establishing a shared foundation is essential for creating collective responsibility. The key going forward is to use this shared foundation to guide future discussions and decisions involving all policies, practices, and procedures that impact learning for all students. I encourage you to use protocols to create an environment in which your staff can have conversations examining professional practice, student learning, and problem solving. It is possible and essential to create a safe learning environment amidst the many pressures and stresses we face each day. It is critical for us not to fall victim to factors that we cannot control, but instead focus on what we can control—*ourselves*. With an internal locus of control, we can create a culture of collective responsibility.

Planning on Protocols

Consider the protocols provided in this chapter, as well as those you already use and any others you discover. In each column, record those you will consider implementing, noting after how effective they were and what changes you can make to make them work for your school.

Protocols for Turning Data Into Information	Protocols for Mission	Protocols for Vision	Protocols for Collective Commitments

References and Resources

AllThingsPLC. (n.d.). *See the evidence: Want proof that the PLC process is working for others and can work for you too?* Accessed at www.allthingsplc.info/evidence on September 22, 2020.

Buffum, A., Mattos, M., & Malone, J. (2018). *Taking action: A handbook for RTI at Work.* Bloomington, IN: Solution Tree Press.

Buffum, A., Mattos, M., & Weber, C. (2012). *Simplifying response to intervention: Four essential guiding principles.* Bloomington, IN: Solution Tree Press.

Cuddemi, J. (2017a, June 20). *Decision making: "How can we get on the same page?"* [Blog post]. Accessed at www.solutiontree.com/blog/decision-making-getting-on-the-same-page on February 2, 2021.

Cuddemi, J. (2017b, August 30). *Creating a culture of commitment* [Blog post]. Accessed at www .allthingsplc.info/blog/view/354/creating-a-culture-of-commitment on January 26, 2021.

DuFour, R. (2015). *In praise of American educators: And how they can become even better.* Bloomington, IN: Solution Tree Press.

DuFour, R. (2016, Summer). Loose vs tight. *AllThingsPLC Magazine*, 33.

DuFour, R., DuFour, R., & Eaker, R. (2008). *Revisiting Professional Learning Communities at Work: New insights for improving schools.* Bloomington, IN: Solution Tree Press.

DuFour, R., DuFour, R., Eaker, R., & Many, T. (2010). *Learning by doing: A handbook for Professional Learning Communites at Work* (2nd ed.). Bloomington, IN: Solution Tree Press.

DuFour, R., DuFour, R., Eaker, R., Many, T. W., & Mattos, M. (2016). *Learning by doing: A handbook for Professional Learning Communities at Work* (3rd ed.). Bloomington, IN: Solution Tree Press.

Fullan, M. (2004). *Leading in a culture of change: Personal action guide and workbook.* San Francisco: Jossey-Bass.

Gruenert, S., & Whitaker, T. (2015). *School culture rewired: How to define, assess, and transform it.* Alexandria, VA: Association for Supervision and Curriculum Development.

Hattie, J. (2012). *Visible learning for teachers: Maximizing impact on learning.* New York: Routledge.

Kotter. (n.d.). *The eight-step process for leading change.* Accessed at www.kotterinc.com/8-steps -process-for-leading-change on September 22, 2020.

Kotter, J. P. (2007, January). *Leading changing: Why transformation efforts fail.* Accessed at https:// hbr.org/2007/01/leading-change-why-transformation-efforts-fail on February 20, 2020.

Kramer, S. V., & Schuhl, S. (2017). *School improvement for all: A how-to guide for doing the right work.* Bloomington, IN: Solution Tree Press.

Lencioni, P. (2012). *The advantage: Why organizational health trumps everything else in business.* San Francisco: Jossey-Bass.

Lezotte, L. W. (1991). *Correlates of effective schools: The first and second generation.* Okemos, MI: Effective Schools Products.

Marzano, R. J. (2003). *What works in schools: Translating research into action.* Alexandria, VA: Association for Supervision and Curriculum Development.

Mattos, M., DuFour, R., DuFour, R., Eaker, R., & Many, T. W. (2016). *Concise answers to frequently asked questions about Professional Learning Communities at Work.* Bloomington, IN: Solution Tree Press.

Muhammad, A. (n.d.). *Changing the culture of an organization* [Video file]. Accessed at https://app.globalpd
.com/search/content/MjY1 on January 27, 2021.

Muhammad, A. (2009). *Transforming school culture: How to overcome staff division.* Bloomington, IN: Solution Tree Press.

Muhammad, A. (2018). *Transforming school culture: How to overcome staff division* (2nd ed.). Bloomington, IN: Solution Tree Press.

Muhammad, A., & Cruz, L. F. (2019). *Time for change: Four essential skills for transformational school and district leaders.* Bloomington, IN: Solution Tree Press.

Patterson, K., Grenny, J., McMillan, R., & Switzler, A. (2005). *Crucial confrontations: Tools for resolving broken promises, violated expectations, and bad behavior.* New York: McGraw-Hill.

Peterson, K. D. (2002). Positive or negative. *Journal of Staff Development, 23*(3), 10–15.

Sparks, S. K., & Many, T. W. (2015). *How to cultivate collaboration in a PLC.* Bloomington, IN: Solution Tree Press.

Williams, K. C., & Hierck, T. (2015). *Starting a movement: Building culture from the inside out in professional learning communities.* Bloomington, IN: Solution Tree Press.

 **Robin Noble, MEd,** is a principal, an author, a consultant, and a presenter with more than thirty years of experience in education. She has served as an elementary school principal, a district instructional coach, a middle school English teacher, and a special education teacher. Robin is the principal of Kearny Elementary School, a K–5 Title I elementary school serving a predominantly low-socioeconomic population in Santa Fe, New Mexico.

During her tenure as principal of Ramirez Thomas Elementary School, Robin successfully led her school through the federally funded Turnaround Model of reform, using the professional learning community (PLC) process as the foundation for the work. The school significantly increased proficiency rates, and, after being named the ninth-lowest-performing school in the state just three years earlier, the school was recognized by the New Mexico Public Education Department as a Top Growth School in 2012. In addition, Robin was recognized with the Award for Student Achievement by the New Mexico School Boards Association for her work with her school community and the advancements in student achievement.

Robin specializes in establishing a PLC foundation to usher in influential changes in schools. Her consulting focuses on the importance of creating a culture of high expectations for student learning, developing common language and commitments toward this goal, and facilitating the development of values and systems that lead to effective collaboration, evidence-based learning, and increases in student achievement. Robin also works with educators to help restore a sense of hope and empowerment in their professional lives by developing pathways toward autonomy, competence, and relatedness in the educational setting.

Robin is the author of *Finding Fulfillment: A Path to Reclaiming Hope and Empowerment for Educators.*

She received a bachelor's degree in education from the University of Central Florida and a master's degree in educational leadership from the University of New Mexico.

To learn more about Robin's work, visit https://yourinternalculture.com or follow @robin_rnoble on Twitter.

To book Robin Noble for professional development, contact pd@SolutionTree.com.

Leveraging Shared Leadership in the Priority School

Robin Noble

Leadership for learning is not a solo act;
it is shared and widely dispersed.

—*Sharon V. Kramer and Sarah Schuhl*

In 2010, as the principal of a low-performing elementary school in priority status, I was given the task of implementing the Turnaround Model of school reform. The U.S. Department of Education (n.d.) under Arne Duncan during the Obama administration initiated this model. The final word that our school would be utilizing the Turnaround Model the following year came from our superintendent shortly after returning from winter break. As many educators know, one of the Turnaround Model requirements is mandated removal of 50 percent of the school's current educational staff. I had just started as the school's principal five months earlier, and I realized quickly that life was going to get harder before it got better. Over the following three months, I would have to help coordinate the criteria and the interviews that all educators in the building would have to participate in if they wanted the chance to continue teaching at the school.

This is just one example of the unique and often excruciating demands leaders face in the too-often desperate quest to improve student outcomes in our lowest-performing schools. I know many of you have faced similar challenges in your own work in priority schools. Looking back, I realize that I could never have gotten through this time of upheaval without the help and support of my guiding coalition, a small group of school leaders that doggedly walked through this time with me. This team's commitment to our collective mission, vision, and each member of the school staff was critical to our success in improving outcomes for students. In addition to their support for the changes in systems and mindsets the Professional Learning Community (PLC) at Work culture and processes facilitated, this team of school leaders was also committed to the emotional and professional well-being of the school educators operating in a climate of high-stakes accountability. It was through this shared leadership model that we found success getting through the initial challenges of the Turnaround Model, as well as the subsequent improvement in our students' educational outcomes for the first time in six years.

Setting up a guiding coalition must be your number-one priority as a school leader. In this chapter, I explain why it is important to leverage shared leadership to avoid isolation, what shared leadership looks like in a PLC, and why shared leadership is so crucial in a priority school.

Avoiding Isolation

As leaders of priority schools, I feel certain that each of you has your own story of trying to find your way through the labyrinth of school-reform initiatives. Taking on the role of principal in a priority school is a commitment that requires both a solid conviction and a strong measure of courage because you consistently face higher levels of public scrutiny, increased district and state or province oversight, and more extensive documentation and reporting than your colleagues in schools without the decidedly undesirable label of *low performing*. In some federal school reform guidelines, principals must even confront the potential of losing their position if they do not or have not created the necessary changes to increase student achievement in a two- to three-year period (U.S. Department of Education, 2016).

The gravity of this accountability can become particularly daunting when principals feel isolated in their responsibility, and research suggests that many do feel isolated. In the 2013 *MetLife Survey of the American Teacher*, 89 percent of principals agreed that "the principal should be held accountable for everything that happens to the children in his or her school" (MetLife, 2013). This is a huge responsibility for any one individual to take on alone! This finding may also explain why the same survey indicates 57 percent of principals in low-performing schools say they "feel under great levels of stress several days a week or more" (MetLife, 2013). This too is a startling statistic. We all realize that operating under high levels of stress for extended periods of time is not a sustainable pattern, and one that can lead to burnout and attrition for these essential school leaders (Franke, 2014).

Statistics like these make it clear why it is important to acknowledge and support priority school principals facing these weighty responsibilities. In the PLC at Work process of school reform, one of the critical supports is through conscientious, intentional development of shared leadership (DuFour, DuFour, Eaker, Many, & Mattos, 2016). Yet the pattern of going it alone, either intentionally or unintentionally, can become the norm for many school leaders. You might be surprised at how many priority schools I visit where the guiding coalition (or another form of leadership team) is absent. This can happen for a number of reasons, including the following.

- The principal has not yet fully acknowledged or realized that he or she needs the support of others to effectively lead change.

- The principal does not know the *how* and *why* of effective shared leadership, including its importance to creating and sustaining change. See chapter 6 (page 93) for more information about this topic.

- The principal concludes that he or she will do better at the heavy lifting and decision making necessary to create change if done individually.

The latter is a particularly tempting strategy for a principal in a school characterized by teacher isolation, staff dysfunction, and lack of relational trust. In these situations, a school leader might not think it wise to extend decision-making responsibilities to staff members who may bring incongruent voices to the table. It harkens back to the adage, "If you want it done well, you better do it yourself." However, in *Simplifying Response to Intervention*, coauthors Austin Buffum, Mike Mattos, and Chris Weber (2012) urge leaders to keep in mind that some of our influential staff members may be individuals "who may traditionally resist change. [Yet the] coalition should also represent all relevant points of view and campus expertise" (p. 20). The reality is that influential staff members are going to have influence in your school regardless. It's far better to have them on your team where you can leverage this influence. As leaders, we must remind ourselves that different voices are not a threat to change—they can actually help bring important insights, balance, and clarity. Sometimes those who seem to represent dissent just need to be heard and recognized.

If there is a guiding coalition, these leaders may default to running its meetings the same way such meetings were led when the leaders were teachers themselves, or simply adopt the meeting protocols established before their arrival at the school. Traditionally, these meetings were characterized as more informational as opposed to focused on goals, data, and the collective decisions of change makers.

In *Learning by Doing*, coauthors Richard DuFour, Rebecca DuFour, Robert Eaker, Thomas W. Many, and Mike Mattos (2016) clearly delineate why shared leadership is so important:

> Those who hope to lead the PLC process must begin by acknowledging that no one person will have the energy, expertise, and influence to lead a complex change process . . . without first gaining the support of key staff members. (p. 27)

This wise and succinct quote explains one of the most important reasons for establishing shared leadership in a priority school: it's impossible to do it alone! The key is knowing and acknowledging this. Unfortunately, leaders don't always get to *knowing* and *acknowledging* until after things start to fray. And without question, if you don't have shared leadership and shared decision making in your school, effective change will begin to do just that. Over and over, the school-reform research reminds us that you can't turn around a school if the educators are removed from the decision-making processes:

> A broad and longstanding consensus in leadership theory holds that leaders in all walks of life and all kinds of organizations, public and private, need to depend on others to accomplish the group's purpose and need to encourage the development of leadership across the organization. Schools are no different. (Wallace Foundation, 2013)

Although the *go it alone* paradigm may sound like a good plan initially, it inevitably sets up a culture of top-down leadership and a management style proven time and again to fail in the arena of organizational change (Pink, 2009). Most educators in schools have been trained to do what they are told by their leaders. This is not a bad thing in and of itself. We do need to follow our leaders. However, when stakes are high and the pressure to show results heightens like they do in priority schools, teachers require a deeper motivation than "follow the leader." Educators in a school community need to be part of the decision-making process that leads to the collective actions they are committing to. Being involved in these decisions is how they build a belief in the work they are doing and the internal motivation to stick to it. Establishing a guiding coalition, building shared knowledge about how to move forward, and then securing a collective commitment to the goals and strategies necessary to meet those goals—this is how we build success. And it's the foundation of the collaborative community of a PLC. Research (Margolis & McCabe, 2006; Pink, 2009) supports the assertion that "when any group of individuals, including educators, loses the ability to define and solve the problems they face, they also lose the drive, motivation, and sense of self-efficacy that keep them moving forward toward their goals" (Noble, 2020, pp. 4–5). When principals attempt to go it alone, it is only a short time before this leads to both principal isolation and a deterioration of genuine teacher input and engagement.

Sharing Leadership in a PLC: Mindsets and Focus

What does shared leadership look like in a PLC priority school community? The Glossary of Education Reform (2013) was published to bring clarity to the vast terminology birthed from the school-reform movement and the federal legislation supporting it. This glossary defines *shared leadership* as "the practice of governing a school by expanding the number of people involved in making important decisions related to the school's organization, operation, and academics" (Glossary of Education Reform, 2013). While this definition's emphasis on shared decision making helps leaders get closer to the construct of shared leadership, in a PLC it goes much deeper. The guiding coalition in a PLC has a very specific purpose and function: to help sustain a school culture committed to high levels of learning for all, and to ensure that each staff member carries out the collective commitments and responsibilities he or she has agreed to accomplish for this goal.

In Kenneth C. Williams and Tom Hierck's (2015) book *Starting a Movement: Building Culture From the Inside Out in Professional Learning Communities*, the education authors define the *function* of the guiding coalition as "creating and sustaining a culture of collective responsibility" with a *purpose* to "unite and coordinate the school's collective efforts across grade levels, departments, and subjects" (p. 18). This is an important clarification. Sometimes school leaders believe they are committed to shared leadership when they share ideas and leadership with one or two key staff members (such as the assistant principal, dean, or another trusted staff member). These *are* important relationships. However, to ensure *authentic* shared leadership, members of the guiding coalition must represent the wider school population, including teacher leaders from different grade levels, subject areas, or department-level teams, as well as support-area representatives such as the counselor, special education department staff, ancillary staff, and instructional coaches. (See chapter 8, page 131, for more on this topic, such as inclusion criteria.)

When members of the guiding coalition represent the school's different areas and functions, the shared understandings and actions are more effectively implemented across all areas of the school community. For instance, when the counselor is an active member of your guiding coalition, insights regarding the impacts of poverty and trauma on the school community and student body can help guide the discussions and decisions regarding what extra social-emotional or behavioral supports your school may need to offer. Likewise, if you have a second-grade representative on your team but not a third-grade representative, the team may miss key transitional needs for students moving from primarily *learning to read* in the lower grades to an emphasis on *reading to learn* starting in third grade. In short, if key members are not present, we can miss critical information in the development of our action plans and goals.

Another important shift Williams and Hierck (2015) capture when defining *authentic shared leadership* is the difference between a leadership team whose priority is relaying information, and a guiding coalition focused on its function and purpose to support sustainable change that leads to increased student learning and success. They describe the information-handling style of a traditional leadership team as operating in the messenger mentality of shared leadership (Williams & Hierck, 2015). In practice, this is when the teacher leaders' primary purpose on the team is either relaying information about concerns members of the school community want the principal to address or solve, or the principal relaying information to the leadership team that he or she wants disseminated to the school community (Kramer & Schuhl, 2017). This information generally relates to school, district, or state or province initiatives that require knowledge and compliance. With a messenger mentality, questions that guide the conversations during leadership meetings may include, "How is our bus duty schedule going to work?" "When will the assembly on Wednesday take place?" "This team is showing up late for duty. What are you going to do about it?" and "Can you please convey this timeline representing the latest mandates on assessment compliance from the state?" It's not that this information is unimportant. It's just that messages to be passed along cannot be the primary focus of a guiding coalition in a PLC. Its purpose is much greater.

If we look at the flip side of this communication cycle, the time when the guiding coalition members return to their team to relay decisions and information requires a shift as well. We've already established that school reform requires necessary change and that this change can be hard. For a team leader communicating necessary change to the team, it might be easy to fall back on, "Hey, I'm just the messenger." Williams and Hierck (2015) say this shift, in a guiding coalition, to shared decision making and collective responsibility requires the team leader to be the *missionary*, not just a messenger. Team leaders communicate and support the necessary change with clear understanding and conviction about the *why* of the change and the confidence to lead their team in the *how* of successfully accomplishing the change necessary to improve student outcomes.

A high-functioning guiding coalition, again, has the mindsets and focused function and purpose of supporting sustainable change. In a priority school embracing the PLC at Work model, there is an urgency that requires a clear understanding among guiding coalition members about these critical mindsets and how they frame their work when they come together as a team. In addition to mindsets, there is the *focus*. Coauthors Sharon V. Kramer and Sarah Schuhl (2017) note when members of the guiding coalition meet, their team "must operate as a model for all of the other collaborative teams in the school" (p. 11). With this responsibility in mind, each time the guiding coalition meets, members focus on the four critical questions of a PLC (DuFour et al., 2016; see page 3). With this focus, the questions that drive their discussions sound more like, "Is what we are currently doing working schoolwide to improve student learning and outcomes?" or "What is our evidence?" And if what they are doing is not working schoolwide, guiding coalition members ask, "What do we need to create, do, or adapt to ensure our students are increasing their learning outcomes?"

As you can see, a guiding coalition's focus looks significantly different than the questions driving the focus in a messenger mentality leadership meeting. A high-functioning guiding coalition must have a relentless focus on learning and the artifacts that confirm this learning is happening in their school each time members meet. It is the only way a school community can turn around a low-performing school with the urgency required in the high-stakes culture of the priority school setting.

Knowing Why Shared Leadership Is So Crucial in the Priority School

I'd like to touch on some of the specific *whys* of shared leadership as they relate to the priority school and clarify why high-functioning guiding coalitions are crucial. Shared leadership has three key functions of significance in a priority school.

1. It addresses the need for collective responsibility and accountability to facilitate urgent change.

2. It addresses the educator's need to feel engaged and competent in the work of school reform.

3. It addresses the educator's need for high social-emotional support.

The Need for Collective Responsibility and Accountability to Facilitate Urgent Change

Let's start with collective responsibility and the urgency for change. In a priority school, there is without question an urgent need to lead, support, and facilitate effective change quickly and collectively. Too many students in a priority school are failing to learn, and the call to turn around this trend as quickly as possible becomes a moral imperative. As you know, the only way to create effective systemic change in a school is to engage key members of the school community in helping lead this change. Members of the guiding coalition help monitor, direct, and support the mindsets and actions that ensure a collective effort to achieve the schoolwide goals for academic growth. Once a school has agreed on a *mission* (why it exists) to ensure this happens, and *vision* (what it must become) for increased student learning, it becomes incumbent on school community members to follow through on their collective commitments (DuFour et al., 2016). It's the only way to realize the school's vision.

This is why your guiding coalition is so important! The members' purpose is to ensure this happens schoolwide with consistency. School leaders must depend on the ability of guiding coalition members to convey a deep understanding and commitment to both the urgency of the school's mission and the importance of the collective actions necessary to fulfill that mission. Guiding coalition leaders solidify these commitments throughout the school community by monitoring their teams' actions, celebrating their successes, and keeping the mission and vision alive and relevant in the teams they represent. They no longer represent the messenger mentality; they communicate and act on the larger ideas and commitments of their school's vision (Williams & Hierck, 2015). It is the complete and total commitment of the guiding coalition members to bring unity of purpose, while coordinating collective efforts in the teams they represent, that allows school-reform efforts to be swift and effective.

The Educator's Need to Feel Engaged and Competent in the Work of School Reform

The next important *why* of shared leadership in a priority school is the need for educators in the school community to have the opportunity to restore a sense of competence and empowerment. In fact, in their self-determination theory, researchers Edward L. Deci and Richard M. Ryan (2012) theorize that (1) the need to feel competent achieving goals and (2) the need to have some form of autonomy in deciding how to attain goals are two of the top innate needs all humans share in their search to find happiness, contentment, and a sense of self-efficacy. On the other hand, in priority schools, there is often a history of top-down mandates birthed out of what I refer to as *fear-based leadership*. Fear-based leadership operates from a fear of failure. It grows out of a hidden uncertainty regarding what actions will actually turn around a school and if the actions can be done at all. This uncertainty can easily turn into an overreliance on compliance and fidelity to programs and textbooks touted as the fix-alls for achievement gaps in priority schools.

Let me clarify here that I'm not suggesting that programs and textbooks are not important tools in our work as educators. However, with an overreliance on programs and textbooks to turn around low performance, schools can ignore the importance of mining the insights, talents, and professionalism of the educators in the school who work directly with the students and the standards they must master. This has led to removing educators from taking part in the decision-making processes that determine what actions and curricula to best utilize to meet the students' unique needs. I continually see this disconnect played out in schools across the country. Every three to five years (sometimes less), after teachers have begun to master the current textbooks, programs, and interventions, the state or district leaders decide that the current resources are no longer sufficient. They then introduce a whole new slate of programs that teachers are required to master. There is often minimal, if any, dialogue with educators about this change or why it's necessary. This cycle is frustrating and demoralizing to educators, who often feel like victims of these continual changes instead of active participants in creating effective change. Over time, this disconnect leads to teacher demoralization and diminishes their motivation to engage in change. As author, businessperson, and keynote speaker Stephen R. Covey (1989) so aptly asserts, "no involvement, no commitment" (p. 143).

It is important to clarify that the trend of removing teachers from the collective decision making and problem solving necessary to turn around a school is not inevitably the school principal's decision. Unfortunately, priority schools are too often the first schools to lose the autonomy to decide what is best for their schools. In many cases, district leaders, responding to the demand for change and innovation to improve school performance, decide to give their A- and B-rated schools autonomy to innovate, but allocate their D- and F-rated schools to follow the program the district leaders identify with fidelity. In this case, a principal can feel like his or her hands are tied. In reality, it is the D and F schools that most need the autonomy and leverage to innovate and meet the needs of their unique student body by determining what curriculum and support they need.

The research on the power and efficacy of collaborative teachers' decision making as they answer the questions of what to do to increase student outcomes cannot be denied (Hattie, 2009). The research on PLCs and collective teacher self-efficacy's impact on increasing student outcomes are prolific (DuFour, 2016). Yet time after time, year after year, schools and districts fall back on fidelity and compliance. PLC at Work is not a program or initiative, but instead, is a process predicated on the belief that the answers to the questions of how to increase learning for all students lies in the collective inquiry and collaboration of the school's educators (DuFour et al., 2016). Again, it's not that all programs and initiatives in and of themselves are bad or ineffective. However, they must become tools in the hands of educators, not the other way around.

One of the first priorities of any school that needs to re-engage staff and facilitate a cultural shift to learning for all is to re-establish the priority of the educator's voice in the decision-making processes. This starts with creating a guiding coalition representative of the educators in the building and establishing shared leadership where all voices are heard and valued.

The Educator's Need for High Social-Emotional Support

Just like the principal, teachers and support staff face increased pressure in priority schools to create and sustain the lasting changes necessary for school improvement. The same stress and potential burnout principals feel in the high-stakes environment is also prevalent in the teachers and other educators in the school (MetLife, 2013).

In Michael A. West's (2012) book *Effective Teamwork*, he clearly delineates two very important areas that need focus and support if collaborative teams are going to be successful: (1) the tasks necessary to meet the team's set goals and objectives and (2) the social, emotional, and other human factors critical to the well-being of its members. In a priority school setting, it is easy to get lopsided on these two critical needs by giving all your attention to goal attainment at the expense of the well-being of the educators who are called on to meet those goals. The reproducible "Collaborative Team Success: Balancing Goals With Well-Being" (page 126) is available for reflection.

I remember being in the throes of implementing the Turnaround Model of school reform for my school. I was the school principal, and goal attainment was definitely a focus that weighed heavily on my mind. We started this reform with only 22 percent proficient in reading and 18 percent proficient in mathematics. Increasing these percentages was a moral imperative all of us took very seriously. I, like many priority school leaders, was asking a great deal of my teachers and staff, and they were absolutely responding to the call. However, I remember a morning when one of the guiding coalition members came to my office and confided in me, saying, "Robin, we're trying our best. We are. But we're feeling overwhelmed and starting to feel as if we are going down with the ship."

He then conveyed how he and his team were overwhelmed with the tasks of learning a new curriculum, keeping up with their flexible groupings, and completing the necessary documentation and artifacts. I was startled by this information and felt terrible that I had not sensed or been aware of the high level of stress this team was experiencing. I immediately met with this team's members with the goal of alleviating some of this stress. We started by identifying all the tasks they were currently trying to complete and writing them on chart paper. Next, we looked at the four critical questions of a PLC (page 3). Using these priorities and the school's collective commitments, we worked together to cross off those tasks that were not a priority and create a manageable list of actions focused on what was most important for student learning. This lightened their burden, alleviated unnecessary stress, and helped refocus their work together as a collaborative team. I learned a great lesson that day: as a school leader, you must keep your finger on the pulse of the well-being of the educators in your building, not just their task completion. When members of the school community are operating under high levels of stress, goal attainment is compromised, and morale suffers.

If I did not have a guiding coalition with members who shared relational trust and a knowledge that I welcomed and acknowledged all voices and concerns, I may never have known the level of stress my teachers were experiencing. In a priority school, tasks and initiatives can begin to pile up, and leaders forget they must balance each member's plate. They can't keep adding without taking some away. Kramer and Schuhl (2017) write, "Leadership consists of both pressure and support" (p. 16). And your guiding coalition members will help you keep this balance if you let them know you care as much about their social-emotional well-being as you do about goal attainment. Writing about the sustainable work of a PLC, authors Richard DuFour and Robert Eaker (1998) echo this balance when they state that in a PLC, "Educators create an environment that fosters mutual cooperation, emotional support, and personal growth as they work together to achieve what they cannot accomplish alone" (p. xii).

As a reminder, this need to balance goal attainment and emotional well-being is just as true for you as the priority school leader. I encourage you to know and make time for those activities and self-care techniques that are most effective at managing your stress. I also encourage you to try to build a coalition of other school leaders that can support you as you support one another. I continue to have a group of principals and school leaders in my district and profession that I can turn to when I feel overwhelmed about the tasks before me. I know I am safe with these individuals and can be honest, and even vulnerable, as I work to navigate the demands and stresses that are associated with the need for high levels of change and an urgency to implement these changes.

Taking Next Steps

The rubric in figure 7.1 will help you determine areas of need with actionable steps and plans for increasing the effectiveness of your shared leadership. See chapter 3 (page 45) for more about loose and tight work, chapter 6 (page 93) for more about collective responsibility, and chapter 10 (page 163) for more about the right work.

In addition to assessing the guiding coalition with the rubric, ask yourself the following questions. These questions can help you consider the state of shared leadership in your school right now.

- **"Do I currently have a guiding coalition?"** If not, make this a priority. It is critical to your success in school reform. Chapters 6 and 8 (page 131) clarify who to include and how this coalition should work.

- If you do have a guiding coalition or leadership team, **"Are members acting as messengers or have they embraced the shifts that exhibit the mindsets and focus of change agents supporting our school's vision and collective commitments?"** To shift away from the messenger mentality, you and your team will need to revisit your team's mindsets, purpose, and function. It is critical that school leaders clarify this shift from a messenger focus to a change agent focus with those who are selected to serve on the guiding coalition and clarify the attributes members bring to this form of shared leadership. Author Lyle Kirtman's (2014) studies of effective school leadership investigate research on over seven hundred educational organizations over a span of thirty years. Kirtman identifies seven competencies present in highly effective school leaders:

    1. Challenges the status quo
    2. Builds trust through clear communications and expectations
    3. Creates commonly owned plan for success
    4. Focuses on team over self
    5. Has high sense of urgency for change and sustainable results
    6. Commits to continuous self-improvement
    7. Builds external networks and partnerships (Kirtman, 2014, as cited in Williams & Hierck, 2015, p. 25)

    When I work to create a guiding coalition, I ask members to reflect on these competencies and identify which ones they feel are strengths and which ones they consider areas of needed growth. We share with one another our strengths and weaknesses, personally and collectively. We then share what area we will work to strengthen and sustain as we take on the responsibilities

	Level 1 Beginning	Level 2 Attempting	Level 3 Practicing	Level 4 Embracing
Leadership Team	Team contains volunteer teachers and staff. Team focuses on every issue and may spend more time on complaints and ideas for first-order change than student learning. Team creates an agenda but does not always follow it and operates using procedural norms.	Team contains previously designated leaders or rotating leaders. Team leads the work of school improvement, but may be focused on first-order change. Team creates agendas for meetings in advance of the meetings and operates using norms.	Team contains teachers with characteristics including change agent, expert, credible, and leader. Team models and leads the work of school improvement. Team creates agendas, shares meeting minutes, and operates using norms.	Team contains teachers with characteristics, including change agent, expert, credible, and leader, and re-evaluates members each year with entrance and exit interviews. Team models, monitors with feedback, and leads the work of school improvement. Team creates agendas and shares minutes electronically while using norms.
Vision and Action	Team looks at data related to student achievement and demographics. A vision statement exists, though the team seldom, if ever, references or addresses it. The team has only loosely agreed on collective commitments and has not written them down. It is focused on goals and not results.	Teams gather and analyze data related to demographics and student learning. The team has established a vision and written it down for each adult in the school. Some staff members work toward it. The team has established collective commitments or goals.	Teams gather and analyze a full picture of data to determine the root issues to address to improve learning. The team has established a vision, which compels those in the building to reach it. The team has established collective commitments and goals.	Teams gather and analyze data from all stakeholders routinely and in a location that leadership can easily access. The team has established a vision and all in the community work toward achieving it. The team has established collective commitments and goals and routinely reviews and updates them as necessary.
Leading the Right Work	Teachers wait to be told what to do (and will do it) but are not clear about what is tight and loose in the work of school improvement. Teacher teams are clear about and address some of the four critical questions of a PLC.	The work of collaborative teams is all designated as tight and teams are on rigid schedules of what to address and when, but may not be clear about why. Teacher teams comply with addressing the four critical questions of a PLC but are still unclear about why.	The principal and teachers are clear about what is tight and what is loose in the work of school improvement. Teachers work to address the four critical questions of a PLC in collaborative teams, using data to determine student learning.	The principal, teachers, and staff are clear about what is tight and loose in the work of school improvement and focus on student learning. Teachers work in collaborative teams to improve student learning using the four critical questions of a PLC and monitor that journey continually.

Source: Kramer & Schuhl, 2017, pp. 25–26.

Figure 7.1: Chart a course focused on a learning rubric.

of leading change. This activity helps clarify that their work on this team is no longer merely as a messenger bringing back information, but as an advocate and gatekeeper of the changes we want to make collectively as a school community to ensure high levels of learning for all of our students.

- **"Do I intentionally select members of the guiding coalition for their ability to lead change?"** Some people have characteristics that equip them to lead a change effort, and these are the people you want on your team. Leaders should not randomly select guiding coalition members in a priority school. Figure 7.2 is a simple tool that I encourage you to review. The blank reproducible "Leadership Team Selection Protocol" (page 127) is also available.

Use the characteristics in each section to determine the most effective members of the leadership team.	
Eagerness to Promote Change List individuals who are committed to school improvement.	**Expertise** List individuals who have demonstrated knowledge and experience that will support school improvement.
Credibility List individuals who are influential among the other staff members.	**Leadership Skills** List individuals who are proven leaders in the school.

Source: Adapted from Buffum et al., 2012; Kotter, 1996; Kramer & Schuhl, 2017.

Figure 7.2: Leadership team selection protocol.

- **"Do I meet with the guiding coalition at least twice a month?"**
  To accomplish change as quickly as possible, the school's guiding coalition must meet regularly. Consider the time and budget allocation necessary to accomplish this. Many districts provide a stipend for shared leadership teams to meet regularly; however, there is not always allocation for the number of people you need for collective representation. To accomplish this goal, you may need to get creative. For example, do you have school improvement grant (SIG) money to allocate? Is there money in your Title I funding to allocate? Can you effectively present to your district the need for full representation and get district funding? You may also want to look at your current schedule and resources. Can you create time in the school day to allow leaders to meet without the need to provide hourly compensation? I've seen all of these used to accomplish the goal of providing all the necessary time and representation.

- **"Do our meeting agendas and conversations focus on the four critical questions of a PLC?"** Those questions are:

  1. What is it we want our students to know and be able to do?
  2. How will we know if each student has learned it?
  3. How will we respond when some students do not learn it?
  4. How will we extend the learning for students who have demonstrated proficiency? (DuFour et al., 2016, p. 59)

- **"Do our meetings center around student data and teacher artifacts that help answer these four critical questions for the school?"** State assessments and district benchmark assessments are important indicators of your school's progress toward its academic goals. However, the data grade-level teams capture about their common formative assessments, as well as the data regarding how students are responding to intervention and remediation groups, will provide the greater focus and leverage you need to close achievement gaps for your students. The reproducible "Data-Analysis Protocol" (page 223) is an excellent tool to introduce to your grade-level and subject-area teams, and then review with your guiding coalition.

- **"Do our meetings end with a plan for how to support the actionable steps members determine necessary to increase student outcomes?"** Action is the only thing that results in change, and you must make actionable steps a priority. Simply having a Next Steps section on your guiding coalition agenda in which the notetaker can capture agreements for next steps, and then following up on them again at each meeting, will help you and your guiding coalition monitor agreed-on actions for effectiveness, adapt when necessary, and celebrate your successes.

- **"Is the most prominent voice in the room during meetings the voices of guiding coalition members, or is it _my_ voice?"** (Spoiler alert—it needs to be _theirs_.) I encourage you to monitor this over the course of a few guiding coalition meetings. Who is doing a majority of the talking? Often, there is a tendency for those in the room to agree with the principal. They will listen to your lead about the *what* and *how* of change, and then follow through. This is what they have been programmed to do. However, this is not what you want. If you don't teach your guiding coalition team members that their voices are just as critical as yours to making decisions, you may never hear important feedback that is critical to successfully initiating collective actions and commitments. Members of the guiding coalition need to know they can disagree and have honest conversations without feeling disloyal to you or other members. Here are some suggestions.

‣ Educate your team leaders about shared leadership in a PLC and why it's so important to you.

‣ Find any chance you can to celebrate and be thankful to those who share their concerns or a different opinion from yours. By doing this, you teach that person, and those in your team watching, that you are not threatened by different opinions and actually welcome them.

‣ Be a good listener. Restate what members suggest, and ask other members for feedback on their perspective. Demonstrate that you are genuinely interested in what they have to say.

‣ Introduce the definition of consensus in a PLC: "Consensus is achieved when (1) all points of view have been not only heard but also solicited and (2) the will of the group is evident, even to those who most oppose it" (Mattos, DuFour, DuFour, Eaker, & Many, 2016, p. 19). This definition makes clear the value and importance of all voices being heard and valued when making decisions about how to move forward collectively.

A commitment that all voices are heard, even when voices go against the grain, honors and supports the collaboration that characterizes a PLC. This is how we learn from one another and have the ability to adapt.

Conclusion

My hope is that you've gained a clearer understanding of why a school's guiding coalition is so critical to supporting and sustaining the vision, mission, and collective commitments of the school community. Ultimately, these members are key players in ensuring a priority school attains the academic goals so important to turning around their school. Guiding coalition members become a problem-solving entity for learning as they work with their teams, along with the school leader, to ensure the processes and practices of the school are creating high levels of learning for all students. The guiding coalition bravely, honestly, and collectively shines a light on the current reality of learning in its school while modeling the commitments and mindsets that create a culture of learning for all. After leading and coaching priority schools for many years, I can confidently assert it is through the passion, commitments, and shared leadership of the guiding coalition members that schools can finally break through the ceiling of low-proficiency rates that plague so many priority schools.

Collaborative Team Success: Balancing Goals With Well-Being

Teams must focus and support two areas if they are to succeed: (1) the tasks necessary to meet the team's set goals and objectives and (2) the social, emotional, and other human factors critical to the well-being of its members (West, 2012). Record all the tasks your team is currently trying to accomplish. Next, review the biggest priorities: the four critical questions of a PLC (DuFour, DuFour, Eaker, Many, & Mattos, 2016) and your school's collective commitments. From there, cross off those tasks that are not a priority and create a new, manageable list of actions focused on what is most important for student learning.

All Tasks the Team Is Trying to Complete	The Four Critical Questions of a PLC	School's Collective Commitments
	1. What is it we want our students to know and be able to do? 2. How will we know if each student has learned it? 3. How will we respond when some students do not learn it? 4. How will we extend the learning for students who have demonstrated proficiency? (DuFour et al., 2016, p. 59)	
Revised Task List:		

Source: Adapted from DuFour, R., DuFour, R., Eaker, R., Many, T. W., & Mattos, M. (2016). Learning by doing: A handbook for Professional Learning Communities at Work (3rd ed.). Bloomington, IN: Solution Tree Press; West, M. A. (2012). Effective teamwork: Practical lessons from organizational research (3rd ed.). West Sussex, England: Wiley.

Leadership Team Selection Protocol

Use the characteristics in each section to determine the most effective members of the leadership team.

Eagerness to Promote Change List individuals who are committed to school improvement.	**Expertise** List individuals who have demonstrated knowledge and experience that will support school improvement.
Credibility List individuals who are influential among the other staff members.	**Leadership Skills** List individuals who are proven leaders in the school.

Source: Kramer, S. V., & Schuhl, S. (2017). School improvement for all: A how-to guide for doing the right work. *Bloomington, IN: Solution Tree Press.*

References and Resources

Buffum, A., Mattos, M., & Weber, C. (2012). *Simplifying response to intervention: Four essential guiding principles.* Bloomington, IN: Solution Tree Press.

Covey, S. R. (1989). *The seven habits of highly effective people: Powerful lesson in personal change.* New York: Simon & Schuster.

Deci, E. L., & Ryan, R. M. (2012). Self-determination theory. In P. A. M. Van Lange, A. W. Kruglanski, & E. T. Higgins (Eds.), *Handbook of theories of social psychology* (pp. 416–436). Thousand Oaks, CA: SAGE.

DuFour, R. (2016). *Advocates for professional learning communities: Finding common ground in education reform.* Accessed at www.allthingsplc.info/files/uploads/AdvocatesforPLCs -Updated11-9-15.pdf on February 10, 2021.

DuFour, R., DuFour, R., Eaker, R., Many, T. W., & Mattos, M. (2016). *Learning by doing: A handbook for Professional Learning Communities at Work* (3rd ed.). Bloomington, IN: Solution Tree Press.

DuFour, R., & Eaker, R. (1998). *Professional Learning Communities at Work: Best practices for enhancing student achievement.* Bloomington, IN: Solution Tree Press.

Franke, H. A. (2014). Toxic stress: Effects, prevention and treatment. *Children, 1*(3), 390– 402. Accessed at www.ncbi.nlm.nih.gov/pmc/articles/PMC4928741/#:~:text=Toxic%20 stress%20results%20in%20prolonged,%2C%20reassurance%2C%20or%20 emotional%20attachments on November 7, 2020.

Glossary of Education Reform. (2013, November 12). *Shared leadership.* Accessed at www.edglossary .org/shared-leadership on February 15, 2020.

Hattie, J. (2009). *Visible learning: A synthesis of over 800 meta-analyses relating to achievement.* New York: Routledge.

Kirtman, L. (2014). *Leadership and teams: The missing piece of the educational reform puzzle.* Boston: Pearson.

Kotter, J. P. (1996). *Leading change.* Boston: Harvard Business School Press.

Kramer, S. V., & Schuhl, S. (2017). *School improvement for all: A how-to guide for doing the right work.* Bloomington, IN: Solution Tree Press.

Margolis, H., & McCabe, P. P. (2006). Improving self-efficacy and motivation: What to do, what to say. *Intervention in School and Clinic, 41*(4), 218–227.

Mattos, M., DuFour, R., DuFour, R., Eaker, R., & Many, T. W. (2016). *Concise answers to frequently asked questions about Professional Learning Communities at Work.* Bloomington, IN: Solution Tree Press.

MetLife. (2013, February). *The MetLife survey of the American teacher: Challenges for school leadership.* Accessed at www.metlife.com/content/dam/microsites/about/corporate-profile /MetLife-Teacher-Survey-2012.pdf on February 10, 2020.

Noble, R. (2020). *Finding fulfillment: A path to reclaiming hope and empowerment for educators.* Bloomington, IN: Solution Tree Press.

Pink, D. H. (2009). *Drive: The surprising truth about what motivates us.* New York: Riverhead Books.

U.S. Department of Education. (n.d.). *Demonstrating that an SEA's lists of reward, priority, and focus schools meet ESEA flexibility definitions.* Accessed at www.ed.gov/sites/default /files/demonstrating-meet-flex-definitions.pdf on February 10, 2021.

U.S. Department of Education. (2015). *Profiles of school turnaround strategies in selected sites.* Accessed at www2.ed.gov/programs/sif/sigprofiles/index.html on November 5, 2020.

U.S. Department of Education. (2016). *Documentation for the school improvement grants public-use data file for cohorts 1–4, school years 2010–11 through 2013–14.* Accessed at www2.ed.gov/programs/sif/data/sy1011-1314.pdf on February 10, 2021.

Wallace Foundation. (2013, January). *The school principal as leader: Guiding schools to better teaching and learning.* Accessed at www.wallacefoundation.org/knowledge-center/Documents/The -School-Principal-as-Leader-Guiding-Schools-to-Better-Teaching-and-Learning-2nd-Ed.pdf on February 10, 2020.

West, M. A. (2012). *Effective teamwork: Practical lessons from organizational research* (3rd ed.). West Sussex, England: Wiley.

Williams, K. C., & Hierck, T. (2015). *Starting a movement: Building culture from the inside out in professional learning communities.* Bloomington, IN: Solution Tree Press.

Gerry Petersen-Incorvaia, PhD, has worked at both school sites and district offices while implementing professional learning communities (PLCs). Gerry is an assistant superintendent for educational services for the Glendale Elementary School District in Glendale, Arizona. He has served as a teacher, principal, university professor, and curriculum and instruction director. While director for curriculum and instruction and assistant superintendent, Glendale Elementary School District became a Model PLC district.

Gerry has trained and presented with Rick Stiggins and Jan Chappuis on assessment, presented with the State Collaborative on Assessment and Student Standards, and written curriculum and presented with Jay and Daisy McTighe on Understanding by Design. Gerry's diverse experiences in schools and districts have invigorated his philosophy that all students have equity of access to a rigorous education.

Gerry earned a bachelor's degree from Luther College and master's and doctoral degrees from the University of Arizona.

To learn more about Gerry's work, follow @DrGerryPI on Twitter.

To book Gerry Petersen-Incorvaia for professional development, contact pd@SolutionTree.com.

Ensuring the District Guiding Coalition and School Learning Team Have Impact

Gerry Petersen-Incorvaia

Leadership that gets real results is collaborative; it's a process that involves building a school leadership team, a **guiding coalition** . . . to lead the school-improvement transformation in what we can almost guarantee to be tumultuous work.

—*Sharon V. Kramer and Sarah Schuhl*

In the fall of 2015, there was discussion in my district (Glendale Elementary School District in Glendale, Arizona) about how to accelerate the right work throughout the district. A lot of structures and alignment were not in place with regard to curriculum, instruction, assessment, and professional development. The educational services' team knew big changes were needed and it would take a large districtwide task force and school task forces to do this work. The team decided to create not only a district guiding coalition but also school learning teams. The school learning teams were similar to a guiding coalition in that they were a diverse group of identified teacher leaders at each school site. Each school had a learning team leader per grade level, and teachers of every diverse population were included. The district guiding coalition was a team of school learning team members who came together at a district level to build their capacity and move the work forward. These two teams—(1) district guiding coalition and (2) school learning team—while learning through job-embedded professional development, helped lead the work at every school site in the district and as an entire school district. It was imperative for this work to happen throughout the entire district. Then, our district was named a Model professional learning community (PLC) district by Solution Tree in the fall of 2018.

Continuous school improvement occurs by harnessing the power within a shared leadership model. In priority schools and districts, *impactful actions* are large-scale movements that require more than just one person or a small group of people to lead the organization through the actions. No superintendent, assistant superintendent, principal or assistant principal, or teacher leader can do it alone. Districts and schools need an all-hands-on-deck approach to shift from isolation to a PLC moving on a continuous positive trajectory that then ensures all students have access to an aligned curriculum, instruction, and assessment system to allow for increased student achievement.

In the PLC at Work process in a priority school or district, building a guiding coalition at the district level and a school learning team (or school leadership team) at the site level are important steps. Although the work of these teams may be similar, the complexity and size of the work is different. When a school or district begins the PLC at Work process or has perhaps been doing *PLC lite* (that is, superficial implementation of PLC principles; DuFour, DuFour, Eaker, Many, & Mattos, 2016), there may not be a guiding coalition, or the work of the guiding coalition may not be the right work to ensure greater student achievement. Ensuring the school learning teams implement district guiding coalition work, with support and monitoring, is the best effective practice. The work moves from support and monitoring structures within the PLC process to identifying and solving problems of practice through a collective inquiry approach. This helps not only build capacity of school staff for the right work but also sustain it. It is imperative to "use the term *school learning team* because in schools in need of improvement, this team works to gain a deeper learning and understanding of the work" (Kramer & Schuhl, 2017, p. 9). Also, organizing the work of a district guiding coalition and a school learning team helps support this work to ensure a positive trajectory of student achievement (Kotter, 2014; Kramer & Schuhl, 2017).

An important shift happens for school staff who are members of the school learning team: the shift from representative to team member and messenger to missionary allows movement from efficiency to advocacy (Williams & Hierck, 2015). These individuals become the champions of this work and help create the sense of urgency needed to move this work forward.

Creating a sense of urgency is an important first step in priority schools. Without this, it can be harder to make progress. There is no time to wait in priority schools or districts; many times they are on the verge of state takeover or massive turnaround efforts.

Sometimes during the implementation process, there is a realization of an all-district need to readdress basic collaborative team work, such as deconstructing or unwrapping of standards or developing common formative assessments. These needs help create the agendas for district guiding coalition professional learning in order to bring back the learning to the school learning team. Author Austin Buffum (2012) agrees:

> Too often, schools rely upon preexisting "leadership teams" to guide the cultural change necessary to operate as a PLC. Members of these preexisting teams have been selected around old paradigms and ways of thinking that are anathema to the real work of PLCs. Even worse, principals sometimes go it alone in attempting to change the culture of their schools, or they only involve staff in ways that appear to be symbolic rather than substantive.

Champions of change are needed to help with a potential cultural shift. Ensuring the guiding coalition and school learning teams have these shifts in mind is important to moving the work forward. These shifts help to shape the *why*, *how*, and *what* of the work.

Organization of a Guiding Coalition and School Learning Team

To make the changes needed in a priority school or to get out of the failure rut may be quite difficult. The people closest to the work can make the change happen at a more rapid pace than those who are not. However, having champions of the work to lead it is an important step and structure in the process. A district guiding coalition and a school learning team that focus entirely and only on the learning at the site is an important structure for a district and school to implement.

Since the real, impactful work occurs at the school site, I recommend organizing the school learning team first. (Remember, similar to a guiding coalition, this term refers to a team solely focused on increasing student achievement for all students.) The school learning team should include grade-level and content team leaders from each team.

Leadership for change is the essence of the work of the school learning team and must include tasks that focus on learning (Kramer & Schuhl, 2017). The criteria for this team follow.

- An eagerness to promote change
- Expertise relevant to the tasks at hand
- High credibility with all stakeholders
- Proven leadership skills

These criteria help identify the characteristics members need. Figure 8.1 (page 134) features interview questions that can help identify someone who would be appropriate for a school learning team.

The school learning team needs to have representation on the district guiding coalition. A district guiding coalition helps change the context or create space for leaders to practice and share effective practices. As educational consultant and author Michael Fullan (2020) explains: "leading in a culture of change does not mean placing changed individuals into unchanged environments. Rather, change leaders work on changing the context, helping create new settings conducive to learning and sharing that learning" (p. 93).

The recommended participants in a district guiding coalition are representatives from every school site. The membership can be flexible, depending on how the district might be able to bring the group together (depending on the room capacity and the capacity of the team leading the professional learning, time, organization, and other contingencies). For rapid and maximum impact, I recommend professional development for all members of a school learning team with the district guiding coalition. This should take

Questions	Phrases to Look for or Listen for in an Answer	
What is your expertise in ensuring all students have access to a guaranteed and viable curriculum?	*Academic diversity* *Differentiation* *Scaffolding* *Collaborative team* *Pacing guide* *Common formative assessments*	*Preassessment* *Checks for understanding* *Intervention* *Extension*
What does rigorous instruction for all students mean to you?	*Teach at high levels for all students* *High expectations* *Differentiation* *Scaffolding*	*Enrichment* *Student access* *Diverse populations* *Collaboration*
Explain a time when you have felt passionate about something to the point of wanting to promote change.	*Personal drive* *Heart* *Mindfulness* *Change process*	Why it is important How they went about the change
What are some of the artifacts you might create in a collaborative team that is working through a learning cycle unit by unit?	*Proficiency map* *Pacing guide* *Common formative assessments* *Lesson plan* *Unit of study*	*Intervention plan* *Preassessment* *Deconstructing or unpacking standards* *Student data trackers*
What does *high expectations to ensure high levels of learning for all students* mean to you? How do you show this in your instruction?	*Diverse populations* *Depth of Knowledge* *Questioning*	*Checks for understanding* *Differentiation* *Collaboration*
What does it mean to be *results oriented*, and how does that impact your work?	*Assessment* *Evaluation* *Performance*	*Implement action* *Data driven* *Student learning*

Part of the work of a school learning team is to have credibility with collaborative team members and colleagues schoolwide. What does this mean to you, and how do you showcase this in your work?	Walk the talk Lead by example Collaboration Efficacy	Influence Support and monitoring Accountability
How do you reflect on your classroom instruction? What data do you use to help with your reflection?	Qualitative and quantitative data Narrative data Observation Performance tasks	Checks for understanding Exit tickets Daily reflection Instructional rounds Observing colleagues
Shifting from being a collaborative team member to also being a member of the school learning team builds the capacity of shared leadership at the school site. How might this affect your perspective of your position on campus?	Learning by doing Leader of the work Professional capacity	

Figure 8.1: Potential interview questions and what to look for in answers.

place as almost like a workshop setting over the course of a year, perhaps four to six hours per month. This district-level team should also include representatives from the departments of educational services or academic services (that is, curriculum, instruction, and assessment; special education; language acquisition; and federal programs).

The purposes of the district guiding coalition and school learning team are similar.

- The district guiding coalition includes school learning team members in order to provide professional learning these members will take back to their school learning team and school staff. It also helps the district educational services or curriculum department keep a pulse on the work at the school site. The number of school learning team members who participate in the district guiding coalition depends on factors such as a district's finances, organizational health, and human capacity. Effective best practice is for all members of the school learning team to participate, which would require, depending on schedules, Saturday professional learning, after-school professional learning, or the use of substitutes and other educational supports to allow for district guiding coalition time.

- The purpose of a school learning team is to create, implement, build capacity for, and support and monitor the right work within continuous school improvement. In underperforming districts and schools, it is important to enact work that accelerates the pace of the right work. A district guiding coalition will focus on helping not just move student achievement forward teacher by teacher, collaborative team by collaborative team, or school by school, but also move an entire district of schools forward.

To increase adult collaboration and student achievement, part of the work of a district guiding coalition and school learning team is to ensure a PLC road map.

The Professional Learning Content

The professional learning for the district guiding coalition is organized in a manner so the school learning team receives a trainer-of-trainer model of professional learning at the district guiding coalition professional development, and can then take the learning back to the campus staff.

As coauthors Terri L. Martin and Cameron L. Rains (2018) state, "The guiding coalition identifies necessary changes and develops implementation plans. Its members understand the change process, help move staff forward positively, and challenge the status quo when necessary" (p. 29). This is the work needed for an all-hands-on-deck approach to continuous school improvement in a priority school and district. This work is easily replicated at district and school-site levels, given that it focuses on the impactful purpose of schooling. It takes time and a diverse group of teachers and administrators, but the benefits help a school and district focus on the teaching and learning of the organization. Table 8.1 lists the right work and not-so-right work of a district guiding coalition and school learning team.

Figure 8.2 (page 138) shows an example of an agenda for the first district guiding coalition meeting. A similar agenda should be in place for school learning teams as well, especially as a professional learning agenda. See the reproducible "First District Guiding Coalition Meeting Agenda Template" (page 142) for a blank version.

While doing the work, when in doubt, always *fail forward*, using the experience to learn and grow (Maxwell, 2000). If too many restraints or nonproblem-solving discussions are not allowing the work to move forward, a school will not find its way on a positive trajectory. *Failing forward* allows for results—results to react to or an opportunity to learn from lessons and progress toward goals. This allows teams to be open to uncertainty, and the process gives educational staff permission to be wrong, reflect, and try again (Henriksen & Richardson, 2017).

How do members of a district guiding coalition or school learning team hold colleagues accountable, support implementation, and accelerate a positive trajectory of

Table 8.1: Work of a District Guiding Coalition and School Learning Team

The Right Work of a District Guiding Coalition and School Learning Team	The Not-So-Right Work of a District Guiding Coalition and School Learning Team
• Providing support, monitoring, and feedback on the work of collaborative teams ➤ Deconstruction of essential standards ➤ Proficiency maps ➤ Common formative assessment creation and implementation ➤ Diverse population support (that is, gifted, special education, English learners) ➤ Schoolwide data analysis • Working through the organization of schoolwide work ➤ Master schedule creation and revision for maximizing collaboration ➤ Response to intervention (RTI) pyramid ➤ Grade-level teachers support ➤ Identifying and solving a problem of practice ➤ Ensuring celebration of progress toward goals and lessons learned throughout the process • Training for leading this work at the school site ➤ Crucial conversations with accountability	• Discussing student behavior and discipline ➤ Office referral forms ➤ Suspension rates • Planning recess, lunchroom, crossing guard, and other duties • Class size • Parent-teacher conferences • Teacher evaluation • Complaints without solution options

results while doing this important work? This work is all done through ensuring *reciprocal accountability*. Coauthors Richard DuFour, Rebecca DuFour, Robert Eaker, Thomas W. Many, and Mike Mattos (2016) suggest the following.

- Build capacity of your guiding coalition to lead the PLC process at multiple levels.

- Turn *regularly scheduled* guiding coalition meetings into a collaborative and collective effort to both celebrate and amplify positive results (rehearse and role-play) and identify and resolve any implementation challenges.

- Call on district coalition team members to *present regular progress reports* to coalition leaders and fellow members on how implementation is proceeding.

Date: August 15	**Time:** 4:00–6:00 p.m.
Learning Targets: • Identify the purpose of the district guiding coalition and the school learning team • Explore the *what* of the right work • Explore the *how* of the right work • Determine how school learning team members will take the work back to the school site and collaborative teams	
Items	**Notes and Reflection for School Learning Team**
Introductions (ten to fifteen minutes)	
Celebrations of progress toward goals and lessons learned throughout the process (five to ten minutes)	
Purpose of the district guiding coalition (twenty to thirty minutes)	
Purpose of the school learning team (twenty to thirty minutes)	
The *what* of the right work (an hour to an hour and a half)	
The *how* of the right work (an hour to an hour and a half)	
Taking the work back to the school site and collaborative teams (an hour to an hour and a half)	

Figure 8.2: Sample agenda.

Figure 8.3 is a rubric for assessing the work of the district guiding coalition and school learning team. Members of these teams may use this rubric as a self-assessment tool, as well as those looking into the work.

Highly Effective	Effective	Somewhat Effective	Ineffective
District Guiding Coalition			
Creates multiple, consistent opportunities for providing feedback to the district office on alignment of curriculum, instruction, assessment, and professional learning	Creates few, inconsistent opportunities for providing feedback to the district office on alignment of curriculum, instruction, assessment, and professional learning	Creates inconsistent opportunities for providing feedback to the district office on alignment of curriculum, instruction, assessment, and professional learning	Creates no opportunities for providing feedback to the district office on alignment of curriculum, instruction, assessment, and professional learning
Reflects regularly on new professional learning and how the implementation of the new learning will occur at the school site	Reflects a few times on new professional learning and how the implementation of the new learning will occur at the school site	Reflects inconsistently on new professional learning and how the implementation of the new learning will occur at the school site	Does not reflect on new professional learning and how the implementation of the new learning will occur at the school site
Provides multiple opportunities for problem solving school site and district issues that prevent the right work of collaborative teams	Provides inconsistent opportunities for problem solving school site and district issues that prevent the right work of collaborative teams	Provides a single opportunity for problem solving school site and district issues that prevent the right work of collaborative teams	Provides no opportunities for problem solving school site and district issues that prevent the right work of collaborative teams
Explores consistently district clarity and coherence with the right work of collaborative teams	Explores often district clarity and coherence with the right work of collaborative teams	Explores a few times and inconsistently district clarity and coherence with the right work of collaborative teams	Does not explore clarity of coherence with the right work of collaborative teams
Celebrates consistently progress toward goals and lessons learned throughout the process	Celebrates often progress toward goals and lessons learned throughout the process	Celebrates inconsistently progress toward goals and lessons learned throughout the process	Does not celebrate progress toward goals and lessons learned throughout the process
School Learning Team			
Takes guiding coalition learning back to the school site by creating and adjusting systems for collaborative teams (including the learning cycle and learning organization tights) and implements all of the work of collaborative teams	Takes guiding coalition learning back to the school site and discusses implementation and rollout of systems, and implements some of the work	Takes some guiding coalition learning back to the school site and discusses implementation but does not implement the work	Does not take guiding coalition learning back to the school site
Monitors artifacts of collaboration	Identifies the work of collaborative teams and creates the templates and artifacts they need	Identifies the work of collaborative teams and expects collaborative teams to create their own templates and artifacts	Expects collaborative teams to create and identify their own artifacts of collaboration
Provides timely, actionable, and poignant feedback to all collaborative teams regarding progress toward goals	Provides timely feedback to all collaborative teams regarding progress toward goals	Provides inconsistent feedback to collaborative teams regarding progress toward goals	Provides no feedback to collaborative teams regarding progress toward goals

Figure 8.3: Rubric for assessing the work.

*Visit **go.SolutionTree.com/PLCbooks** for a free reproducible version of this figure.*

Given the rubric criteria in figure 8.3, it is important to identify issues with implementation and develop next steps to support the effective best practices. The reproducible "Issues and Next Steps" (page 143) helps organize this work.

Collective Inquiry to Solve a Problem of Practice

Once school collaborative teams are on the same page, doing the right work, and moving forward, digging deeper is needed within a continuous-improvement model for a school and a district. Identifying, problem solving, implementing a solution for, and reflecting on a problem of practice is an effective next step. A *problem of practice* comes out of the instructional rounds literature and is a problem a school identifies as at odds with the tight alignment of curriculum, instruction, assessment, intervention, and professional learning (Fowler-Finn, 2013). A problem of practice is observable and actionable and connects to continuous school improvement; hence, a problem of practice can be identified in every organization until everything is working perfectly, effectively, and at high levels.

Some examples of a problem of practice follow.

- A highly flooded RTI pyramid (too many students needing Tier 3 intensive support)

- Primary students not grade-level ready for the state-assessed grade levels (for example, not reading by third grade)

- Not enough students on pace to graduate (lack of courses, grades, or state assessment requirements met)

- A lack of purposeful planning for rigor, pacing, and mastery

- A shift from instruction for only gifted and general education to *all* students

The reproducible "Problem of Practice Identification Template" (page 144) is for working from data points to find the problem of practice.

The instructional rounds literature lends itself to a group of people building capacity to solve a problem the school may be facing (Fowler-Finn, 2013). The following six steps are a sequential path to identifying and solving a problem of practice.

1. The site administration meets with its school learning team. During this meeting, everyone analyzes multiple data points and identifies core areas or root causes for the data.

2. The school learning team identifies one core area or root cause that, if solved, would have the highest leverage impact on student achievement. The school learning team shares this information with its collaborative teams to ensure the problem of practice is a target. The school learning team then shares suggestions, ideas, and problem solving with the district guiding coalition.

3. The school learning team charts out possible strategies that may include people, time, resources, organization, and supports that will help solve the problem of practice. The school learning team shares this information with its collaborative

teams to ensure all ideas are collected and a sense of urgency and focus is schoolwide (vertical and horizontal). Then the school learning team shares this plan with the district guiding coalition for suggestions, ideas, and problem solving.

4. The school learning team chooses which strategies to implement, and develops and implements an action plan. Part of this action plan should include data points to analyze the impact of the strategies. The school learning team's task is to support and monitor implementation of the action plan.

5. After implementing the plan and collecting the data points, the school learning team analyzes the data and asks, "Are the strategies having a positive impact on the data? Does the school continue with these strategies? Are new strategies needed? Is a revision or tweak to the plan needed? Do the data still identify the same problem of practice? Do the data showcase a different problem of practice? Are there celebrations in the data to show the school is on the right track?" The school learning team then shares evidence of implementation with the district guiding coalition for suggestions, ideas, and problem solving.

6. Repeat steps 1–5 to solve the problem of practice. Celebrate the small wins. Progress toward the goals and lessons learned throughout the process as a school learning team and district guiding coalition.

The process also works with a district guiding coalition and even with districtwide professional development with school site or district office administration. The important piece is that the problem of practice should be based on the multiple data points that tell a story of an underlining issue that may be preventing increased student achievement.

Conclusion

When there is alignment of practice, there is alignment of access for students to an aligned curriculum, instruction, and assessment system. This helps all students reach high levels of learning. As a school district and a school site, it is important to remember and implement structures that ensure this alignment is in place and, at the same time, grows shared leadership throughout the organization.

Once the district guiding coalition and the school learning teams are doing the right work, it leads to a process for supporting and monitoring the identified work. When whole schools and districts move forward with a focus on student achievement, it shows in the student learning and real results. When a district and school site implement these two leading teams, it is important to remember that in a continuous-improvement model, there are moments of looking at current reality and problem solving to get even better. It is also important to remember that it is not about being right or wrong, but about doing better for students. This is the epitome of continuous school and district improvement.

First District Guiding Coalition
Meeting Agenda Template

Date:	Time:
Learning Targets:	

Items	Notes and Reflection for School Learning Team
Introductions (ten to fifteen minutes)	
Celebrations of progress toward goals and lessons learned throughout the process (five to ten minutes)	
Purpose of the district guiding coalition (twenty to thirty minutes)	
Purpose of the school learning team (twenty to thirty minutes)	
The *what* of the right work (an hour to an hour and a half)	
The *how* of the right work (an hour to an hour and a half)	
Taking the work back to the school site and collaborative teams (an hour to an hour and a half)	

Issues and Next Steps

	Identified Issues With Implementation	Next Steps
District Guiding Coalition		
School Learning Team		

Problem of Practice Identification Template

Data Point One:	Data Point Two:	Data Point Three:

What Data Point to:

Issues in Practice	Possible Problems of Practice *(Root causes of the listed issues)*	Identified Problem of Practice *(Yields the highest leverage for increasing student achievement)*
Policies:		
Procedures:		
Processes:		
Curriculum:		
Instruction:		
Assessment:		
Professional Development:		

Source: Adapted from Fowler-Finn, T. (2013). Leading instructional rounds in education: A facilitator's guide. *Cambridge, MA: Harvard Education Press.*

References and Resources

Buffum, A. (2012, July 6). *Who is steering your school's bus?* [Blog post]. Accessed at www
.allthingsplc.info/blog/view/188/who-is-steering-your-school-bus on September 23, 2020.

Dewey, J. R. (2018, June 27). *Do the right work: Develop your PLC road map* [Blog post].
Accessed at www.allthingsplc.info/blog/view/371/do-the-right-work-develop-your-plc
-road-map on September 23, 2020.

DuFour, R., DuFour, R., Eaker, R., Many, T. W., & Mattos, M. (2016). *Learning by doing:
A handbook for Professional Learning Communities at Work* (3rd ed.). Bloomington, IN:
Solution Tree Press.

Fowler-Finn, T. (2013). *Leading instructional rounds in education: A facilitator's guide*. Cambridge,
MA: Harvard Education Press.

Fullan, M. (2020). *Leading in a culture of change* (2nd ed.). San Francisco: Jossey-Bass.

García, H. (2015, July 1). *Avoiding the "PLC lite" scenario* [Blog post]. Accessed at www.solutiontree
.com/blog/avoiding-the-plc-lite-scenario-2 on November 25, 2020.

Henriksen, D., & Richardson, C. (2017). Teachers are designers: Addressing problems of
practice in education. *Phi Delta Kappan, 99*(2), 60–64.

Kotter, J. P. (2014). *Accelerate: Building strategic agility for a faster moving world*. Boston:
Harvard Business Review Press.

Kramer, S. V. (2015). *How to leverage PLCs for school improvement*. Bloomington, IN: Solution
Tree Press.

Kramer, S. V., & Schuhl, S. (2017). *School improvement for all: A how-to guide for doing the right
work*. Bloomington, IN: Solution Tree Press.

Martin, T. L., & Rains, C. L. (2018). *Stronger together: Answering the questions of collaborative
leadership*. Bloomington, IN: Solution Tree Press.

Maxwell, J. C. (2000). *Failing forward: Turning mistakes into stepping-stones for success*.
Nashville, TN: Nelson.

Sinek, S. (2009). *Start with why: How great leaders inspire everyone to take action*. New York: Portfolio.

Williams, K. C., & Hierck, T. (2015). *Starting a movement: Building culture from the inside out
in professional learning communities*. Bloomington, IN: Solution Tree Press.

 **Rebecca Nicolas, EdD,** is the principal of Fern Creek High School in Louisville, Kentucky. Her work focuses on implementation of the professional learning community (PLC) process and integration of collaborative teams.

Prior to her current role at Fern Creek, Rebecca was an assistant principal at the high school and an English teacher and assistant principal at Doss High School also in Louisville, Kentucky. She has twenty years of experience working in schools with student at-risk populations. Her work at Fern Creek includes developing integrated response to intervention (RTI) practices, using data in developing effective teams, and inclusion of nontraditional students in highly rigorous courses. As one of the few examples of an urban turnaround high school in Kentucky, Fern Creek has received recognition as a Model PLC school, has been a runner-up for the 2016 DuFour Award, and has won the 2016 National Preparedness Leadership Initiative School Innovation and Change Award and 2017 DuFour Award.

Rebecca earned a bachelor's degree in English from Centre College in Danville, Kentucky; a master's degree in English from Wake Forest University in Winston-Salem, North Carolina; and a doctoral degree in educational leadership from Spalding University in Louisville, Kentucky.

To book Rebecca Nicolas for professional development, contact pd@SolutionTree.com.

Monitoring Productivity Instead of Activity

Rebecca Nicolas

> Embracing accountability does not mean that
> the school ranks and penalizes teachers and
> students; it means identifying learning needs and
> realizing learning opportunities because everyone
> is accountable for the learning of each student.
> It means there is a healthy culture of adults and
> students learning from the data and the narrative that
> a school produces. It means learning comes first.
>
> —*Sharon V. Kramer and Sarah Schuhl*

Running a school is a loud business. There is so much noise on any given day, demanding your time and attention. There is so much to do, and it all needs to be done *right now*: staffing shortages, parent complaints, facility limitations, district mandates, technology challenges, student behavior, teacher training. The activity—the static—is louder for priority school principals. In addition to all the standard demands of running a school, priority school leaders face the additional challenge of turning around the culture and climate of the school to ensure they are supporting teachers and challenging students in ways they may have never done before. This is a monumental task, but you are committed. You know the key to successfully leading your school is to become a professional learning community (PLC) by rewriting the script for your school, your teachers, and your students. You know you must set up the environment to provide a guaranteed and viable curriculum, always working toward the goal of ensuring high levels of learning for all.

As a school leader, you take the right steps, attend the trainings, and read the books. You head back to school, organize a guiding coalition, and craft a mission and vision to guide your efforts. You fall asleep at night with your dog-eared copy of coauthors Richard DuFour, Rebecca DuFour, Robert Eaker, Thomas W. Many, and Mike Mattos's (2016) *Learning by Doing* by your bedside. You manipulate the master schedule to provide extra planning. You firmly establish tight expectations for who meets where and when. There is no question you and your school have made the commitment to follow the PLC process. Now, surely, a true PLC will flourish!

As a school leader in a PLC, there are tight (or non-negotiable) tasks that are strictly your responsibility. You understand this and establish collaborative teams as the primary organizational units of your school, using the funding and supports at your disposal to ensure fidelity. You definitely assign teachers to teams and provide them time and space to meet. You ensure teams have the tools and training they need to do the right work. These are tasks for administrators, and while a teacher team could come together despite less-than-ideal conditions, you know that a school leader greatly increases the chance of teacher teams working effectively when he or she ensures the tight tasks remains tight (DuFour et al., 2016).

After setting up the conditions for teams to be successful, it may be tempting for some school leaders to sit back and let that PLC magic happen. After all, the *loose* of the tight/loose relationship is the fun part. This is when teachers meet to determine essential standards, plan instruction, administer assessments, and pore over data. This is when teachers challenge themselves to become better teachers and their peers encourage them to take risks. This is when interventions come to life and students get access to extensions and enrichment. This is when students are learning at levels so impressive, their teachers have to post about it on Twitter and write blogs about the life-changing impact of it all.

After all, that's what is supposed to happen. But sometimes it doesn't. Sometimes teachers are resistant to the idea of collaboration and sit sulkily through their weekly meetings. Sometimes, teachers have the best intentions but can't come together to get a common formative assessment off the ground. Sometimes team members love one another but use their time together as a minifaculty meeting, talking about the abuse of hall passes and the price of the replacement bulbs for the overhead projector. And sometimes teams play PLC, flirting with the idea of the four critical questions (DuFour et al., 2016; page 3), "going on a few dates" with critical question one or two, but never quite committing to the next steps it takes to pull off critical questions three and four. Consultant, author, and former administrator and teacher Tesha Ferriby Thomas (2019) confirms the importance of leadership in ensuring teams press on: coached teams are more likely to focus on student learning versus other conversations unrelated to learning than uncoached teams. It is critical that school leadership engage in helping teams focus on the right work.

So what then? How can a school leader ensure fidelity in the day-to-day workings of a PLC?

There are many ways teams can lose their way, even if school leadership has created the environment they need to be successful. The commitment of the guiding coalition must be to continue to engage in the process, identifying challenges, providing support and resources to the teams as they move toward a more comprehensive understanding of the process. It is the responsibility of the guiding coalition to hold collaborative teams accountable to expectations (Kramer & Schuhl, 2017). If collaborative teams are the primary units of organization for a school, the leadership team must be collaborative, working through the challenges of providing a guaranteed and viable curriculum along with teacher teams, always toward the goal of learning for all.

Archetypes of Teacher Teams

When a leader looks out over the teams that characterize his or her organization, a few archetypes may emerge. While each team is competent (or dysfunctional) in its own way, all teams usually share common characteristics that can help a school leader diagnose their challenges and design next steps. All PLCs exist on a continuum of implementation, and some of the following descriptions of teams merely describe points on the journey. However, if teams are not afforded constant support and feedback (page 163), it is likely they will remain in their current state, never fully realizing their role in the PLC process. As a leader, you may have encountered one of the following teams. If you are reflective, you may have to admit that you've participated in one too.

- Lost and confused team
- Bless-your-heart team
- Cute and compliant team
- Logs and hogs team
- Busy bees team

As a school leader, it is tempting to look at the variety of teams that populate your PLC and feel defeated. In this essentially human enterprise, humans can certainly mess up plans with their very human failings. Maybe they don't understand the process, maybe they don't care, or maybe they are eying the school district down the road that doesn't ask its teachers to do anything more than what they've always done.

However, I urge you not to feel defeated. Instead, consider the power of your own team, the team of leaders and coaches you assemble to engage in the process, right alongside your teachers. This is the team that works through the four critical questions (just like a teacher team), but has, for its data, the products each team creates during time together. This is the team that can meet teachers and teams where they are in the process and provide targeted support and feedback to move each team closer to its goals.

The following descriptions may characterize teams in your building, teams with whom you've worked, or teams on which you actively participate. None of these are unsalvageable, but all need help moving toward a greater level of effectiveness.

The Lost and Confused Team

These team members may or may not show up for meetings, and no one really knows why. Did they have some other meeting? Did they forget about this meeting? Are they hiding in the copy room? It's hard to say, but it's pretty clear not all team members value their time together. On this team, members are unclear about what activities they should be doing during their time together, so they end up talking about everything and nothing at all. It doesn't really matter what members discuss because there is no coherent link between the last meeting, this one, and the next one. No one is keeping track of progress toward team goals. There is no evidence their time together is having any impact on student learning. There is also no communication between team members when they are not required to be together. You won't find them poring over data during a planning period, and they don't eat lunch together or create long-term plans during the summer. Team members comply with your expectations to meet during a set time, and they put in their time and move on, usually teaching in the exact same way they have always taught, untouched by the PLC process except for a "lost" hour each week.

The Bless-Your-Heart Team

After encountering the lost and confused team, the bless-your-heart team may feel like a balm to your wounded PLC spirit, but don't be seduced by their generally affable dispositions. While these team members are more pleasant to be around, they pose an equally thorny challenge for the school leader who is trying to support teams. The bless-your-heart team members are eager to meet and seem to enjoy their time together, but they while away the minutes completing paperwork and checking off housekeeping details. The team members are genial with one another but often seem uncertain how to hold one another accountable for team norms. The team is open to trying new things in theory, but can't seem to collect data in a systemic way, and are hard-pressed to say what is actually working in regard to student learning. This team *wants* to do the right thing, but honestly can't really articulate what the right thing is or how the members intend to do it. They are trying, bless them, but they are no closer to realizing the vision of the PLC than the lost and confused team down the hall.

The Cute and Compliant Team

The cute and compliant team is a social media–friendly group whose tweets and Facebook posts create the impression that they are a high-flying collaborative juggernaut. And to be fair, this team is meeting some expectations—like always filling out their agenda on time and bringing common data to the table. Members of the team celebrate everyone's birthday and throw themed baby showers when appropriate. There are snacks at every meeting, and if they are feeling particularly ambitious one summer, members may buy matching T-shirts for everyone on the team, announcing their solidarity and commitment. Team members like one another and they are not afraid to say it, tossing off shout-outs in the faculty spotlight newsletter and declaring themselves *work husbands* and *work wives*. At every meeting, there is lots of lively discussion, but it never moves beyond the surface or asks the hard questions about evidence or progress toward goals. As a leader, this team may not feel like your biggest problem, but they are a challenge, nonetheless, and need your support to move toward a place where all that enthusiasm actually impacts student learning.

The Logs and Hogs Team

This type of team is particularly challenging in that the experience, enthusiasm, and collaboration level of the individual members is so uneven. This dysfunction often happens when you appoint the most veteran teacher team leader, rather than choosing a team member who can truly engage his or her peers in the work. This team has at least one member who talks all the time (a *hog*) and one member who doesn't talk at all (a *log*). The team leader may treat the rest of the team members like his or her employees, not fully empowered members of a collaborative unit. Team members divide duties and engage in work share rather than discussing challenges together. Someone is inevitably put in charge of running copies for the group and does it quietly, hoping to spend enough time in the copy room that the meeting will be almost over when he or she returns. Team members have been known to tattle on one another to administrators when they violate norms. They have no loyalty to one another and the guiding coalition's imposition of tight expectations are the bonds that keep the team intact. Because this team can't find a way to truly invest everyone in the process, someone is usually frustrated and someone has usually checked out.

The Busy Bees Team

This team is perhaps the most challenging for a school leader because its dysfunction is so difficult to spot. Sitting with this team can actually feel quite affirming. When district-visiting dignitaries show up to audit your implementation of the PLC process, you may usher them straight to the room where this team is meeting, because at first glance, they seem to be killing it. This team is always busy creating assessments, posting data, and talking about student performance. Team members love comparing their data with the rest of the team, especially when their students outperform the rest of the team members' students. (A red flag that the team is full of busy bees: they say things like *my students* instead of *our students*.) The team's agenda is chock full of activities and they always have a long to-do list. The team has lots of new ideas and fun stories about the students who are successfully learning in their classes. The team knows they need to plan for interventions, but there is always so much to do, so they keep pushing it off for next time. They never quite find the time to grapple with the answers to critical questions three and four: "How will we respond when some students do not learn it?" and "How will we extend the learning for students who have demonstrated proficiency?" (DuFour et al., 2016, p. 59).

The Instructional Leadership Team

The creation of an instructional leadership team (ILT) is a critical component in ensuring the fidelity of your organization to the principles of the PLC process. Coauthors Sharon V. Kramer and Sarah Schuhl (2017) find, "The single most important task a principal can do to ensure high levels of learning for students and adults is to build a leadership team" (p. 9). This requires a collective commitment of all team members and an understanding of the iterative process of data analysis and intervention. When an ILT embraces this process, members reaffirm the schoolwide commitment to becoming a PLC. An ILT that uses the four critical questions to ground its work models best practice and sets the tone for teacher teams.

To clarify, an ILT is not just a group of school leaders who meet to discuss the needs of the school and the events on the week's agenda. At Fern Creek High School, we have that team. It meets every Monday after school and consists of the principals, the counselors, the athletic director, the mental health counselor, the special education leader, and the instructional coaches. The agenda includes pep rally and gym use, whether to buy new uniforms for the band, and anti-bullying assembly plans. We talk about eighth-grade open house, the senior prom, and how much we have in textbook allocation for the rest of the year. This meeting is necessary, but it doesn't fit the definition of an ILT. Our ILT meets every Thursday after school and only includes the personnel who work directly with teams and teachers as they refine their commitments to the PLC process. For us, that is our principal, assistant principals, and instructional coaches—that's it. Our scope is narrow and purposeful. Other schools may include other members based on expertise and interest, but we limit who is participating to maintain confidentiality in discussing teacher and team effectiveness.

Our ILT has undergone multiple revisions through the years, but our vision has always been to truly capture the state of specific teacher teams and the school's commitment to the PLC process. At this meeting, ILT members use data to make decisions and use the collective expertise of the members to design team interventions. The next steps the ILT generates are then shared with each team's facilitator and then monitored over time. ILT members are as systematic in monitoring our progress as we ask our teacher teams to be. We believe in the process, and we believe in learning for all and follow the vision of Kramer and Schuhl (2017) who state: "The leadership team must operate as a model for all of the other collaborative teams in the school" (p. 11).

Early iterations of our ILT fell prey to the same pitfalls many teacher teams do as they begin this work. When teacher teams come together, but don't have data to ground members' conversations, they often find themselves talking about individual students, groups of students, the administration, or the state of the nation—often in a less-than-flattering way. For many teachers, their first impulse on sitting down with other teachers at the end of a long day is commiseration, not collaboration. Sharing frustrations and venting about challenges is a natural part of a conversation in any workplace, but it can't be the work of a collaborative team.

The ILT is no different. If you don't have data about teams to ground your conversation, it is likely you will talk about individual teachers, classrooms, or the state of the candidates you interviewed that week. These conversations may be cathartic, but they don't move teams to a deeper implementation of the PLC process or create opportunities for increased student learning. The question we faced as an ILT was just what data we should use to focus our efforts. We started with anecdotal classroom observation data. We tried to limit ourselves to talking about how teams were doing, but usually descended into diagnosing what ailed a particular teacher, not necessarily in relation to his or her team. We then tried to analyze agendas, but quickly realized that teams could competently fill out agendas that did not necessarily reflect the work they actually accomplished during team time. We tried about seven different versions of agendas in seven years, until we realized our team, like any other, had to focus on the four critical questions to truly ground our work. It was that realization that led us to our current version of our ILT—one that focuses on team productivity over team activity. The following section talks about what data we monitor and how it aligns with those four critical questions.

Activity Versus Productivity

Recall the busy bees team description from earlier in this chapter (page 151) and the need to focus on productivity comes into sharper focus. After years of working with our teachers and teams to refine the PLC process, many could use the language of the PLC quite effectively. Members knew how teams were supposed to look and they knew what would satisfy any administrator who happened to sit in a team meeting on any given week. They were content with being busy and without attending critically to what they were actually producing as a result of their time together as a team. This is not to say these teachers were engaged in some nefarious plot to get out of doing the work. They felt like they were working and working hard. However, when teachers would speak regarding their level of satisfaction with their team and the time members spent collaborating, they would always express a greater commitment after their team had done something particularly *productive*. It was at that point our ILT experienced the revelation that being productive results in actual products. It's right there in the word *productive*. Then we decided to monitor *product*ivity over activity and transformed our work as an ILT.

The products our ILT now monitors are categorized by the four critical questions. This was a natural extension of the norm we had for teams that wanted to spend their time acting like they were running a minifaculty meeting. When we would go into meetings and the members' discussion focused on dress code violations or the lack of toilet paper in the upstairs bathroom, it was our ILT members' norm to ask, "What critical question are we discussing right now?" The team would usually realize it had gotten off track and move toward a more relevant topic. As an ILT, we wanted to take a close look at the products a team was generating with regard to which critical question it aligned with.

For example, if a team was actively working on unpacking essential standards, we could see the templates members were using and discern the team was grappling with critical question one. If a team was looking at data from a common formative assessment, we would determine members were working on critical question two. We designed our agendas so teams would make that connection too, linking the products from a team meeting with the corresponding critical question and showing evidence of their work. Work products constitute evidence for this process. Figure 9.1 (page 154) shows an example of a completed agenda. The reproducible "Team Agenda Template" (page 159) is offered as a blank version.

Each week, the team facilitator indicates the products the team generated or refined during its time together. A member of the ILT may be in the meeting, but it is not required. If an ILT member is present, he or she is often a silent observer of the process and should not be considered a member of the team.

It is critical for each ILT member to understand his or her role in the process. "Leaders have to balance their attention between defining and achieving the specific task of their group, building and maintaining as a team, and meeting the needs of and developing the individuals within it" (Bungay, 2011, p. 229). If an administrator is in the meeting room,

Team Members: Geometry teachers—Smith, Thomas, Hanson, Brown	Date: September 1
Team Members Present: Smith, Thomas, Hanson, Brown	
Planning Activities (Check all that apply.)	

Critical question one: What is it we want our students to know and be able to do? ☐ Curriculum guides ☒ Pacing of power (or priority) standards ☐ Student-friendly learning targets ☒ Assessment design and planning ☐ Lesson plans ☐ Rubric design or scoring protocols Other:	**Minutes and Notes** • Review team norms. • Review essential standard document, and determine additional examples of rigor needed for essential standard one. • Enter common formative assessment one and two into GradeCam (see https://gradecam.com). • Review state assessment data from last spring (last year's class).
Critical question two: How will we know if each student has learned it? ☐ Common formative assessments data ☐ Student writing samples ☐ Student projects ☐ Rubrics ☒ Student results from district or state summative assessments ☐ Teachers' observation and anecdotal evidence Other:	
	Curriculum Status Check (How is our pacing?) On track
Critical question three: How will we respond when some students do not learn it? ☐ Analysis protocols ☐ Daily, weekly, and long-term interventions planning ☐ Time built into the schedule ☐ Recovery plans ☐ Multiple ways to reassess Other:	
	Additional Support • Hanson needs a new projector bulb. • Brown's classes are still not showing up in GradeCam.
Critical question four: How will we extend the learning for students who have demonstrated proficiency? ☐ Enrichment plans ☐ Extension plans ☐ Student choice ☐ Student leadership opportunities ☐ Community partnerships ☐ Celebrations and recognitions Other:	

Source: © 2020 by Fern Creek High School, Louisville, Kentucky. Used with permission. Adapted from DuFour et al., 2016.

Figure 9.1: Sample team agenda.

teachers will often defer to his or her judgment and look for approval in making decisions. It's not always easy to hold your tongue as you watch teams work, but the time for you to provide feedback is later. Your job at the meeting is to monitor the conversation and products the team generates, and to be as unobtrusive as possible while you do it.

The ILT member gathers data over several weeks of team meetings and then brings that information to the ILT on an established schedule. For our ILT, each member is responsible for three or four teams. Each week, the ILT members discuss the data from two or three teams. Therefore, each team comes up for discussion every four weeks or so, and the feedback team members receive helps refine their work over the course of the school year. Figure 9.2 shows an example of an ILT schedule.

Weekly Meeting—Thursdays 2:30–3:30 p.m.		
Team Members—Principal, assistant principals, instructional coaches		
Team	Observer	Agenda Presentation Dates
Algebra I	AP one	January 9
English II	Principal	January 9
Biology	Coach	January 23
Algebra II	Coach	January 23
Computer Science	AP two	January 30
English I	Principal	January 30
Algebra III	Coach	February 6
English III	AP three	February 6
English IV	Principal	February 13

Figure 9.2: Sample ILT schedule.

At the ILT meeting, the member presenting data for the week will have three to four agendas comprising the data the rest of the ILT members will analyze. Using the agenda that focuses on the four critical questions (see figure 9.1), it becomes apparent if a team is stalled at critical question one for an extended period of time. Over time, it will also be clear if a team has an understanding of how the PLC process is indeed a *process*. If members are not producing artifacts that reflect all four critical questions, it might become obvious that they have fallen a little too much in love with one part of it. For example, a team might really enjoy looking at the common formative assessments data, but it doesn't do much with these data if there are never any products that reflect members' engagement with critical questions three and four.

As with any team, your ILT will probably have members with varying levels of expertise and engagement. If one of the assistant principals is the locker-and-buses guy and one of your coaches is too shy to talk, you may have a log and hog on your team. Consider this, though:

> For a team to work well, members need the knowledge and skills to do the tasks that are required. For example, if a leadership team will analyze data, provide professional development, and serve as communication conduits, then members need strong skills in these areas. (Aguilar, 2016, p. 278)

The beautiful part of an ILT is that the process to create it includes how to train all the participants (school leaders) on how to be productive members of a data-based team. The process requires all school leaders to become experts in the language and components of the process so they can help teacher teams become more productive as well. The norms for your team are just as important as the norms for your teacher teams, and the process you use to analyze data must require all members to own that data and work toward generating next steps. Figure 9.3 shows the agenda for our ILT, which is pretty simple.

Team Data (ten to fifteen minutes)

1. The presenting member distributes copies of the last three or four agendas from the teacher team for analysis.

2. The presenting member discusses any additional observational data, strengths, challenges, and previous goals of the teacher team.

3. ILT members ask clarifying questions about the agendas and observational data.

Data Analysis and Next Steps (ten to fifteen minutes)

1. The ILT analyzes the data and determines next steps.

2. The presenting ILT member creates and posts a four- or five-week short-term SMART goal (O'Neill & Conzemius, 2006) for the teacher team.

Source: O'Neill & Conzemius, 2006.

Figure 9.3: Sample ILT agenda.

Using this format, the ILT members can analyze the data from two or three teams a week. Depending on the size of your school, this will result in SMART goals for the team that will stretch for four or five weeks until the next time that team comes up for review. SMART goals keep the ILT member and teacher team members on track for next steps with regard to team functionality. In fact, "not only do collaborative teams represent the optimum setting for the pursuit of meaningful SMART goals, but SMART goals also represent an essential tool in developing powerful collaborative teams" (DuFour et al., 2016, p. 102).

Some teams are better than others at crafting SMART goals (page 59), so it's important to train teams in what a good SMART goal looks like. The following are *nonexamples* of ILT and teacher team SMART goals.

- We need to spend more time together.

- We need a new facilitator.

- We need the principal to buy us a book about teams.

- We need common planning.

- We need common data.

While some of these are worthy needs, they are not SMART goals. *SMART goals* describe what the team will do, in what timeframe, and how members will know if they are successful. The following are some examples of SMART goals.

- By December 1, biology team members will collaborate to create five common assessments. Then, the team will upload the data from these common assessments within forty-eight hours.

- By October 15, world civilization team members will collaboratively create norms and commit to reviewing them at the beginning of each team meeting.

- By the end of the calendar year, the English III team will create and upload two samples of student work for each performance level on the writing rubric.

- By January 1, the career and technical education team will have data from at least four common formative assessments about the employability section of the Kentucky Occupational Skill Standards Assessment exam.

Perhaps the most critical part of the process is not the identification of next steps for a team, but the conversation that a member of the leadership team has with the team or team facilitator to move the team forward. These conversations should be collaborative, not punitive. This may seem obvious, but I once had a revelatory conversation with a principal who was eager to know, "What do you *do* to them when they don't _____" (fill in the blank with unpack essential standards, design and implement common formative assessments, implement interventions, and so on). I was taken aback by the implication that I had some ready punishment waiting for a team or teacher who was not working effectively. The goal shouldn't be for the school leader to do anything *to* a team that needs support, but that he or she will initiate a conversation about next steps.

Coauthors Richard DuFour and Mike Mattos (2013) explore the idea of being purposeful rather than punitive in their article, "How Do Principals Really Improve Schools?" The conversation the leadership team member will have with team members is based on the data the leadership team collects over time and is usually positive and purposeful about where the team is heading. The data cycle mirrors the feed-forward principles leadership experts and coauthors Nancy Frey and Douglas Fisher (2011) describe, including an analysis of misconceptions and errors to better craft support. The implications for next steps aren't something the school leader cooks up as punishment. Next steps are usually obvious when the data present a clear picture of the team's trajectory. The reproducible "Instructional Leadership Team Template" (page 160) helps our ILT keep track of the insights they glean from the data-analysis session to document our next steps.

Conclusion

Every organization that commits to becoming a PLC eventually realizes that being a PLC is not a destination, but a trajectory of learning that you refine over time. Leaders in a priority school must commit to the process despite the noisy demands that each day brings. Becoming a PLC is the most challenging and rewarding work a school can engage in. Guiding that work will forever change you as a leader and require you to demonstrate an unwavering commitment to the right work. The ILT members must actively engage in the iterative data-analysis cycle to ensure they provide feedback and support as teams encounter new challenges and move toward deeper implementation. The systems you implement to ensure fidelity to your school's collective commitments must hold each individual (including you and your school leaders) accountable for high levels of professional learning. Accountability systems that monitor productivity will bring you closer to understanding the current state of your teacher teams and illuminate the way forward.

The dysfunctions that can beset any team are likely to occur within an ILT without the collective commitments necessary to sustain the work. I urge you to not let this dysfunction discourage you. As a leader in a priority school, you will always have the opportunity (and quite frankly some compelling justifications) to say why this process is too hard, takes too long, or is too messy. Do not be discouraged! This is not only work you can do but also work you *need* to do. It is the moral imperative of any school, made all the more compelling because your students so desperately need you to ensure learning for all. Take on the challenge. Commit yourself to *learning by doing*, refining your practices as you go, and keeping your eye on the right work.

Team Agenda Template

Team Members:	Date:
Team Members Present:	

Planning Activities (Check all that apply.)	
Critical question one: What is it we want our students to know and be able to do? ☐ Curriculum guides ☐ Pacing of power (or priority) standards ☐ Student-friendly learning targets ☐ Assessment design and planning ☐ Lesson plans ☐ Rubric design or scoring protocols Other:	**Minutes and Notes**
Critical question two: How will we know if each student has learned it? ☐ Common formative assessments data ☐ Student writing samples ☐ Student projects ☐ Rubrics ☐ Student results from district or state summative assessments ☐ Teachers' observation and anecdotal evidence Other:	**Curriculum Status Check (How is our pacing?)**
Critical question three: How will we respond when some students do not learn it? ☐ Analysis protocols ☐ Daily, weekly, and long-term interventions planning ☐ Time built into the schedule ☐ Recovery plans ☐ Multiple ways to reassess Other:	**Additional Support**
Critical question four: How will we extend the learning for students who have demonstrated proficiency? ☐ Enrichment plans ☐ Extension plans ☐ Student choice ☐ Student leadership opportunities ☐ Community partnerships ☐ Celebrations and recognitions Other:	

Source: © 2020 by Fern Creek High School, Louisville, Kentucky. Used with permission. Adapted from DuFour, R., DuFour, R., Eaker, R., Many, T. W., & Mattos, M. (2016). Learning by doing: A handbook for Professional Learning Communities at Work (3rd ed.). Bloomington, IN: Solution Tree Press.

Instructional Leadership Team Template

Agenda dates:

Team SMART goal:

Observer notes:

Next steps for facilitator:

Next steps for the team:

References and Resources

Aguilar, E. (2016). *The art of coaching teams: Building resilient communities that transform schools*. San Francisco: Jossey-Bass.

Bungay, S. (2011). *The art of action: How leaders close the gaps between plans, actions, and results*. Boston: Nicholas Brealey.

DuFour, R., DuFour, R., Eaker, R., Many, T. W., & Mattos, M. (2016). *Learning by doing: A handbook for Professional Learning Communities at Work* (3rd ed.). Bloomington, IN: Solution Tree Press.

DuFour, R., & Mattos, M. (2013). How do principals really improve schools? *Principalship*, *70*(7), 34–40.

Frey, N., & Fisher, D. (2011). *The formative assessment action plan: Practical steps to more successful teaching and learning*. Alexandria, VA: Association for Supervision and Curriculum Development.

Kramer, S. V., & Schuhl, S. (2017). *School improvement for all: A how-to guide for doing the right work*. Bloomington, IN: Solution Tree Press.

O'Neill, J., & Conzemius, A. (2006). *The power of SMART goals: Using goals to improve student learning*. Bloomington, IN: Solution Tree Press.

Thomas, T. F. (2019, December). *The implications of instructional coaches' participation in professional learning community collaborative team meetings*. Doctoral dissertation, University of Michigan–Flint. Accessed at https://deepblue.lib.umich.edu /bitstream/handle/2027.42/152356/ThomasT2019.pdf?sequence=1&isAllowed=y on September 23, 2020.

Sarah Schuhl, MS, is an educational coach and consultant specializing in mathematics, professional learning communities (PLCs), common formative and summative assessments, priority school improvement, and response to intervention (RTI). She has worked in schools as a secondary mathematics teacher, high school instructional coach, and K–12 mathematics specialist.

Schuhl was instrumental in the creation of a PLC in the Centennial School District in Oregon, helping teachers make large gains in student achievement. She earned the Centennial School District Triple C Award in 2012.

Schuhl designs meaningful professional development in districts throughout the United States. Her work focuses on strengthening the teaching and learning of mathematics, having teachers learn from one another when working effectively as collaborative teams in a PLC, and striving to ensure the learning of each student through assessment practices and intervention. Her practical approach includes working with teachers and administrators to implement assessments for learning, analyze data, collectively respond to student learning, and map standards.

Since 2015, Schuhl has coauthored the books *Engage in the Mathematical Practices: Strategies to Build Numeracy and Literacy With K–5 Learners* and *School Improvement for All: A How-To Guide for Doing the Right Work*. She is a coauthor (with Timothy D. Kanold) of the *Every Student Can Learn Mathematics* series, *Mathematics at Work™ Plan Book*, and the *Mathematics Unit Planning in a PLC at Work* series.

Previously, Schuhl served as a member and chair of the National Council of Teachers of Mathematics (NCTM) editorial panel for the journal *Mathematics Teacher* and is secretary of the National Council of Supervisors of Mathematics (NCSM). Her work with the Oregon Department of Education includes designing mathematics assessment items, test specifications and blueprints, and rubrics for achievement-level descriptors. She has also contributed to a middle school mathematics series and an elementary mathematics intervention program.

Schuhl earned a bachelor of science in mathematics from Eastern Oregon University and a master of science in mathematics education from Portland State University.

To learn more about Schuhl's work, follow @SSchuhl on Twitter.

To book Sarah Schuhl for professional development, contact pd@SolutionTree.com.

Providing Feedback
on the Right Work

Sarah Schuhl

Leadership for learning is a combination of
exerting pressure and providing support.

—*Sharon V. Kramer and Sarah Schuhl*

Two months into coaching and supporting a priority middle school, the work that had started strong with a focus on student learning and clear principal leadership began to steer off course. Collaborative teams were scheduled to meet twice weekly during their common planning time. Teams had been learning how to make sense of standards, create common assessments, and analyze data for meaningful interventions and extensions. As an instructional leader, the principal knew she needed to attend team meetings and provide supports and feedback; however, she found herself spending most of her time addressing behavior issues and security concerns or attending district meetings. In addition, guiding coalition meetings were not happening with regularity because she quickly cancelled them when scheduling conflicts arose. As a result, teachers started coming late to team meetings, if at all, and did not see value in the work because, without feedback, they too focused more on student behaviors or upcoming school events than on student learning. In frustration, the principal looked at me and exclaimed, "This is impossible!"

Unfortunately, I have seen this scenario play out in many of the priority schools I have had the opportunity to work with—elementary, middle, and high school—and it was an issue in my own school district as well. Leadership matters in a priority school, and, despite best intentions to focus on teaching and learning, there are often many valid pressing issues needing attention. If only a principal's role in leading a priority school came with a clear road map! Regardless, a leader's minute-to-minute decisions impact teachers and students alike and show what that leader most values. How does a principal make sure to spend energy on the right work—that which grows student learning?

It is all too easy for the hard work of student learning to fade into the background. Staff know students need to learn, but the leader's and teachers' *actions* may say otherwise. The work to improve a school is larger than any one person, which this quote points out:

> No single individual can develop the improvement process, communicate the process adequately to large numbers of people, discover and remove obstacles, identify the specific support individuals will need to succeed in the initiative, anchor the process in the organization's culture, and create the small wins necessary to sustain the process. (DuFour & Fullan, 2013, p. 24)

We gained traction and started improving student learning in the middle school referenced at the start of this chapter when we created a shared leadership model—one that repurposed the guiding coalition to lead *with* the principal. Together, they led the work of collaborative teams and gathered and analyzed schoolwide data to inform decisions and next steps. Each collaborative team also had a team lead who was the liaison between the team and principal or guiding coalition and responsible for sharing the work and student learning of his or her team.

Leading a priority school starts with clarity. Consider how clear or unclear your expectations are for collaborative teams, the guiding coalition, or your own administrative team. Former school administrator and education author Mike Schmoker (2004) says, "Clarity precedes competence" (p. 85). Until collaborative teams, the guiding coalition, and all stakeholders can articulate their work, they may flounder on their path to improve learning in the school. Research professor Brené Brown (2018) writes, "Clear is kind. Unclear is unkind" (p. 44). At times, you will have to conduct difficult conversations to reinforce expectations and refocus staff to ensure student learning. Feedback given to staff works best when it aligns with clearly defined expectations.

This chapter clarifies the work of collaborative teams and the guiding coalition so feedback can continue to grow the learning of the adults and students in the building. Throughout the chapter, strategies to give meaningful feedback are also explored. Grant Wiggins (2012) shares seven keys to effective feedback teachers can give students to grow their learning, which also works for effective feedback given to adults. Wiggins (2012) states, "Helpful feedback is goal-referenced; tangible and transparent; actionable; user-friendly (specific and personalized); timely; ongoing; and consistent."

How does your school culture embrace feedback about clearly articulated goals and actions? In a healthy learning culture, feedback to teachers and teams is seen as an opportunity to celebrate or learn rather than data that might be used negatively in an evaluation. As Wiggins (2012) explains, feedback to clearly articulated goals or expectations also gives the feedback relevance and purpose. For staff moving to align their work to the school's priorities, clarifying the work of teams in learning cycles is one of the first steps.

The Work of Teams in Learning Cycles

Clarifying the work teams must accomplish and supporting those teams through feedback requires that teams have at least one hour of designated time during the school week to address the four critical questions of a professional learning community (PLC; DuFour, DuFour, Eaker, Many, & Mattos, 2016). Without time as a collaborative team to make sense of standards students must learn, create common assessments, and develop interventions or extensions, teachers will soon become frustrated and resent any feedback on their work.

Once time is established for each team to meet, clarifying what work to accomplish becomes critical. Sharon V. Kramer and Sarah Schuhl (2017) note:

> Ultimately, collaborative teams must be clear about the right work and know what specifically their leaders are holding them accountable to in terms of actions. Leaders, in return, must look for evidence of those team actions and provide meaningful feedback to nurture the learning of teams. (p. 148)

Teams work to routinely address student learning through unit-by-unit learning cycles. A *unit* is a chunk of time in which a team addresses specific standards. In some courses, the standards might correlate with chapters in a textbook, and in other disciplines, the standards might be grouped into periods of time lasting about three to four weeks in duration.

Together, and with the help of district pacing documents (if possible) such as a proficiency map, scope and sequence, or curriculum map, teams determine the standards students will learn in each unit and the unit's start and end dates. In this way, teams begin to answer the first critical question of a PLC (page 3). Often, there are too many standards for students to learn well, especially if students are below grade level. Many educators and researchers write about the need in a course or grade level to rank the standards in order of importance and focus on those deemed most essential (Ainsworth, 2013; Buffum, Mattos, & Malone, 2018; DuFour et al., 2016; Reeves, 2002; Wiggins & McTighe, 2011). Teams can rank the identified standards for each unit as need-to-know (or priority or essential), important-to-know, or nice-to-know (Schuhl, Kanold, Deinhart, Larson, & Toncheff, 2020).

Figure 10.1 (page 166) shows a learning cycle model teams can use to determine their work before, during, and after each unit. The model starts with a clear focus on the standards that the grade-alike or course-alike team expects students to learn. For singleton teachers, the focus is on common skills students learn in a unit with a team-created rubric for scoring. Teachers will still plan units and determine, as a team, when to give assessments on the common skill so they can analyze student learning and instructional practices.

- **Before the unit:** In figure 10.1, the first four boxes starting at the top and moving clockwise, identify the team actions required *before the unit begins*. The gray shaded circle encompasses teacher and team actions during the unit, and the last boxes show team actions once the unit ends. Each of these team actions provides an opportunity for you, as a leader (as well as your guiding coalition), to monitor and support the work of teams. Ideally, teams will collectively unwrap standards and create common assessments with scoring agreements *before the unit begins* so each teacher can plan more focused and effective lessons.

  Teams post on a calendar when members will give common formative assessments (mid-unit) on the need-to-know standards and common

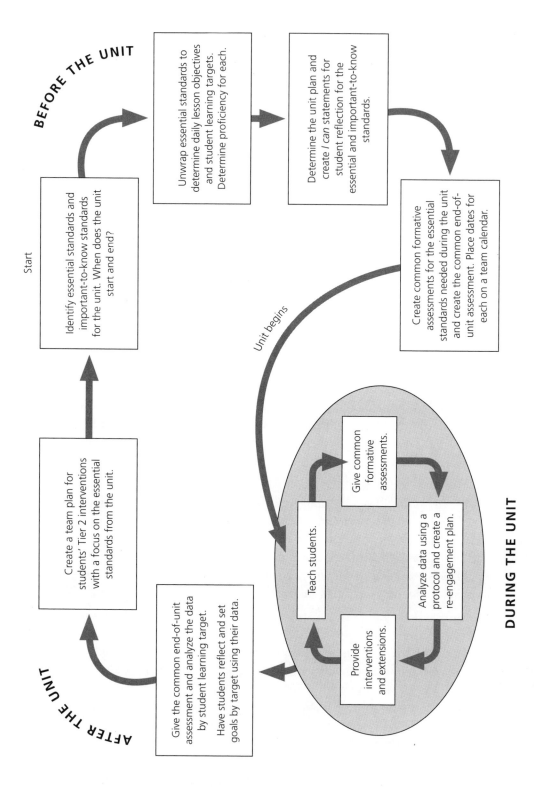

Source: Adapted from Buffum et al., 2018; DuFour et al., 2016; Kanold & Larson, 2015; Putnam City School District, Oklahoma City, Oklahoma.

Figure 10.1: Team learning cycle.

end-of-unit (summative) assessments on the need-to-know and important-to-know standards. Teams plan to never teach more than ten days without analyzing and responding to student learning data, whether from a mid-unit common formative assessment or a common end-of-unit assessment.

- **During the unit:** Teachers on the team instruct, give short common assessments mid-unit on one or two learning targets, and re-engage learners as needed while discussing the effectiveness of instructional practices. Interventions may be provided for Tier 1 and Tier 2. Some teams will plan their full unit and place dates for assessments and topics for instruction on a calendar, and others may separate a unit into ten-day learning cycles as described in chapter 13 (page 213). Regardless of how teams plan for student learning, teams should never teach more than ten days without giving a common mid-unit or end-of-unit assessment to gather data related to student learning and instruction.

- **After the unit:** Teams analyze assessment data from the culminating common end-of-unit assessment to determine how to best re-engage students in learning during all-student classroom-based Tier 1 instruction or targeted Tier 2 interventions. Teams also work to ensure students are reflecting on their learning and setting goals using common assessment data during and after each unit.

As a principal, consider how to provide clarity to teachers about their work in collaborative teams through your feedback during team meetings, through the artifacts teams produce, or via classroom walkthroughs. You can share feedback orally in real time through observations and questions or write it for teams to consider or celebrate.

Leading the work of teams also means it is important to look for and remove roadblocks so you can help teams grow the practices that most impact student learning. It is easy for a collaborative team to spend too much time identifying essential standards and then unwrapping them. In fact, teachers can get lost in this process and eventually stop because they do not see the relationship to student learning when their time is solely spent unwrapping standard after standard. A consequence is the team never really addressing the four critical questions designed to improve student learning.

This, in part, is what had happened in the middle school I referenced earlier in this chapter. Thankfully, the principal identified the frustration from spending so much time unwrapping standards and created a solution: teams already had a list of essential standards that identified when students should be proficient with each. She asked teacher teams to address essential standards on a unit-by-unit basis, rather than making sense of all of them at once. That way, teams were challenged to clarify an essential standard or two, create common assessments, analyze data, and respond to student learning and instructional practices on only those one or two essential standards in a given unit. Then, they could continue with the next essential standards in the next unit. Together, teams gave short or long common assessments at least every ten days to check on student learning and marked those dates on a calendar. The work became more manageable, and teams refined their ability to answer the four critical questions with each unit throughout the year.

One benefit to teams creating common assessments is they discuss student proficiency with standards in the unit and the instructional strategies that will help students learn. Figure 10.2 shows the relationship in a unit between team common mid-unit and end-of-unit assessments and the individual work of a teacher in the classroom designing daily lessons, checking for understanding (indicated with check marks), and providing opportunities for students to revise or strengthen their learning through formative feedback (indicated with Fs).

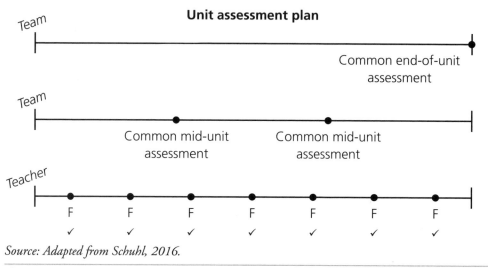

Source: Adapted from Schuhl, 2016.

Figure 10.2: Team and teacher assessment plan.

Clarifying the work of teams before, during, and after a unit—with a focus first on the learning cycle using essential standards on ten-day cycles—grows routines. Routines, in turn, lead to teams regularly and consistently doing the right work related to student learning. What type of feedback can a leader give to teams to grow their productive routines?

Leadership Feedback to Collaborative Teams

The heart of learning happens in the classroom every day as students learn from instruction and feedback. Just as feedback is critical to student learning (Hattie, 2012), feedback is also critical to teachers' and teams' learning. As a leader, consider how you might answer the following questions.

- What is it you want teams to know and be able to do?
- How will you give feedback on what you most value and that grows student learning?
- How can you use your guiding coalition to monitor the work of collaborative teams and provide feedback?
- How can you give feedback at team meetings?

- How can you give feedback after walkthroughs of the team members' classrooms?
- How can you give feedback using artifacts in team folders?

The critical work of teams is to grow student learning. In light of that, what should be the focus of your feedback to teams? What feedback helps wandering teams stay focused on improving every student's learning? How can you give feedback in a meaningful and productive manner?

At the middle school where the principal initially struggled to find time to attend meetings and provide feedback, she and I strategized options for her to monitor the teams' work. At times she might give feedback during team meetings or give feedback using walkthroughs of team members' classrooms. The principal also began looking at team artifacts with the guiding coalition and her administrative team. Each of these provides an opportunity for a leader to grow the learning of teachers and, in turn, students.

Give Feedback to Teams Using the Guiding Coalition

Two of the guiding coalition's critical responsibilities are to (1) lead the work of collaborative teams to impact student learning and (2) identify roadblocks to collaborative teams' answering the four critical questions of a PLC (page 3). In fact, your guiding coalition should often ask the critical questions with a shift from *students* to *collaborative teams* (DuFour et al., 2016).

1. What do we want *collaborative teams* to know and be able to do?

2. How will we know if each *collaborative team* has learned it?

3. How will we respond when some *collaborative teams* do not learn it (or are not doing it)?

4. How will we extend learning for *collaborative teams* that have demonstrated proficiency?

Each member of the guiding coalition is also a member (or liaison) of a collaborative team. As part of the agenda, you might ask guiding coalition members if they can bring an example of work from their teams to share with one another and learn from. During a meeting, members might share examples of unwrapped standards to targets, common assessments, rubrics, or a team's data analysis with an intervention plan. In turn, members can ask each other questions and gather ideas that can strengthen the impact on student learning for their own team. The guiding coalition can also celebrate the growth in team products and determine any professional development needed to support teams. The goal is to learn from one another and make the work of teams more efficient and effective. The reproducible "Leading the Right Work" (page 173) shares the work of the guiding coalition and collaborative teams in answering the four critical questions and addressing meeting agenda topics.

As a leader, consider how your guiding coalition is monitoring the work of teams in a productive way. Working together, the guiding coalition gives and receives feedback that doesn't simply acknowledge the completion of the task, but comments on the quality of the work addressing the four critical PLC questions during their meetings in a way that grows student learning.

Teams create products during their meetings that provide an opportunity for meaningful feedback and learning. There was large growth in the work of teams at the middle school when the principal required them to store their products, or *artifacts*, in an electronic folder system the team organized by unit. That let the principal and the members of each collaborative team and the guiding coalition access all the documents for learning, planning, feedback, and reflection. Such a system also meant teams could grow their work one year to the next, despite staff turnover.

Consider how you and your guiding coalition might provide clarity about the products teams need to produce when addressing student learning. What protocol are teams using to unwrap standards, create common assessments, analyze data, determine effective instructional practices, and clarify interventions and extensions? Protocols lend themselves to quality team products and teach teams how to do each task through their questions or templates. Visit **go.SolutionTree.com/PLCbooks** for free reproducible versions of these protocols from *School Improvement for All* (Kramer & Schuhl, 2017).

Simply telling teachers what to do and expecting it to be done can be frustrating for you, the principal, and also the teachers. Additionally, it minimizes the learning opportunities through feedback and fails to create equitable and consistent expectations across grade-level or course-alike teams at a school. Consider how to use your guiding coalition to clarify how teams address the four critical questions and, most importantly, how you will celebrate the work of teams along the way.

Give Feedback to Teams During Team Meetings

Using the guiding coalition to create clarity for collaborative teams is one way to provide feedback to teams. Another is through attending weekly team meetings to provide real-time feedback and clarification. When teams meet, they complete agendas and create products. A leader sitting in a team meeting can quickly provide meaningful feedback to teams. What are you hearing at team meetings? What do you observe teams doing at meetings or in their digital folders? Challenge teams to discuss the work in terms of standards students are learning. Some questions to consider as you meet with teams follow.

- How often are you observing teams discuss standards and student proficiency of each standard?
- How often are teams creating common assessments with scoring agreements?
- How often are teams completing a data-analysis protocol to do the following?
  - ‣ Analyze effective instructional practices.
  - ‣ Determine which students learned and which did not learn *yet*.
  - ‣ Make instructional decisions about what to do next as a team in class (Tier 1) or during Tier 2 interventions.
- How often are teams celebrating the learning of students because of their collective efforts?

The reproducible "Evidence of Doing the Right Work Feedback Form" (page 174) shows some possible actions you might see teams do before, during, and after completing a unit in their learning cycle. It is a checklist or observational tool that you can use at team meetings to give feedback to the teachers on the team. There is value in recognizing the hard work of teams and providing feedback to deepen their work.

Give Feedback to Teams Using Classroom Walkthroughs

You can also use the third column in the reproducible "Evidence of Doing the Right Work Feedback Form" for giving feedback to a team after classroom walkthroughs across team members' classrooms. You will see evidence of the work of teams in classrooms through common learning targets and standards, equitable instructional practices, and even the sharing of students for interventions and extensions, when appropriate. Consider the following questions during team walkthroughs.

- Are the teachers referencing the same learning targets?

- Can students articulate what they are learning?

- Are students taking assessments at the same time?

- How are students reflecting on their learning during the unit and after each assessment?

- Are teachers teaching the same general concept (is pacing the same)?

- What similarities, if any, are observable as part of instruction? Are the expectations of reasoning similar across the classroom for each concept learned?

Consider how to gather data about the work of teams to determine any needed professional development. Which teams may need support with the skills needed to be effective? Which teams need help to remove roadblocks so they can do the required work that improves student learning? Again, the reproducible (page 174) provides a template for providing feedback to a team and collecting data about the work of teams through team meetings and classroom walkthroughs.

When teams are doing the right work, students experience equity of expectations across the grade level or course. You are also growing shared leadership across the school with team leaders and your guiding coalition.

Conclusion

As a leader, the growth of teams is a charge, but not one solely on your shoulders. Consider how you, with your guiding coalition, can provide clarity for the work of collaborative teams and supports through feedback. Also consider how feedback at team meetings and through walkthroughs will strengthen the learning of teams and students.

There will be missteps and roadblocks to teams doing the right work on your journey to improvement. Remember, that is when there is an opportunity to learn and refocus. The middle school that struggled to get past time spent on behavior and district meetings systematically addressed issues with policies, procedures, and practices. They now focus on the work of collaborative teams and student learning using the four critical questions of a PLC. It did not happen overnight, and it did not happen without some missteps along the way.

Teachers will be frustrated with collaborative team meetings when they are not focused on student learning and linked to teaching in the classroom. And guiding coalition meetings will be a problem if things like a backpack policy dominate a month's worth of time. Consider how you will clarify the work of collaborative teams and your guiding coalition. This shared leadership provides an opportunity for you to give feedback to teams to grow leaders and to strengthen and celebrate the right work.

Last, and certainly not least, the middle school principal was amazing at growing teacher teamwork through celebration. Celebration is feedback. Celebrate because the work is hard. Celebrate because it is the right work. Celebrate because you will see more students learning. Together, you and your staff will make an amazing difference in the lives of students.

Leading the Right Work

Guiding Coalition	Collaborative Teams

Lead Creation of School Foundations
• Create a mission.
• Create a vision.
• Create collective commitments.
• Create schoolwide SMART goals.
 	
Analyze Data
• Monitor progress toward SMART goals and the accompanying action steps.
• Monitor student learning and behavior data.
• Plan celebrations.
 	
Remove Roadblocks
• Identify roadblocks and brainstorm solutions. Consider possible issues with the following.
  ➤ Master schedule
  ➤ Collaboration time
  ➤ Resource allocation
  ➤ Protected time for Tier 1 core instruction
  ➤ Time and personnel for Tier 2 interventions
  ➤ Plan for Tier 3 remediations
• Identify needed staff professional development.
• Keep focused on the tights, or non-negotiables.
 	
Identify Academic and Behavior Consistencies
• Identify core instructional practices needed across the school.
• Identify schoolwide expected behaviors.
 	
Monitor the Work of Collaborative Teams
• Share artifacts and provide feedback.
• Celebrate student learning resulting from the work of teams.
• Determine what is tight and loose for all teams.
• Identify next steps and needed professional development.
	Create Team Foundations
	• Create a vision.
	• Create norms.
	• Create SMART goals with action steps.
	
	Question one: What is it we want our students to know and be able to do?
	• Identify essential standards.
	• Unwrap essential standards and plan for the common assessments of each.
	• Create proficiency maps (pacing guides) to include every course or subject state or provincial standard.
	• Create unit plans for instruction and assessment of standards in each unit.
	• Create student learning targets for each unit.
	
	Question two: How will we know if each student has learned it?
	• Create common mid-unit and end-of-unit assessments before the unit begins.
	• Determine scoring agreements for common assessments and clarify student proficiency.
	• Calibrate scoring of common assessments.
	• Analyze data from common assessments as a team by standard or learning target.
	
	Questions three and four: How will we respond when some students do not learn it and how will we extend learning for students who have demonstrated proficiency?
	• Collectively respond to common assessment data by answering the following.
	  ➤ Which instructional practices worked?
	  ➤ Which students learned or did not learn?
	  ➤ What are the trends in learning as shown in work?
	  ➤ How will students reflect on their learning and set goals?
	• Create a team plan to re-engage students in learning identified targets whether they need intervention or extension.

Source: Adapted from Buffum, A., Mattos, M., & Malone, J. (2018). Taking action: A handbook for RTI at Work. Bloomington, IN: Solution Tree Press; DuFour, R., DuFour, R., Eaker, R., Many, T. W., & Mattos, M. (2016). Learning by doing: A handbook for Professional Learning Communities at Work (3rd ed.). Bloomington, IN: Solution Tree Press; Kramer, S. V., & Schuhl, S. (2017). School improvement for all: A how-to guide for doing the right work. Bloomington, IN: Solution Tree Press.

Evidence of Doing the Right Work Feedback Form

When monitoring the work of teams at a team meeting or classroom walkthrough, check the specific evidence observed for each appropriate team action. Circle a rating in the rightmost column to give feedback to the teachers on the team about the quality of their work.

Before the Unit			
Team Actions	**Team Meetings With Artifacts**	**Walkthroughs Across Team Classrooms**	**Rating**
Identify and make sense of the standards for the unit and establish pacing and student learning targets.	☐ Check pacing—identify start and end dates for the unit and the essential and important-to-know standards students will learn. ☐ Unpack essential standards and determine student-friendly learning targets. ☐ Determine what a student must know and be able to do to be proficient with the standards in the unit. ☐ Identify tasks and instructional strategies to use in order for students to learn the standards in the unit. ☐ Determine dates on a calendar for common mid-unit and end-of-unit assessments.	☐ Teachers reference the same learning target with students during the lesson. ☐ Students can articulate the learning target to one another. ☐ Same general pacing of the lessons is evident. ☐ Same general rigor of tasks and student engagement are evident.	Embracing Practicing Attempting Beginning

page 1 of 4

Develop common mid-unit and end-of-unit assessments.	☐ Determine the essential standards or targets to assess mid-unit. ☐ Determine the essential and important-to-know standards to assess at the end of the unit. ☐ Create common assessments with common scoring agreements. ☐ Determine proficiency scores or performances on the common mid-unit or end-of-unit assessment for each learning target or standard. ☐ Confirm dates to give each common mid-unit or end-of-unit assessment.	☐ Students take common assessments on the same day. ☐ Students take the common assessment under the same conditions (notes, calculator, extra time, and so on). ☐ Students can explain the learning targets and the expectations for meeting proficiency with each learning target on the assessment.	Embracing
			Practicing
			Attempting
			Beginning

Feedback:

During and After the Unit			
Team Actions	**Team Meetings With Artifacts**	**Walkthroughs Across Team Classrooms**	**Rating**
Discuss effectiveness of instructional practices and try new practices.	☐ Identify effective instructional strategies to use during lessons. ☐ Discuss how to differentiate instruction during the unit or for specific tasks or standards. ☐ Determine how to address prerequisite skills while teaching grade-level content in the unit. ☐ Plan effective strategies for teacher feedback during whole- or small-group parts of lessons. ☐ Share common misconceptions students may have and plan to address each one.	☐ Teachers give some common differentiation and feedback to students. ☐ Observe time in lessons for small-group discourse that provides student-to-student feedback and teacher-to-student feedback with student action. ☐ Teachers use research-based instructional strategies in lessons throughout the unit in all classrooms. ☐ Teachers use similar tasks (equivalent rigor) in lessons to teach a standard. ☐ Teachers teach grade-level content during the lesson.	Embracing Practicing Attempting Beginning
Analyze data from common assessments and make a team plan to re-engage learners.	☐ Identify as a team the students who learned or did not learn yet. ☐ Calibrate scoring of common assessments. ☐ Discuss effectiveness of instructional practices using student work from assessments. ☐ Complete a data-analysis protocol and document Tier 1 and Tier 2 plans to re-engage students in learning.	☐ Teachers re-engage students using Tier 2 interventions to address learning needs by standard. ☐ Teachers re-engage students similarly in learning activities in each classroom (Tier 1 interventions and extensions). ☐ Teachers share students across their team during Tier 1 to re-engage learners by targeted learning need.	Embracing Practicing Attempting Beginning

page 3 of 4

Students analyze data and set learning goals.	☐ Discuss how to give feedback to students from their assessments for continued learning. ☐ Develop a protocol or template for students to fix or embrace their errors from the common assessments and identify what they have learned and what they have not learned yet. ☐ Determine a protocol or template for student goal setting based on their evidence of learning.	☐ Students complete their reflection, goal, and tracker using common assessment data and formative feedback. ☐ Students create a learning plan in each classroom and take action on that plan.	Embracing
			Practicing
			Attempting
			Beginning
Feedback:			

Source: Adapted from Kanold, T. D., Toncheff, M., Larson, M. R., Barnes, B., Kanold-McIntyre, J., & Schuhl, S. (2018). Mathematics coaching and collaboration in a PLC at Work. *Bloomington, IN: Solution Tree Press.*

page 4 of 4

References and Resources

Ainsworth, L. (2003). *Power standards: Identifying the standards that matter the most.* Denver, CO: Advanced Learning Press.

Ainsworth, L. (2013). *Prioritizing the common core: Identifying specific standards to emphasize the most.* Englewood, CO: Lead + Learn Press.

Brown, B. (2018). *Dare to lead: Brave work, tough conversations, whole hearts.* New York: Random House.

Buffum, A., Mattos, M., & Malone, J. (2018). *Taking action: A handbook for RTI at Work.* Bloomington, IN: Solution Tree Press.

DuFour, R., DuFour, R., Eaker, R., Many, T. W., & Mattos, M. (2016). *Learning by doing: A handbook for Professional Learning Communities at Work* (3rd ed.). Bloomington, IN: Solution Tree Press.

DuFour, R., & Fullan, M. (2013). *Cultures built to last: Systemic PLCs at Work.* Bloomington, IN: Solution Tree Press.

Hattie, J. (2012). *Visible learning for teachers: Maximizing impact on learning.* New York: Routledge.

Kanold, T. D., & Larson, M. R. (2015). *Beyond the Common Core: A handbook for mathematics in a PLC at Work, leader's guide.* Bloomington, IN: Solution Tree Press.

Kanold, T. D., Schuhl, S., Larson, M. R., Barnes, B., Kanold-McIntyre, J., & Toncheff, M. (2018). *Mathematics assessment and intervention in a PLC at Work.* Bloomington, IN: Solution Tree Press.

Kanold, T. D., Toncheff, M., Larson, M. R., Barnes, B., Kanold-McIntyre, J., & Schuhl, S. (2018). *Mathematics coaching and collaboration in a PLC at Work.* Bloomington, IN: Solution Tree Press.

Kramer, S. V., & Schuhl, S. (2017). *School improvement for all: A how-to guide for doing the right work.* Bloomington, IN: Solution Tree Press.

Mattos, M., DuFour, R., DuFour, R., Eaker, R., & Many, T. W. (2016). *Concise answers to frequently asked questions about Professional Learning Communities at Work.* Bloomington, IN: Solution Tree Press.

Reeves, D. B. (2002). *The leader's guide to standards: A blueprint for educational equity and excellence.* San Francisco: Jossey-Bass.

Reeves, D. (2020). *Achieving equity and excellence: Immediate results from the lessons of high-poverty, high-success schools.* Bloomington, IN: Solution Tree Press.

Schmoker, M. (2004). Learning communities at the crossroads: Toward the best schools we've ever had. *Phi Delta Kappan, 86*(1), 84–88.

Schuhl, S. (2016, July). *Creating useful common assessments.* [Conference presentation]. Professional Learning Communities at Work Institute, Atlanta, GA.

Schuhl, S., Kanold, T. D., Deinhart, J., Larson, M. R., & Toncheff, M. (2020). *Mathematics unit planning in a PLC at Work, grades 3–5.* Bloomington, IN: Solution Tree Press.

Wiggins, G. (2012, September). *Seven keys to effective feedback.* Accessed at http://www.ascd .org/publications/educational-leadership/sept12/vol70/num01/Seven-Keys-to-Effective -Feedback.aspx on March 16, 2021.

Wiggins, G., & McTighe, J. (2011). *The understanding by design guide to creating high-quality units.* Alexandria, VA: Association for Supervision and Curriculum Development.

 **Michelle Marrillia** has seventeen years of experience as an educator and is an assistant principal of Fern Creek High School in Louisville, Kentucky. As an instructional coach, staff developer, and professional learning community (PLC) coordinator at Fern Creek, Michelle helped move the school from a persistently low-achieving school in 2010 to a proficient school in 2015.

In 2017, Fern Creek won Solution Tree's prestigious DuFour Award and $25,000 prize. Created in honor of PLC architect Richard DuFour, the award credits high-performing schools that demonstrate exceptional levels of student achievement. In 2016, Fern Creek received the School Innovation and Change Award through the National Preparedness Leadership Initiative.

Michelle specializes in training instructional coaches in PLCs, creating differentiated professional learning programs for beginning and sustaining successful PLCs, implementing response to intervention (RTI) systems, developing teacher leaders, and using PLCs to support turnaround efforts in schools with at-risk populations.

Michelle earned a bachelor's degree in biology from Georgetown College and a master's degree in teaching from the University of Louisville. She also received her school administration certification in instructional leadership at Spalding University in Louisville.

To learn more about Michelle's work, follow @michellemarrill on Twitter.

To book Michelle Marrillia for professional development, contact pd@SolutionTree.com.

Giving All Teachers the Coach They Deserve

Michelle Marrillia

> The world is a changing place, requiring knowledge
> and skills much different from those in years past.
>
> —*Sharon V. Kramer and Sarah Schuhl*

When I work with schools, I start by asking these questions: "Do you have an instructional coach in the building?" If the answer is *yes*, then I ask, "What does he or she do all day?" My favorite answer to this question was at a workshop in California. A principal quickly raised her hand and shouted out, "She makes us better educators each day!" The teachers at the table nodded in agreement, and then the coach beamed and responded, "It is a team effort. We work together well." That was it. That was the gold star answer! Now how do we make that happen for all schools?

During a time of high-stakes accountability and teacher shortages, it is more important than ever for schools to have structures in place that assist and value every teacher's work. Providing quality professional development is key to improving teaching and learning. However, in my experience, the single day, stand and deliver traditional model of professional development does not yield a high-impact change in teacher practices. As the popularity of instructional coaching increases, principals have the opportunity to shift from *sit, get, and forget* teacher development sessions to a more individualized model of teacher support. This professional development is high impact, as coaching improves the quality of teachers' instruction "by as much as—or more than—the difference in effectiveness between a novice and a teacher with five to 10 years of experience" (Kraft & Blazer, 2018). Yet, meeting every teacher's needs can be a daunting task for even the most experienced instructional coach.

Ideally, schools have multiple coaches to guarantee that every teacher receives frequent, quality coaching, although the reality is that often teacher improvement falls on the shoulders of one coach. As the ratio of coach to teacher increases in a school, the effectiveness of the coaching decreases (Kraft & Blazer, 2018). Clearly articulating coaching roles and responsibilities will enhance the impact of the instructional coach and strengthen collaborative teams. However, even the best coach cannot implement or sustain a successful professional learning community (PLC) alone. If school improvement is going to be long lasting, then school leaders must embrace a coaching mindset to support teachers and teams.

This chapter will address the key components for both instructional coaches and school leaders to design a successful coaching plan that supports *every* teacher.

- Defining the instructional coach's roles and responsibilities in the PLC

- Creating a leadership team that embraces a coaching mindset

- Implementing a coaching plan that provides continuous feedback and support for every teacher

- Creating a meaningful and realistic coaching schedule

Defining the Instructional Coach's Roles and Responsibilities in the PLC

University of Kansas Center for Research on Learning associate Jim Knight (2016) defines instructional coaches as partners who work "with teachers to analyze current reality, set goals, identify and explain teaching strategies to hit the goals, and provide support until the goals are met." In a PLC, coaches expand this approach when working with teacher teams.

Creating a master schedule that allows teacher teams to collaborate is fundamental to the success of a PLC and is also critical to a comprehensive coaching model. Coaches can achieve greater results by beginning with a team-oriented approach, followed by individual coaching for teachers who need more time and support.

Every effort of an instructional coach must center on teacher support and improvement, and defining the coach's roles and responsibilities is critical to the school-improvement process and student success. Principals must support the coach's work and communicate that work frequently to both the faculty and other building administrators for the coach to succeed. In a PLC, coaches should do the following.

- Act as the lead for the team facilitators.

- Provide ongoing formal and informal professional learning.

- Monitor the work of the collaborative teams to ensure fidelity (of the PLC actions).

- Provide nonevaluative, nonjudgmental support to teams and teachers.

Ultimately, when determining the roles and responsibilities of an instructional coach, a strong administrator knows the job description should focus on two simple things: (1) instruction and (2) all things that support instruction.

It is important to note that the instructional coach cannot lead this charge until he or she is well versed in foundational PLC work. To assist coaches, school leaders can set aside time for instructional coaches to prepare by attending conferences, visiting Model PLC schools, facilitating mentorships with other instructional coaches, and allowing for planning and research during the day. These practices will strengthen the coach's PLC knowledge base, help that person build collaborative relationships with other coaches and, ultimately, benefit teacher teams.

Act as the Lead for Team Facilitators

A successful coach understands the teachers, not the coaches, should facilitate the teacher teams. However, the coach can help build capacity in the PLC by creating a clear communication structure for the team facilitators and collaborative team members. A team facilitator increases the collaborative team's effectiveness when given the right training, resources, and feedback. Coaches equip the facilitators by leading regular trainings on the essential elements of the PLC and team dynamics.

The coach might use a tool like that in the reproducible "Collaborative Team Agenda Template" (page 192) as part of the communication structure. At Fern Creek High School in Louisville, Kentucky, our common team agenda is based on the four critical questions (page 3). Meeting facilitators are tasked with taking minutes from each meeting and ensuring the form is appropriately stored on a shared drive.

Our instructional coach typically provides four facilitator trainings based on this agenda, which includes the four critical questions (DuFour, DuFour, Eaker, Many, & Mattos, 2016). These trainings assist our facilitators in becoming more expert in the PLC process and enable them to facilitate their teams effectively. For example, in a session designed around question one, the coach may focus on essential standards. Depending on the team's expertise, the coach may differentiate training on learning how to unpack team-determined essential standards and creating proficiency maps or simply learning how to access state standards and local curriculum frameworks. The coach provides other tools, templates, and support for facilitators according to their current needs.

In the early days of our school turnaround efforts, we hosted monthly facilitator meetings. Because the PLC process was new to everyone in our school, we often felt as if we were generating as many questions as we were answers. These trainings were critical to our improvement process at the time. However, after several years, we were able to eliminate the monthly trainings and focus on the four critical question foundational trainings. We used the additional time to provide individual support to assist facilitators in preparing for team meetings and *data days* (full-release days when teacher teams meet to review student data and create plans for next steps). Our instructional coach created a schedule to meet with every facilitator one-to-one to help plan release days, set goals, and reflect. This individual coaching was key to ensuring our teams were doing the right work.

Provide Ongoing Formal and Informal Professional Learning

The coach's second role is to provide ongoing formal and informal professional learning that aligns to the school's mission and vision. When school leaders view the instructional coach as a valuable member of the school leadership team and the guiding coalition, the coach plays a role in determining why the school exists and where the school is going. This is central to successfully helping teams see the connections between their work and overall school improvement. A skilled coach will not only facilitate professional learning for content teams but also initiate collaboration among vertical and cross-curricular teams to meet the goals of the whole school.

It is a widely accepted practice that many of the formal professional development sessions in a school will fall to the instructional coach. Administrators may lean heavily on coaches to assist and collaborate on schoolwide faculty retreats or monthly after-school sessions. While there is value in formal, whole-school professional development, high-impact professional learning also takes place in the less formal conversations between the coach and teachers. When coaches build strong relationships with teachers and teacher teams, meaningful informal professional learning can seemingly happen anywhere and anytime.

Monitor Collaborative Teams' Work to Ensure Fidelity

Another of their foci becomes monitoring the collaborative teams' work and ensuring the fidelity of PLC actions. When principals safeguard time and space for coaches to meet with teacher teams, it allows coaches to become increasingly familiar with the teams' activities and products. When the coach is invested in observing teams and examining agendas and work products, opportunities for rich conversations become frequent and more authentic because the coach is viewed as a part of the collaboration process. This allows the coach to set the stage for a continuous feedback loop between the teachers and school leaders as well.

As coaches seek to better understand where each collaborative team is on its PLC journey, they consider what is necessary to support each team because:

> It is difficult to overstate the importance of collaborative teams in the improvement process. It is even more important, however, to emphasize that collaboration does not lead to improved results unless people are focused on the right work. Collaboration is a means to an end, not the end itself. (DuFour et al., 2016, p. 12)

A coach can help teams determine what products to produce at each level of the PLC process, provide resources, and help foster a community of reflective practitioners within the school. The collaborative team agenda also functions as a tool for principals and coaches to discuss the team's productivity. For example, if a team only produces products that align to critical question one—determining learning targets, discussing instructional strategies, and planning assessments, for example—then the coach or principal would assume that the team may need support analyzing data or planning interventions. Additionally, if the agendas reveal that the team never plans for student extension activities, then the coach can provide assistance in planning in this area. Ideally, collaboration continues with teams, and the coach can help team members reflect on these agendas and determine the gaps on their own.

It is important to note that a team's needs can vary greatly in a school. A ninth-grade English language arts team may be highly effective and need little support, while the ninth-grade algebra team down the hall may be struggling just to administer a common formative assessment. Some teams naturally work well together, and others try to make excuses not to meet. Determining these individual team needs allows the coach to develop support plans specific to assisting each team improve instruction and student outcomes.

Provide Nonevaluative, Nonjudgmental Support to Teams and Teachers

Finally, an instructional coach provides teachers nonevaluative, nonjudgmental support. Research supports the correlation between strong professional environments and increased rates of teacher improvement (Kraft & Papay, 2014). The best coaches promote a culture that allows teams and teachers to take risks and ask for feedback on instructional practices. The teams' work then focuses on how to apply what they are learning to future outcomes to improve learning for all.

Creating a Leadership Team That Embraces a Coaching Mindset

Early in my instructional coaching career, I remember a strong, well-respected teacher saying to me, "You and the administrators only focus on the new and struggling teachers. If you want the good teachers to be great, then you have to coach us too" (E. Canale, personal communication, March 14, 2014). She was absolutely right; as leaders of a priority school, we had to make changes to ensure every teacher was receiving quality feedback and opportunities to grow professionally. We also knew that it was going to take more than one coach and another administrator or two to provide the support needed to meet the lofty school-improvement goals we had in mind, because "While coaches are instructional leaders that facilitate, model, and execute the professional development, school administrators still play a major role in the process" (Johnson, 2016). We thought that if the principal and coach collaborated to develop an instructional leadership team (ILT) with members who participate in team and individual coaching, every teacher in the school would benefit.

At Fern Creek High School, we examined our ILT and determined we could more effectively provide quality feedback and support to our teacher teams. We had a young staff, newly formed teams, and an ever-changing student population, all of which contributed to increasing our commitment to giving every teacher a quality coaching experience.

Our ILT consists of the principal, assistant principals, and instructional coaches who do weekly learning walks and monitor the work of the collaborative teams. Each ILT member is assigned two or three collaborative teams. We attend their meetings, schedule time with our teams' facilitators, and do follow-up learning walks and coaching sessions for the teachers on our teams. Our learning walk protocol allows time for the ILT members to meet with the teachers on their assigned collaborative teams. The teachers choose what type of data to collect and which learning walk form they prefer. The ILT member commits to doing a learning walk one time per week and typically it is unannounced, unless the teacher requests a specific day and time. Weekly, the ILT collaborates on how to best meet the needs of teams who seem to be lacking forward momentum. Using the ILT share form in figure 11.1 (page 186), we determine what to do next to support the team. Those next steps are made through a coaching lens and based on observations, conversations, and each team's work products. Figure 11.1 is an example of how an ILT member may use the shared document to gather data, share and record next steps, and

Facilitator: Johnna	Date: October 2, 2020
Team Name: Senior Math	ILT Member: Anthony
Here's what. *What do the agendas reveal about the team's productivity?*	*What do you observe in the classroom and team meetings?*
Agendas • The team is bringing data to the meetings. • They meet with fidelity. • There is no evidence of a data-analysis protocol to determine which students need more time and support. • They are not documenting any next steps toward recovery and extension on standards. • There is no evidence that the team is using common measures to determine proficiency on essential standards. The rubric is generic and can be applied to any standard.	Observation • The team worked through the unit planner for chapter 2 during their common planning after-school meeting for two weeks. (Instructional coach was present for two of three meeting times.) • They spent time unpacking the essential standards for unit 2; this led to much discussion and questions about what the standards mean. • They discussed needing more support to differentiate lessons.
So what? *What do these data reveal about the team?*	
They need a deeper understanding of how to unpack essential standards and why it is important.	They were open to working with the coach and seem to be moving in the right direction toward addressing the four critical questions.
Now what? *Together, the ILT generates next steps for the team.*	*What are the next steps for the ILT member working with this team?*
ILT • Can members start grading their common formative assessments together for twenty minutes each week? It will help to calibrate their scores and ultimately build more authentic rubrics. • As they are trying to build a better differentiated Tier 1 system, can they incorporate peer-to-peer learning walks for ideas?	ILT Member • Meet with the facilitator to set goals and timelines. • The agendas and minutes do not reflect what is taking place in the team meetings. Can we work together to plan the agenda before the next meeting? Do you want me to take the minutes when you meet next week? • Share with ILT in four weeks.
Facilitator Reflection and Next Steps	**Additional Notes**
• There is a planned agenda for the Tuesday meeting and I will take the minutes. • Team members will bring ten ungraded common formative assessments each to the team meeting on Tuesday to score together using the rubric they created at the end of last week. They will repeat this for all upcoming common formative assessments. • They will use the data-analysis protocol during their common planning on Thursday after grading all common formative assessments. They are planning a recovery and extension workshop based on that data on Friday. • The coach will videotape two teachers during that time, and the team will watch the videos together and discuss what they learned from the workshop model that week.	As part of the embedded professional development time, the coach suggests all teachers do learning walks. The mathematics department is doing one on a team member and one on a non-team member. Many teachers are visiting classes with another teacher, coach, or supervising administrator.

Figure 11.1: ILT share template example.

ultimately provide support for the facilitator and team. The reproducible "Instructional Leadership Team Share Template" (page 194) is a blank version.

This intentionality allows weekly coaching opportunities for teams and individual teachers. Shifting our ILT from a monitoring-only mindset to a coaching mindset led to richer conversations about teacher improvement, highlighted areas of concern, and created a structure to determine next steps for increasing academic achievement. This expanded the coaching footprint in the entire school.

Implementing a Coaching Plan That Provides Continuous Feedback and Support for Every Teacher

Coaches and principals in a PLC collaborate to create a comprehensive professional development plan that ensures instructional support on three levels: (1) whole school, (2) group, and (3) individual teacher. This differentiated approach allows every teacher to receive the coaching he or she needs to improve student achievement.

Whole-School Coaching Plan

So often in a priority school, the pressures of staff turnover, initiative overload, and state test scores overwhelm administrators and teachers. It is the instructional coach's job to anchor the school in the foundational work of the PLC. DuFour and colleagues (2016) state the school's fundamental purpose is to ensure all students learn at high levels. Strong leaders understand to increase student learning, they must promote continual adult learning as well.

When we take time to gather teachers in a large group, we need to ensure they leave with a valuable learning experience. Avoid being a school leader who pulls teachers away from precious planning, collaborating, or family time to deliver information you can just as effectively communicate in an email. Instead of meeting just to meet, approach every faculty meeting as a full-staff coaching opportunity. Is every member of the staff clear on the school's mission and vision? Does the staff use a common language when discussing standards, assessments, and data? Is it time to celebrate?

Creating a meaningful, whole-faculty gathering requires intentionality and clarity on the meeting's purpose. As leaders, we would be disappointed to find a teacher without a thoughtful plan that includes a learning objective, instructional strategies, and opportunities to assess for the day. Yet, at times, we fall into a trap of meeting with our faculty just because it is the second Tuesday of the month; it's just what we do. As leaders, we must ensure we are providing professional development that "happens with, not to, teachers" (Yaron, 2017).

Leaders can collaborate with instructional coaches to provide quality learning opportunities for the whole faculty, when necessary, that continue to connect and reinforce the big ideas of the PLC and support the specific collective commitments of the school.

Group Coaching Plan

Whether a staff are just beginning their journey as a PLC or are veterans of the PLC process, a coach can provide critical feedback to teacher teams. Coauthors Anthony Muhammad and Luis F. Cruz (2019) state, "When school leaders effectively link the why and who aspects of change with a discussion centered on 'What do we do next?' they formulate a more comprehensive vision of next steps" (p. 67). When coaches frequently meet with teacher teams, opportunities to ensure all teachers have a critical understanding of the *why* become more frequent and authentic. A skilled coach knows his or her job is to capitalize on those moments to increase the overall capacity of the teacher and team. I believe these moments are also when leaders and coaches have the most opportunity to build trust with teachers. I have heard it said it's hard to sound genuine over a microphone, meaning as leaders and coaches, when standing in front of the large group and explaining our motives, it is more difficult to make the connections necessary to have the long-lasting dedication and resilience the staff need to achieve their mission and vision. However, when school leaders and coaches are sitting in small groups discussing the *why* and answering concerns, being transparent, and holding one another accountable—that is setting the stage for all students to learn.

Intentional time and focus with teams will allow the coach to build an embedded professional-learning schedule based on teachers' current needs. Understanding that coaching teams "improves teacher effectiveness several teachers at a time" (Many, Maffoni, Sparks, & Thomas, 2018, p. 19), a savvy coach will maximize time and opportunity to work with teacher teams weekly. Just like teacher teams need data to determine next steps, a coach collects learning walk and team data to determine what embedded professional learning will assist teachers to meet the school-improvement goals. An effective way to provide data to teams is to do individual learning walks in the days following their collaborative team meeting. It allows the coach an opportunity to see the team's plans in action and then offer feedback about implementation. This often leads to conversation starters that help the whole team improve instructional practices.

Individual Teacher Coaching Plan

The focus of individual teacher coaching is based on specific teacher needs connected to the work of his or her collaborative team. Coaches working with individual teachers should engage in a coaching cycle that consists of a planning meeting, scheduled observations, and follow-up conversations that focus on reflection.

Creating a Meaningful and Realistic Coaching Schedule

Time management is critical to ensuring all teachers have access to quality coaching. Consider these seven key components when preparing a meaningful and realistic coaching schedule.

1. Planning and preparation time

2. Team time

3. Classroom observations

4. Coaching conversations

5. Professional learning and development (schoolwide, and by department and collaborative team)

6. Collaboration in the ILT and among team facilitators, the principal, and district leaders

7. Other duties as assigned

Figure 11.2 (page 190) shows an example of what an instructional coach's weekly schedule might look like.

The shaded blocks show how a coach can meet with two collaborative teams (algebra I and geometry), observe all of the classroom teachers on those teams, and then meet with the teams again to provide group feedback. The coach then schedules follow-up time for individual teachers who may need extra time and support. The coach also begins the team coaching cycle for algebra II with the plan to complete the coaching cycle in the following week. The strength of creating a schedule similar to figure 11.2 is twofold. First, the teachers have multiple points of access to the coach, and second, the coach still has time in the week to support the data day, provide a lunch-and-learn professional development and additional learning walks, and plan daily.

Members of the ILT can use a similar schedule to ensure they are meeting with their assigned teams and completing coaching cycles with their assigned teachers. For the building administrators, I suggest following this schedule for only one team per week. This intentionally cultivates the coaching mindset for all and reinforces that faculty and administrators are allies in the school-improvement process.

It is important to note that all members of the ILT may not have the same number of teams to support. A challenge we faced during implementation was creating a more realistic timeframe to do this work. We were fortunate our leadership team members believed in what we were trying to accomplish, but all the other responsibilities of their jobs were becoming a barrier to fully supporting the individual teachers on their coaching team.

We quickly realized it was just as important to differentiate the coaching schedule for each ILT member as it was to differentiate professional development for the teachers. For example, when we started to create our coaching teams, every ILT member had the same number of teachers. About six weeks into the process, we adjusted so the assistant principal (who was in charge of ninth-grade discipline) had fewer teachers on his team. He does about twice the amount of discipline than the assistant principal who oversees twelfth grade, so he needed a more workable schedule. We dropped his coaching team to half of his original list. This provided him time to invest in his teachers without the pressure of sacrificing the other responsibilities of his job. We also worked with the instructional coach to help when the principal and assistant principals had a particularly

Class	Monday	Tuesday	Wednesday	Thursday	Friday
Period one 7:40–8:30 a.m.	Planning and Prep Research	Data Day: Biology		Learning Walks	**Teacher K–L Observation** (fifteen minutes each)
Period two 8:35–9:25 a.m.	**Collaborative Team Time Algebra I** Common Plan (Teachers A–D)		**Coaching Conversations** as needed (Teachers A, B, C, or D)	**Collaborative Team Time Algebra II** Common Plan (Teachers K–O)	Principal-Coach Planning Meeting
Period three 9:30–10:20 a.m.	Learning Walks	**Teacher A–B Observation** (fifteen minutes each)	**Teacher G–H Observation** (fifteen minutes each)	Planning and Prep Research	**Teacher M–O Observation** (fifteen minutes each)
Period four 10:25–11:15 a.m.	**Coaching Conversations** Teachers E–F (fifteen minutes each)	Planning and Prep Research	Planning and Prep Research	**Collaborative Team Time Geometry** Common Plan (Teachers G–J)	**Coaching Conversations** as needed (Teachers G–J)
Period five 11:20 a.m.–12:30 p.m.	Lunch Duty	Lunch and Learn: Schoolwide Professional Development	Lunch Duty	Lunch Duty	Lunch Duty
Period six 12:35–1:25 p.m.	Meet With Biology Team Facilitator to Review Data Day Agenda and Materials	**Teacher C–D Observation** (fifteen minutes each)	Learning Walks		Planning and Prep Research
Period seven 1:30–2:20 p.m.		Biology Data Day Work Product Share	**Teacher Observation I–J** (fifteen minutes each)	Check-In With Mathematics Department Chair	Learning Walks
After School 2:30–3:30 p.m.	Leadership Team Meeting	**Collaborative Team Time Algebra I, Geometry (Teachers G–J)** (thirty minutes each)		ILT	Facilitator Training and Check-In

Figure 11.2: Sample coaching schedule.

difficult week. The instructional coach was able to provide feedback to teachers when their assigned coach was unable to visit their classrooms.

Administrators can no longer rely on the antiquated idea that instruction and student outcomes will improve with one yearly formal evaluation or informal classroom visits. Instructional coaches and principals must work together to build instructional leadership capacity in the school. However, building a strong ILT takes time and patience.

A key component to the improvement process is understanding that many building leaders may lack the necessary training to effectively coach teachers. The idea of planning, observing, and reflecting with teachers can be intimidating for some school leaders and completely foreign to others. Coaches can provide the support and training for these school leaders by embedding professional learning time into the ILT meetings on topics such as the following.

- Holding crucial conversations

- Providing feedback and support

- Setting team and teacher goals

- Planning and reflecting conversations

Principal-with-coach learning walks can provide great support for school leaders who are looking to improve their coaching skills. Collecting data on a teacher learning walk versus giving comments on a formal evaluation are very different types of feedback for many administrators. Meeting with teachers, determining look-fors, observing a class, and having a coaching conversation together can be empowering to a school leader.

Conclusion

As an instructional coach and then as an administrator in a former priority school, I understand the many daily distractors school leaders and teachers face. There is always something waiting in the wings and rarely do we feel like experts when we are starting something new. Looking back, it was the teachers who were the drivers of what has come to be our coaching plan. They wanted to help students, they sought out other professionals to share ideas, and they were asking for feedback to improve their practice. Therefore, as our commitment to becoming a successful PLC grew, so did our determination to provide quality feedback to every teacher. Ultimately, we knew our PLC could not be fully realized until we embraced a learning-for-all mindset that included supporting and giving every teacher the coach he or she deserves.

Collaborative Team Agenda Template

Team:	Date:
Team Members Present:	

Planning Activities (check all that apply)	**Minutes** (Products)
Critical question one: What do we want students to know and be able to do?	
☐ Prioritize standards.	
☐ Determine learning targets.	
☐ Design and plan assessments.	
☐ Plan lessons ensuring equity in classrooms.	
☐ Design rubrics and scoring protocols.	
☐ Analyze instructional strategies.	
Critical question two: How will we know when each student has learned it?	
☐ Analyze common formative assessment data.	
☐ Analyze student work (student writing samples or projects).	
☐ Analyze student results from school, district, state, or provincial summative assessments.	
☐ Analyze teachers' observation and anecdotal evidence.	
☐ Ensure equitable scoring and calibration.	
Critical question three: How will we respond when some students do not learn it?	
☐ Review assessments.	
☐ Provide meaningful feedback.	
☐ Analyze strategies.	
☐ Plan daily, weekly, and longer-term interventions.	
☐ Plan academic advising.	

page 1 of 2

Critical question four: How will we extend the learning for students who have demonstrated proficiency? ☐ Plan extension (standards beyond essential). ☐ Plan enrichment (student choice and passion projects). ☐ Plan student celebrations and recognitions.	
Short-term SMART goal: Team goals are based on student academic outcomes.	
Stretch SMART goal: Year-long team goal tied to school goals.	
Additional support: Ensure interventions and extension. Plan academic advising. Other: _____	
Team notes:	

Instructional Leadership Team Share Template

Facilitator:	Date:
Team Name:	ILT Member:

Here's what. *What do the agendas reveal about the team's productivity?*	*What do you observe in the classroom and team meetings?*
Agendas	Observation

So what? *What do these data reveal about the team?*	

page 1 of 2

Now what?	
Together, the ILT generates next steps for the team.	*What are the next steps for the ILT member working with this team?*
ILT	ILT Member
Facilitator Reflection and Next Steps	Additional Notes

References and Resources

DuFour, R., DuFour, R., Eaker, R., Many, T. W., & Mattos, M. (2016). *Learning by doing: A handbook for Professional Learning Communities at Work* (3rd ed.). Bloomington, IN: Solution Tree Press.

Johnson, K. G. (2016). Instructional coaching implementation: Considerations for K–12 administrators. *Journal of School Administration Research and Development, 1*(2), 37–40. Accessed at https://files.eric.ed.gov/fulltext/EJ1158169.pdf on November 19, 2020.

Knight, J. (2016, December 19). *What do instructional coaches do?* Accessed at https://instructionalcoaching.com/what-do-instructional-coaches-do on November 19, 2020.

Kraft, M. A., & Blazar, D. (2018). *Taking teacher coaching to scale.* Accessed at https://educationnext.org/taking-teacher-coaching-to-scale-can-personalized-training-become-standard-practice on November 19, 2020.

Kraft, M. A., & Papay, J. P. (2014). Can professional environments in schools promote teacher development? Explaining heterogeneity in returns to teaching experience. *Educational Evaluation and Policy Analysis, 36*(4), 476–500.

Kramer, S. V., & Schuhl, S. (2017). *School improvement for all: A how-to guide for doing the right work.* Bloomington, IN: Solution Tree Press.

Many, T. W., Maffoni, M. J., Sparks, S. K., & Thomas, T. F. (2018). *Amplify your impact: Coaching collaborative teams in PLCs at Work.* Bloomington, IN: Solution Tree Press.

Muhammad, A., & Cruz, L. F. (2019). *Time for change: Four essential skills for transformational school and district leaders.* Bloomington, IN: Solution Tree Press.

Spiller, J., & Power, K. (2019). *Leading with intention: Eight areas for reflection and planning in your PLC at Work.* Bloomington, IN: Solution Tree Press.

Wong, H., & Wong, R. (2015, March). *Effective teaching: Teacher effectiveness and human capital.* Accessed at https://www.teachers.net/wong/MAR15 on October 6, 2020.

Yaron, L. (2017, May 9). The five Ws of quality professional development. *Education Week.* Accessed at https://edweek.org/tm/articles/2017/05/09/the-five-ws-of-quality-professional-development.html on August 30, 2020.

 **Michael Roberts** is an author and consultant with over two decades of experience in education. Michael has been an administrator at the district level as well as serving as an on-site administrator at the high school, middle school, and elementary levels. He is the author of *Enriching the Learning: Meaningful Extensions for Proficient Students in a PLC at Work* and *Shifting From Me to We: How to Jumpstart Collaboration in a PLC at Work*.

Prior to becoming the director of elementary curriculum and instruction in Scottsdale, Arizona, Michael was the principal of Desert View Elementary School (DVES) in Hermiston, Oregon. Under his leadership, DVES produced evidence of increased learning for all students each year from 2013–2017 and met the challenges (a rising population of English learners, and a dramatic increase in the number of trauma-affected students) for 40 percent growth over four years.

Michael also served as an assistant principal in Prosser, Washington, where he was named the 2010–2011 Three Rivers Principal Association Assistant Principal of the Year. In 2011–2012, Michael was a finalist for Washington State Assistant Principal of the Year.

Michael earned a bachelor's degree in elementary education from Washington State University and a master's degree in educational leadership from Azusa Pacific University.

To learn more about Michael's work, visit his website at www.everykidnow.com, follow @everykidnow on Twitter, or follow @everykidnow on Instagram.

To book Michael Roberts for professional development, contact pd@SolutionTree.com.

Challenging Proficient Students

Michael Roberts

> This work is too big for any one teacher. It will take the
> collective responsibility of administrators, teachers,
> support staff, parents, and community members to
> address the necessary second-order change. Along
> the way, adults must always be learning.
>
> —*Sharon V. Kramer and Sarah Schuhl*

It's late September and the state department of education has just released the school report cards. The superintendent is sitting in her office and reading the bad news. Once again, the state has labeled the district as a failing district for all to see. Tomorrow, this will be reported in the local paper, it will hit social media, and the community will again throw up its collective hands and take full aim at the district and its employees for not fixing the same issues that have existed for the last five years. To make things worse, now the state is threatening to take over the district and dismiss the school board and the superintendent. The pressure is on.

As a result, the superintendent orders the principals and teachers to "teach those kids to read and do fundamental addition and subtraction or else." "Bubble kids," the students who are near scoring proficiency on the state assessment, are to receive the most attention. After all, if they can get over the hump and score in the proficient range, the final report card score for the district will rocket up. The students who are scoring in the lowest quartile on the state assessment will also receive a lot of instructional focus. It looks bad for the district to have 45 percent of its students "minimally proficient," "far from proficient," or "in need of support."

There can be no disagreement—these students need additional time and support; they need to be supported in acquiring prerequisite skills. However, struggling students are not the only students in the building. The segment of the student population who are forgotten in this scenario are those who regularly demonstrate proficiency. When a district or school commits to learning for all students, proficient students cannot be forgotten.

There are *four* critical questions of a professional learning community (PLC; page 3). When the state puts pressure on a school to improve scores, the focus is on questions one, two, and three. Essential standards are selected, common formative assessments are written, and interventions are considered. However, question four—"How will we extend the learning for students who have demonstrated proficiency?"—is rarely asked, much less answered (DuFour, DuFour, Eaker, Many, & Mattos, 2016, p. 59).

By not intentionally planning for students whose learning needs PLC question four can answer, leaders are shortchanging their school and students they serve. By intentionally planning to extend student learning beyond standards that have been deemed essential to student success and into standards that are "nice to know," schools communicate to students that high levels of learning will be rewarded. Teachers raise their expectations for students, the students get excited to learn, and often, negative behaviors decrease.

Outside the school, many states offer bonuses to a district or school based on how many students are advancing into the "highly proficient" or "mastery" range on the district's report card. With benefits available for both students, through higher engagement, and schools, through bonus points states hand out for each student who scores in the highly proficient range, one must ask, "Why is question four so rarely addressed in priority schools?" Leaders struggle to find resources that will help staff build effective extensions, and leaders often do not fully understand the benefits—schoolwide or districtwide—that come from students extending their learning beyond proficiency.

This chapter will explain the organizational benefits of extensions, as well as how to focus on extensions, find resources to support extension building, and the potential of leveraging the bonus points that states award to highly proficient students to raise a school's score.

Knowing the Organizational Benefits of Extension

When extensions are discussed in school, any number of ideas pop into educators' minds. So, for clarity's sake, an *extension* is instruction that takes the student's learning beyond what the core instruction has provided (Roberts, 2019). In other words, once teams have selected the standards all students must master, the remaining standards can be grouped into important-to-know and nice-to-know standards. Students receive extension when they have mastered the essentials of a grade level or subject and are provided instruction on these other standards. This often happens while students who need more time to master essential standards are provided time for extra practice or instruction on essential skills and standards. By continuing to advance proficient students' learning, teacher teams can keep these students engaged and avoid them slipping into boredom (Roberts, 2019).

Educator and author Carol Ann Tomlinson (2015) points out that when students are extended, it helps teachers as well. Extensions redefine the expectations staff have for student learning. These expectations translate into some of the most powerful effects on student learning, as John Hattie (2009) discovered in his meta-analysis. *Collective teacher efficacy*, which Visible Learning Plus (as cited in Waack, n.d.), a professional learning program based on Hattie's research, defines as "the collective belief of the staff of the school/faculty in their ability to positively affect students," carries a 1.57 effect size and is the single greatest accelerator of student learning. When leaders facilitate this belief in staff, staff may be more willing to meaningfully discuss all students' learning needs, not just needed extensions but also interventions. When this happens, teachers raise their estimates of what students can do, and teacher estimates of achievement carry a 1.29 effect size (Hattie, 2009). By improving just both of these effects, students will learn at a quicker pace and more students will be successful (Hattie, 2009).

Once teams begin taking advantage of collective efficacy and thus have a higher estimate of what the students can accomplish, the whole school paradigm begins to change. For instance, when I began working with a school struggling with negative student behaviors, those student behaviors (rather than student learning) became the focus of the school. This misplaced focus dropped the collective efficacy of the staff and their expectations of what the students could learn. In spite of all this, the staff knew there must be a better way to support the students they cared about.

We began working in September to focus on determining what was essential for all the students to learn and how we would assess those essential standards (related to critical questions one and two, page 3). The leadership team decided the essential standards selected by the teacher teams would be placed in notebooks for the students to use. The students were then given the notebooks and put in charge of monitoring their own learning. We regularly assessed students, and when they reached proficiency, students marked the standard they had become proficient on. Students who struggled on the assessment were given additional time and support.

What the school was not prepared for was how the students took to the notebooks and how much the notebooks motivated students. According to the principal, almost all negative behaviors disappeared, and learning time was maximized. Staff came back together quickly to organize important-to-know and nice-to-know standards because over half the student body had demonstrated mastery over the essential standards by January. These important-to-know and nice-to-know standards multiplied the number of students succeeding, as they continued to be enthusiastic about learning. This 350-student preK school typically produced three to six emerging readers a year. The year we implemented the notebooks, the school had twelve emerging readers by January and expected another thirty by the end of the year. This is an example of extension working.

The lessons from this school can be applied universally. Staff became very clear on what was essential and how to assess it. They provided additional time and support for students who were not yet proficient. But do not discount the staff's willingness to come together and dig into nonessential standards to keep the proficient students' learning moving forward. Imagine what would happen to student motivation if, once they completed the essential standards notebook, the teachers had them become student aides or asked them to wait until their peers caught up. The enthusiasm the students had for the notebooks would have waned as they realized the notebooks were all they would learn, and once students completed the essential learning, the negative behaviors would return because the proficient students would have nothing meaningful to do.

When a team works together, be it as a high school geometry or first-grade team, to establish not only essential standards but also where the students' learning progression will go once the essentials are mastered, it maintains student enthusiasm for learning (Roberts, 2019). When students are enthusiastic about learning, it is very easy for staff to expect a lot from them. Especially in a priority school, that expectation is one of the most powerful things a teacher can do for his or her students.

Providing Focus on Extensions

Maharishi Mahesh Yogi (BrainyQuote, n.d.) once said, "Whatever we put our attention on will grow stronger in our life." This simple idea—focusing on where one should improve—applies not only to the individual but also to the organization. Often in priority schools the focus is on the students who have not yet attained proficiency, those lacking serious prerequisites, and those whose behavior is an obstacle to learning. These students dominate administrators' time and thoughts, as well they should. However, a school should focus on supporting all students' learning, not just those who are below proficiency. It is only by adopting the *learning for all* stance that systematic, permanent change is possible.

How does a priority school make that shift? It starts with publicly stating all students can and will learn and then setting out to prove it. Tomlinson (2015) lays out evidence that when teams plan extensions for students who are proficient *before* planning interventions, the interventions are more effective and the staff's expectations of student learning increases. This may occur because once the teams plan rich extensions of learning for students, it redefines for them what students can accomplish, essentially raising the bar of expectations for all students. Tomlinson (2015) provides a compelling reason for a leader who may feel there are only a handful of students who will demonstrate proficiency on any given standard: push staff to build extensions for these students not only because doing so supports their learning but also because *all* students benefit from higher expectations and more thoughtful interventions. These more thoughtful interventions provide more intentional scaffolding to "enable less advanced students to access those rich learning experiences" (Tomlinson, 2015). Hattie's (2009) research supports Tomlinson's assertion when he cites several large effect sizes that tie directly to teachers planning meaningful extensions. For example, teachers' estimates of student achievement, which increases with the writing of extensions, carries a 1.29 effect size. Extensions increase student effort, which carries a .79 effect size (Hattie, 2009).

Once the administrator has begun to shift staff's thinking about building extensions, he or she should bring the staff back to the data. In priority schools, data is often a four-letter word. Leaders try to spin it, and teachers ignore it. This is done for a reason—it's usually bad. These educators are working hard, and they care about the students they support. But, in spite of their best efforts, the students are not getting the results they crave. I have been a long-term coach in many priority schools and have witnessed how, once these sites are labeled *underachieving*, the staff tend to shy away from discussing data in any meaningful way. The administrator must not allow staff to drift away from the data, for there is always good there. A successful organization must face the "brutal facts"

(Collins, 2001, p. 13). Priority schools see their data as one big lump of brutal. However, as a leader, you need to examine *where* students are struggling and also celebrate where the staff and students are succeeding. It is around those student successes extensions need to be built.

We all have biases, and those biases affect how we work with others (Weichel, McCann, & Williams, 2018). In the case of priority schools, the bias may not be around race, gender, or socioeconomic status but based on the school itself. After all, how can a student who attends a failing school be proficient to the point that he or she needs meaningful extensions? However, the data will tell a different story. Even in a school that resides on a given state's "double secret probation list," there are pockets of proficiency. Expand these pockets. Ask staff to focus on those successes with their teams and with those students. If the adults focus on it, it will grow.

Consider business as an example. Why do some ideas stick around and become part of an organization's DNA (like Southwest Airlines becoming the low-fare airline or Nintendo making the switch from manufacturing playing cards to building video games), while other ideas simply drift away? For ideas to become ingrained in any organization, they must be simple, unexpected, concrete, credible, emotional, and attached to a story (Heath & Heath, 2008). One would be hard-pressed to find something simpler and more unexpected than a group of students beating the odds and becoming proficient readers or excellent mathematicians in a priority school. Yet, the data are both concrete and credible. When the school shares the data that proficient students are producing, these stories are emotional for teachers. After all, most of us got into education to change students' lives for the better, and here are students you see in the halls every day, creating the possibility for better lives for themselves.

When an administrator pushes collaborative teams during their meeting time to dig into the data these students produce, he or she makes it clear extensions are something worth focusing on. The staff can identify key points to support student progress along the way. The learning leader on campus needs to facilitate staff sharing these best practices across a campus and expanding on them. The leader would assume the role of facilitator, guiding staff in what to share and with whom. This builds staff confidence and builds connections, and in no time at all, these shared best practices become standard operating procedure.

Finding Resources to Support Extension Building

At one priority school, I met with a first-grade group of teachers. They were explaining to me that no matter what they did, their students were not learning. I asked if they identified the standards and skills in first grade that had the most impact on the students' education going forward. They said they had. I asked if they had created common assessments they could use to judge students' success on those standards. They said they had. I asked what extensions they were using to further learning for students who demonstrate proficiency. No one said anything for a minute or two. Then one teacher said, in her class, students demonstrating proficiency in reading were extended by teaching the students who could not yet read. This is a typical example of a team not getting the results they hoped for because they were not effectively answering the four critical questions of a PLC (DuFour et al., 2016; page 3). They had discussed what they wanted their students to know and how they would determine if students had reached proficiency, but they had not answered questions three or four. There was no systematic plan for students who were not yet proficient, and students who were proficient were an afterthought.

I tell this story not to embarrass anyone or to make light of any hardworking, caring teacher, but merely to point out that because of a lack of training for most staff and a lack of expectations that these students will be intentionally extended, practices like these are so very common. Being an ad-hoc student aid is often the best idea many administrators and teachers have for students who are proficient. In spite of any best intentions, this is not an extension. Some educators will argue that if a student can teach something, he or she truly understands it. It is true that evaluating, analyzing, and applying are all part of teaching and occupy higher levels of educational psychologist Benjamin S. Bloom's (1956) taxonomy. However, very few students are trained to analyze other students' errors and evaluate the best way to correct those errors—especially when the student in question is six years old. Often these student-to-student sessions break down into one student simply saying, "Write down seven; the answer is seven," or the proficient student taking a book from the other student and saying, "I'll read it to you." I have worked with well-meaning teachers in priority or other schools who say, "Kids like helping other kids," and this is often true. But these proficient students are not advancing their own learning during this time. At best, the proficient student is simply staying busy, and at worst, a social wedge is being formed between students deemed to be smart enough to help and students deemed to be "not smart" and in need of help. This division can exacerbate social issues that many proficient students have. Gifted student researcher Deirdre V. Lovecky (1995) notes that some students in these situations will not develop appropriate social skills for their age. For example, proficient students used as ad-hoc aides may begin substituting monologues for conversations, constantly interrupt peers, and insist on their own agenda (Lovecky, 1995).

How do we get around this and other activities that have long taken the place of meaningful extensions? By creating time in the master schedule for extensions and by providing meaningful professional learning about what extensions are and how they can advance proficient students' learning. As staff are being trained on how to build effective, systematic interventions, they should also consider how to expand the process to include students who need extensions. For example, during the time teachers provide interventions, a group of students can engage in meaningful activities.

In addition to needing professional learning, teams will need to know what resources will help them effectively build extensions. For this, leaders should direct staff back to where their essential standards came from: their state standards. To make this happen, teams can sort their standards into the following groups.

- Essential to know and do
- Important to know and do

- Worth being familiar with
- Nice to know (Gregory, Kaufeldt, & Mattos, 2016, p. 79)

Teams will build their essential standards around the essential-to-know-and-do group. All students will be guaranteed that they receive additional time and support to ensure they are successful on these standards. Students who attain proficiency on these standards can then receive extensions around the important-to-know-and-do or the worth-being-familiar-with groups; teams could even venture into the nice-to-know standards. However, because they have been identified as being the lowest priority standards, teams should not worry too much if they cannot introduce them to the students. Refer to these standards as *extension standards*. Teams now have a logical, standards-based progression to continue students' learning.

When teams create these extensions, they need to ensure proficient students see their extensions as different work, not more work. Teams should use the extension standards to build unique skills for proficient students, engage the students in an area of high interest, or use the extensions to build social connections. These three types of extensions—skills, interest, and social—will provide teachers with the differentiation and choices they need to create engaging extensions for all proficient students. Skills extensions should focus on introducing students to new skills that may help them (for example, writing and performing plays based on a folktale they have read). Interest-based extensions should take advantage of an area of high interest for the students (for example, recontextualizing mathematics problems into creating a fashion line or the number of supplies needed for exploring Mount Kilimanjaro). Social extensions focus on having students work in groups to develop greater peer understanding and deepen peer bonds.

When I was a principal of a Title I school in Oregon and we were trying to find resources on how best to build extensions for students, we found relatively little. However, I have written a book dedicated exclusively to effectively and meaningfully answering critical question four—*Enriching the Learning: Meaningful Extensions for Proficient Students in a PLC at Work* (Roberts, 2019)—and another book also answers this question: *When They Already Know It: How to Extend and Personalize Student Learning in a PLC at Work* (Weichel et al., 2018).

One step that will help teams is to include planning for a meaningful extension in their lesson plan. Figure 12.1 (page 206) is an example of a completed form. Teams can use this form when planning extensions for their students. The reproducible "Skill Extension Planning Template" (page 209) is offered as a blank version.

Using Bonus Points for School Score

All administrators should be familiar with the state scoring matrices that create their district's or school's eventual rating, which they will share with the public. Although the score on the report card is never the be-all-end-all, educators do themselves a great disservice if they do not understand how their state assigns grades. This is especially true

Essential Standard: 3.OA.A.1—Interpret products of whole numbers, e.g., interpret 5 × 7 as the total number of objects in 5 groups of 7 objects each. *For example, describe a context in which a total number of objects can be expressed as 5 × 7.*

Date to Begin Extension: November 1, 2020

Date to Conclude Extension: November 15, 2020

Type of Extension: Interest

Team Member Delivering Extension: Smalls

Extension Standards	Extension Students	Formative Assessments During Extension
3.OA.A.3—Use multiplication and division within 100 to solve word problems in situations involving equal groups, arrays, and measurement quantities, e.g., by using drawings and equations with a symbol for the unknown number to represent the problem.	Charles Rob Arjun Jon Penny Sofia Camila	Group-created story Individual solutions to peers' stories
3.OA.A.4—Determine the unknown whole number in a multiplication or division equation relating three whole numbers. *For example, determine the unknown number that makes the equation true in each of the equations 8 × ? = 48, 5 = _ ÷ 3, 6 × 6 = ?.*	Kavya Carlos Tristan Stefani Mikhail Glenn Juan V.	Group-created story Individual solutions to peers' stories

Source: Adapted from Roberts, 2019.

Source for standard: National Governors Association Center for Best Practices & Council of Chief State School Officers, 2010.

Figure 12.1: Planning template example.

of priority schools, where every point on the report card will help lift the F grade, the *needs improvement* label, or whatever designation the state uses. After digging into how individual states score schools, many administrators are surprised at the emphasis these scoring matrices place on moving proficient students to the *beyond proficient* or *highly proficient* level.

Many states give what amounts to bonus points to schools that extend students' learning beyond proficiency. Here are a few random examples of how states award bonus consideration to schools with students in the *beyond proficient* range.

- **Arkansas:** As of 2019–2020, schools earn zero points for students who are in the *in need of support* range. Districts and schools get half a point for students in the *close* range. Those students who fall in the *ready* or *exceeding* range earn one full point for their respective school. However, if the number of students in the *exceeding* range is greater than the number of students in the *in need of support* range, each student in the *exceeding* range earns 1.25 points instead of 1.0 (Arkansas Department of Education, 2018).

- **Arizona:** As of 2019–2020, at the elementary level, 50 percent of a district and school's score comes directly from a student's year-to-year growth. The secondary level student growth makes up 20 percent of a school's final score. At both levels, a student scoring in the proficient range is only 20 percent of the score. If a school does not extend students once they achieve proficiency, the growth indicator is left largely untouched as the students stop growing without meaningful extensions, and that can cause a district's or school's score to quickly drop (Arizona State Board of Education, n.d.).

- **Ohio:** According to *Guide to 2019 Ohio School Report Cards* (Ohio Department of Education, 2019), the performance index measures all students' achievement, instead of measuring only whether they reach proficiency. "Districts and schools receive points for every student's level of achievement. The higher the student's level, the more points the school earns toward its index" (Ohio Department of Education, 2019). The guide goes on to point out that high schools earn extra points for Advanced Placement (AP) tests that students score a 3 or better on and International Baccalaureate (IB) tests that earn a 4 or better (Ohio Department of Education, 2019). The more a student is extended beyond proficient, the higher the report card score for the school.

- **South Carolina:** Students who *meet expectations* earn their school two points, while those who *exceed expectations* receive three points for their school. Essentially, for every student a school has extended from the *meets* to the *exceeds* range, a school receives a bonus point (South Carolina Education Oversight Committee, 2019).

- **Texas:** In the student achievement domain, a student who scores in the *approaches grade level* range counts in the *approaches grade level or above* column. A student who meets grade level counts in the *approaches or above* column and the *meets grade level expectations or above* column. A student who achieves the mastery level will have his or her score counted in the *approaches or above*, the *meets or above*, and the *mastery* levels. In other words, a student who is on grade level will have his or her score count in two columns, while students who have been extended to the mastery level will have a score that registers three times for a school (Texas Education Agency, 2020).

I strongly encourage you to reach out to your state or provincial department of education or visit the department's website to be sure that you fully understand what creates the score or label assigned to your district or school. As reviewing the systems set up in these examples show, priority schools can quickly shed the *failing* label by extending proficient students in meaningful ways and earning the extra points the state awards for content mastery.

Conclusion

Ensuring proficient students are not forgotten when teams plan to advance all learners is vital to a district and school. The whole learning organization benefits from intentionally building extensions, because extensions will redefine what staff expect from students. When a learning leader provides resources to staff, along with the expectations that these green students have their learning advanced, staff are reminded that not all the data being produced in the school are negative. This will help bolster staff morale. When proficient students find they are given different, challenging work, their engagement and excitement will grow. Not only will districts and schools accrue these benefits from intentionally extending students, but the more students a priority school places in the top range of a governing body's matrix, the sooner the district or school can exit double secret probation.

Skill Extension Planning Template

Essential Standard: _____

_____

_____

_____

_____

Date to Begin Extension: _____

Date to Conclude Extension: _____

Type of Extension: _____

Team Member Delivering Extension: _____

Extension Standards	Extension Students	Formative Assessments During Extension

Source: Roberts, M. (2019). Enriching the learning: Meaningful extensions for proficient students in a PLC at Work. *Bloomington, IN: Solution Tree Press.*

References and Resources

Arizona State Board of Education. (n.d.). *A–F letter grades.* Accessed at https://azsbe.az.gov /f-school-letter-grades on January 8, 2021.

Arkansas Department of Education. (2018). *Arkansas Department of Education rules governing the public school rating system on annual school performance reports and the school recognition program.* Accessed at http://adecm.arkansas.gov/Attachments/ade_334_--_Rules_ Governing_the_School_Rating_System_143220.pdf on November 17, 2020.

Bloom, B. S. (Ed.). (1956). *Taxonomy of educational objectives: The classification of educational goals; Handbook I: Cognitive domain.* New York: McKay.

BrainyQuote. (n.d.). *Maharishi Mahesh Yogi quotes.* Accessed at https://brainyquote.com/ quotes/maharishi_mahesh_yogi_140776 on November 19, 2020.

Collins, J. (2001). *Good to great: Why some companies make the leap and others don't.* New York: HarperBusiness.

DuFour, R., DuFour, R., Eaker, R., Many, T. W., & Mattos, M. (2016). *Learning by doing: A handbook for Professional Learning Communities at Work* (3rd ed.). Bloomington, IN: Solution Tree Press.

Gregory, G., Kaufeldt, M., & Mattos, M. (2016). *Best practices at tier 1: Daily differentiation for effective instruction, elementary.* Bloomington, IN: Solution Tree Press.

Hattie, J. (2009). *Visible learning: A synthesis of over 800 meta-analyses relating to achievement.* New York: Routledge.

Heath, C., & Heath, D. (2008). *Made to stick: Why some ideas survive and others die.* New York: Random House.

Kramer, S. V., & Schuhl, S. (2017). *School improvement for all: A how-to guide for doing the right work.* Bloomington, IN: Solution Tree Press.

Lovecky, D. V. (1995). Highly gifted children and peer relationships. *Counseling and Guidance Newsletter, 5*(3), 2, 6–7.

National Governors Association Center for Best Practices & Council of Chief State School Officers. (2010). *Common Core State Standards for mathematics.* Washington, DC: Authors. Accessed at www.corestandards.org/assets/CCSSI_Math%20Standards.pdf on April 1, 2020.

Ohio Department of Education. (2019, September). *Guide to 2019 Ohio school report cards.* Accessed at http://education.ohio.gov/getattachment/Topics/Data/Report-Card-Resources/ Report-Card-Guide.pdf.aspx on November 17, 2020.

Roberts, M. (2019). *Enriching the learning: Meaningful extensions for proficient students in a PLC at Work.* Bloomington, IN: Solution Tree Press.

South Carolina Education Oversight Committee. (2019). *2018–2019 accountability manual.* Accessed at https://eoc.sc.gov/sites/default/files/Documents/Acct%20Manual%202018- 19/AccountabilityManual%20FY%202018-19.FINAL_.pdf on November 16, 2020.

Texas Education Agency. (2020). *2020 accountability manual.* Accessed at https://tea.texas .gov/sites/default/files/Chapters%201-11%202020%20Accountability%20Manual.pdf on November 16, 2020.

Tomlinson, C. A. (2015, January 28). Differentiation does, in fact, work. *Education Week.* Accessed at www.edweek.org/ew/articles/2015/01/28/differentiation-does-in-fact-work .html on September 23, 2020.

Waack, S. (n.d.). *Collective teacher efficacy (CTE) according to John Hattie.* Accessed at https:// visible-learning.org/2018/03/collective-teacher-efficacy-hattie on March 25, 2020.

Weichel, M., McCann, B., & Williams, T. (2018). *When they already know it: How to extend and personalize student learning in a PLC at Work.* Bloomington, IN: Solution Tree Press.

 **Tamie Sanders** has worked in education for over thirty years. After teaching at the middle school level, she entered school administration and made it her mission to improve student achievement. She has become known for her ability to implement successful professional learning communities and to utilize the school-improvement model to produce immediate improvements in student achievement. Through her leadership as a principal and district executive director of secondary schools, she has proven that school and district turnaround is eminently achievable. She took the lowest-performing school in the state of Oklahoma to a B+ rating in just two years.

Tamie has presented research about U.S. Grant High School to the Oklahoma City Public Schools District and the Oklahoma State Department of Education and presented to educators at Vision 2020 Institutes offered by the Oklahoma State Department of Education. She has received a citation for exemplary academic performance from Oklahoma state senator Al McAffrey and was featured in *Stars of Education* magazine, published by the Foundation for Oklahoma City Public Schools, as a principal making dramatic changes at a low-performing school.

Tamie earned a bachelor's degree in secondary education from Oklahoma State University and a master of education degree in administration, curriculum, and supervision from the University of Oklahoma.

To book Tamie Sanders for professional development, contact pd@SolutionTree.com.

Taking the First Five Steps in High School Improvement

Tamie Sanders

The mission of any school should include working
toward grade-level or higher learning for all students.

—*Sharon V. Kramer and Sarah Schuhl*

It was October on a chilly, overcast day at U.S. Grant High School in Oklahoma City, Oklahoma, when I recognized, along with a team of leaders and counselors, that 204 of our 264 seniors were ineligible to graduate that year as they were not meeting graduation requirements. These data, among other sets of data, were what made our school a school-improvement site. The work ahead was not going to be easy, but the community and our students needed us to get it right. The desperate need for our school to reach high achievement for all learners was the priority, and there was no time to focus on anything but this very thing. Many issues would pull for our attention, but we had to find a way to remain laser focused on high academic achievement for all. The lessons I was able to learn with my team are vital to school leadership.

Perhaps the greatest challenge facing high school principals who want their schools to improve is the overwhelming number of students not mastering content standards and thus not performing at grade level. The inverted Response to Intervention (RTI) at Work™ pyramid in figure 13.1 (page 214) has Tier 1 at the top (Buffum, Mattos, & Malone, 2018). In a high-performing high school, most students are able to master or exceed mastery of essential grade-level standards. Few students are at Tier 3, the smallest part of the pyramid, needing intensive remediation in universal skills. However, in an underperforming school, mastery is not typical. Students who have not yet mastered grade-level skills make up the bulk of the pyramid in this case, and the students who meet or exceed mastery make up a very small portion in Tiers 1 and 2. This structure easily allows for instructional interventions and supports because the number of students needing them is manageable. However, in underperforming schools, academic achievement is not typical. The bulk of students are bunched into the tip of the pyramid at Tier 3,

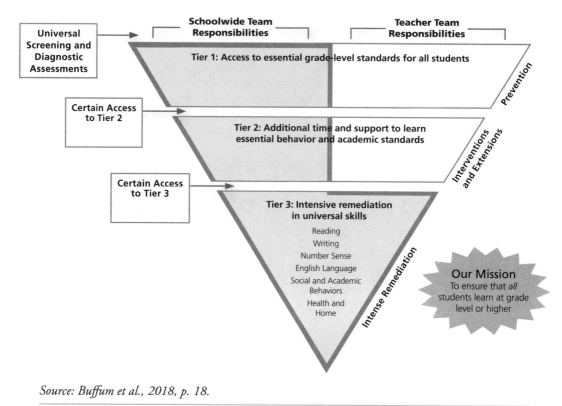

Source: Buffum et al., 2018, p. 18.

Figure 13.1: The RTI at Work inverted intervention pyramid.

it becomes exceedingly more difficult—but still possible—to provide large numbers of students with academic interventions and supports, because the principal must then allocate and provide additional resources, class sections, and teachers. Additionally, there is much more data to collect and analyze in order to accurately identify which students and which areas need support.

As a high school principal, where do you start? What are your first steps to ensure success for all students? It is often said that high schools are the last frontier in developing successful collaborative practices that improve schools. High school teachers are content specialists and are not accustomed to collaborating. Staff must remember, however, that "the adults must work together collaboratively in order to ensure that students will learn. No one individual has all the knowledge or skills to meet the varying needs of students. This requires a collective effort" (Kramer, 2015, p. 14).

Leaders are tasked with ensuring systems and practices that not only support collaboration but also demand it. While they build collaborative structures, high school principals balance a never-ending list of expectations. Ultimately, high school students are the primary benefactors of leaders planning well and taking necessary steps toward improvement. Unorganized schools in which ineffective leadership decisions are made do not fool students. Student success is what being a high school principal is all about, but how do you get there? What are the first steps in creating a successful improvement plan? Where do you start?

In this chapter, you'll explore the first five steps that make immediate impacts in high school leadership.

1. Making time in the schedule for teacher collaboration
2. Taking care of teacher placement and development
3. Letting data drive response to intervention tiers
4. Celebrating students and staff
5. Progress monitoring through ten-day learning cycles

This chapter looks at how these five first steps support both district and school leaders in deepening their understanding and immediately applying this knowledge to support successful high school improvement. Taking action to immediately impact school success is job one for readers of this chapter.

Making Time in the Schedule for Teacher Collaboration

In high schools, one of the first tasks on the road to improvement is to create the time for teachers to work in collaborative teams. The four critical questions require teachers to actually have the time to do their work together (DuFour, DuFour, Eaker, Many, & Mattos, 2016). Administrators who ignore this very important first step of creating the time for collaborative teams to meet during the instructional day are creating a pothole on their road to improvement.

One of the most important aspects to consider when scheduling this time is master scheduling. How many groups of teachers can I feasibly allow to collaborate each day? How can I protect the integrity of this collaborative time when I have a high number of teachers absent every day and a shortage of substitutes, thus making it almost necessary to have teachers cover other classes? How can I provide collaborative time to elective teachers so that they may focus on addressing literacy standards through their content?

This explains why the use of time is so important: "Scheduling reflects a school's priorities. If collaboration is a priority, and it should be, then the schedule will reflect the time necessary to actually do the work of the team" (Kramer & Schuhl, 2017, p. 22). As you read and think about how you allocate time in your school, consider this: time should be a variable, not a fixed asset. In other words, you have the luxury of determining how adults and students use the minutes in the school day. Consider your own personal bias about time. Do you think about time as something that you, as a leader, can adjust and use to the benefit of your students and staff, or does it more typically feel like a box that has been drawn around you and holds you back from being more effective? In school-improvement work, not having enough time is a common reason high school principals give when asked why they have not created time for teachers to collaborate or have not provided a better master schedule for students to learn. The interesting dilemma is that these schools have the same number of hours as the high school in the next community, which has found a way for teachers to collaborate and students to have highly effective schedules. The difference is the way leaders consider time—as fixed asset or a variable.

In a high school where students are struggling to perform on grade level, additional time for support and supplemental instruction must be built into the master schedule. Use annual cohort data to identify the students in need of support and add sections of support classes in the identified areas. These additional sections will come at the sacrifice of others. As school leader, you will have to make hard choices. Eliminating sections of courses that have low enrollment may be the answer. Combining upper-level classes or eliminating an elective with low enrollment may be options to open sections for support classes. Utilizing additional funding sources such as Title I to add staff may also be an option.

Coauthors Richard DuFour and colleagues (2010) remind us:

> Despite the popularity of the term *professional learning community*, the *practices* of a PLC continue to represent "the road less traveled" in public education. Many teachers and administrators prefer the familiarity of their current path, even when it becomes apparent that it will not take them to their desired destination. (p. 7)

These road bumps and potholes can deter the strongest, most committed leaders from creating the changes needed in their schools to improve learning for students.

When building a schedule, you must embed time for educators teaching the same content in the daily schedule strictly for collaboration. You must also fiercely protect this time, as the demands of a school day, combined with the many moving parts, will constantly fight to use this time for other, lower-impact tasks. If the time is not protected, it will be lost. This time must be highly structured with agendas and norms. All agenda items should be tied to instruction and student growth. The ten-day learning cycle (page 221) will drive the nuts and bolts of this time to ensure productivity and drive student growth, but the first step is creating the time and protecting it as sacred time. The responsibility falls on you, the principal—the instructional leader—to model what matters most and define actions required to achieve student growth.

Consider this: teachers were working very hard in an Oklahoma City school. They were spending weekends and long hours each day with big hopes for the students. The leaders kept putting another system of support, template, or protocol in the hands of teachers to do what they thought was supporting the work. At the end of the day, the teachers just felt frustrated and were greatly disappointed with the results of the data, which they deciphered together during lunch or after school. Everyone was exhausted and frustrated. The teachers and staff were doing many of the right things to collaborate. For example, they were attempting to answer questions such as, "What is it students need to master?" and "What will it look like when they do?" However, they never really seemed to ascertain which students were not mastering standards because they always ran out of time. It was clear that well-intentioned educators with some strong structures in place could not do the work necessary for student achievement without more time in the day to do it. The following year, the master schedule was purposefully and intentionally built with time for collaboration in mind, and student achievement drastically improved. In other words, the leader created collaborative time in the master schedule first and then protected it as he or she built the rest of the schedule. Beyond that, teachers and staff felt like they were able to do the work without constantly feeling frustrated, overwhelmed, and discouraged.

Consider these questions.

- Do teachers and staff have designated time in the day for collaboration? Is this time sufficient for the work needed to grow students academically?

- What time can you shift or refocus to be more effective?

- If you gave teachers more time, what elements of collaboration would improve?

When you create dedicated collaborative teacher time, the adults in the building will be able to work interdependently to meet the needs of students. It is now time for you, as the high school principal, to turn your attention to a review of how time is used for students. What kind of schedules are you creating? How effective are your transitions? How is time built into your daily schedule for interventions? Do teachers have enough time to teach, or are your classes too short? Begin by determining how many students need support by looking at the previous year's student-performance data. Use these data to determine the number of additional sections needed in the master schedule to provide all students the support they need. Another option is to provide weekly flexible scheduling for students. You can apply this flex schedule in different ways. An assembly schedule could be used periodically to shorten all class periods to allow for intervention time. You should determine the length and frequency based on need. Flex Friday could be used to provide additional intervention and extension time based on formative assessment results.

Taking Care of Teacher Placement and Development

How do you decide who teaches what courses and which students? What is your current reality? Perhaps you are reading this as a small high school principal and want to shout at this book that you have no choice who teaches what course or which student because you do not have much say in hiring, or because you have few teachers with qualifications suited to teach other courses. In reading this section, it will be important to have a positive mindset about how you can grow and develop teachers, as well as ensure that the best possible placements are made in the interest of your students.

Most states and provinces have established what students are required to know and be able to do, as well as age-appropriate skill bands illustrating when these skills must be mastered. Regardless of seniority or politics in a given school, you should purposefully determine teacher placement with student mastery and proficiency as the main priorities. The number of standards must be reduced to those with the highest priority. Highest priority would be given to those standards tested most frequently and those standards that have the highest number of questions on the end of the year assessment. This single action will ensure that teachers have enough time to teach these essential standards to the mastery level and ensure highlighted achievement levels on any state or national assessment.

The same process for essential standards can be overlaid on essential teacher placement. When placing a teacher in a particular grade band and content area, consider the questions of endurance, leverage, and readiness for the subject area when assessing the teacher's current strengths and weaknesses. For example, suppose a school has a dynamite leadership teacher, which is an elective. This teacher works very hard and always develops engaging lessons. Students want to be in her class, and the data tell you her students improve as writers in her classroom. This teacher is also certified to teach English. The school's English data on the ACT is the lowest subcategory. Because students need the ability to read and write critically to succeed not only in school but also in many aspects of life, this teacher will have a greater effect on all students if she teaches English 11 the following year, rather than teaching leadership again. The skills all students will have access to (as opposed to the elective group who chose her course) will better meet the test of endurance, leverage, and readiness.

Once the art of placement is perfected as much as it can be, a growth mindset (Dweck, 2016) is essential for leaders as they work to develop the teams of teachers in a building. As Sharon V. Kramer and Sarah Schuhl (2017) explain, "the neediest schools experience the most difficulty in attracting and retaining leaders and teachers. . . . The constant change of principals and teachers eliminates the consistent focused efforts necessary to improve schools" (p. 2). All people can learn. As a high school principal, you have the responsibility to ensure the adults in your building feel valued and supported.

Creating a long-term professional learning plan and developing short-term learning opportunities responsive to your teachers' needs will increase the impact you will have in developing effective teachers. Principals can leverage team meetings or the guiding coalition in this effort. Teachers, especially new teachers, need dedicated coaching, modeling, and expertise sharing. The Professional Learning Community (PLC) at Work process supports these in your school, and as the leader, you must do everything you can to guide and lead your teachers' development. Should an educator not desire to grow or not believe in the vision and mission of the school, that person may find a better placement somewhere else. In the meantime, work to develop all teachers as they are working with all students.

Much of teacher development is best achieved when coaching alongside a teacher in the classroom after areas of growth are identified through the PLC process, informal walkthroughs, or observations. It is vital to take inventory of every available resource in the building to grow teachers. Every educator can grow and develop in new ways. Think outside the box. What positions can be repurposed or adjusted to support teaching and learning? Who is the best staff member to work with each educator? How will we measure and monitor growth? At the end of the day, the instructional leader is responsible for the learning in every classroom. Should an educator be unwilling or unable to improve instruction where needed, that educator cannot continue working in the classroom with students when the school is striving for academic achievement.

Consider the following questions.

- Which teachers have the best relationships with students?
- Is this teacher a quality instructor who engages students in their learning?
- How does a particular teacher perform under pressure?
- Is this teacher a natural leader or collaborator?
- Does this teacher understand the ten-day learning cycle?

Letting Data Drive Response to Intervention Tiers

From formative assessments to benchmarks, concrete evidence will drive instructional adjustments and student placement for interventions. Collaborative teams use data to understand what students need next in order to succeed, and this includes next steps for instruction, reassessment, and interventions. The evidence provides teachers with an essential learning: that tiers of intervention are about *who* and *what*. Identifying a student and knowing what he or she needs is in the data. In other words, the right students need to be engaging in the right interventions to master the skills and standards each student needs. The right teacher needs to be the one crafting and delivering the interventions based on data evidence. Progress monitoring by school leaders is necessary to ensure the right interventions are implemented as well as delivering the desired outcomes. Reassessment of student learning, which will provide additional data points to measure growth and proficiency, is the only way to measure the effectiveness of the intervention.

During the school day, the principal monitors teachers' data use. These data inform the various tiers of student interventions. Observing and considering the rigor and overall quality of teachers' formative assessments help truly identify which students are in each tier so the teams can provide each student the appropriate interventions and supports.

These teams must meet a minimum of twice a week, but most high school schedules can support daily collaborative meeting time. This time must be sufficient to unpack standards, develop formative assessments, share instructional strategies, desegregate data, and develop interventions for students. Evidence must drive decisions for all tiers of instruction, and school leaders must consistently evaluate data to ensure leaders are not making decisions arbitrarily or without research and evidence from student outcomes.

How can you support teachers in becoming more evidence-based in their practices if they aren't already? What conversations do you, as the high school principal, need to hear when you walk into a collaborative team meeting? As the leader, you can support this work by providing a common template or protocol and by having an expectation that teams will use this template to understand their data in a continuous cycle of improvement. The reproducible "Data-Analysis Protocol" (page 223) is a blank resource your teams can use.

Celebrating Students and Staff

Don't forget relationships. At every level, relationships play a crucial role in school improvement. Affirmations, shout-outs, recognition, and praise need to be specific, constant, genuine, and meaningful because this work is hard, and teachers and students need to know you appreciate them.

What you celebrate models and communicates what you value. Ensure celebrations align directly with the drive to academic achievement and any other specific goals of a particular site. Celebrations should start small with small wins, building confidence in a struggling student population. Examples of small wins might look like students who demonstrate incremental growth from the beginning-of-the-year assessment to the middle-of-the-year assessment; a student who traditionally struggles in geometry but correctly answers a question out loud in front of his classmates; a student who never attempts the bell work activity, but who decides to do it that particular day; or a student who helps a struggling peer understand the content.

Confidence must be built consistently and with intention. Additionally, students feel the pressure as educators press for academic outcomes. They desire to do well, which comes with a feeling of stress. This stress can be a healthy motivator, but it is important to be mindful of in the celebration plan. Both students and educators alike work harder and are happier when they feel like they belong and are part of a team. It is vital for the administration to have relationships with staff, staff to have relationships with students and administrators, and administrators to have relationships with students. Consider this:

> When the relationships among teachers in a school are characterized by high trust and frequent interaction—that is, when social capital is strong—student achievement scores improve. We also found that even low-ability teachers can perform as well as teachers of average ability if they have strong social capital. Strong social capital can go a long way toward offsetting any disadvantages students face when their teachers have low human capital. (Venables, 2018, pp. 33–34)

Consider these questions.

- What do you celebrate in your school, both small and large?
- How do you show teachers that you notice and appreciate their efforts?
- Do you give teachers specific praise for growing professionally?

Progress Monitoring Through Ten-Day Learning Cycles

As collaborative teams work together to plan units of study, instruction, and assessment, their work focuses on the four critical questions of PLCs (DuFour et al., 2016; page 3). The collaborative team must address critical question number one, "What do we want students to learn?" prior to instructional planning. When considering what you want students to learn, consider education author Maria Nielsen's (as cited in AllThingsPLC, n.d.) content standards categories: boulders, rocks, and butterflies. Essential standards are boulders. These are the standards all students must master because they provide the solid, sturdy, foundational knowledge required for students to progress in their learning. Rocks are the standards that lean on the boulder for support. They fit in the remaining spaces after the boulders are in place. Butterflies, on the other hand, are the would-be-nice-to-know standards. Butterflies fly over the boulders and the rocks and maybe land on them for a time, but they are not essential.

The ten-day learning cycle is a plan for instruction, assessment, and intervention. The cycle is implemented only for essential standards. The reproducible "Ten-Day Learning Cycle Checklist" (page 226) is a tool your team can use. Here is a brief description of the ten-day learning cycle.

- **Day one:** Unpack essential standards. Unpacking ensures teachers are crystal clear on what students need to know and be able to do with that content. It is important that teachers teaching the same content unpack standards together to ensure a common understanding of the rigor involved in the 21st century standards. This process is ongoing.

- **Day two:** Create common formative assessments. The collaborative teams must develop them at the same rigor of the standard. If the standard uses the verb *analyze*, for example, the students must be asked to analyze.

- **Day three:** Create a lesson plan using unpacked essential standards. Lesson plans must be intentional, targeting those rigorous skills and concepts utilizing the data-analysis reproducible to look deeply into the data to see, at the student level, who has mastered what is required.

- **Days four through seven:** Teach a lesson plan. Teachers utilize best practices and skills learned through collaboration to deliver content and skill lessons in a meaningful way with scaffolding.

- **Day eight:** Give a formative assessment and analyze that data; create an intervention lesson with differentiated instruction. From the intervention data, develop intervention groups. Teachers must plan specific intervention and extension activities.

- **Day nine:** This is an intervention day. Split classes into two groups: *got it* and *didn't get it yet*. Develop extension activities to honor the learning of students who have already mastered the standard (page 199).

- **Day ten:** Reassess the *didn't get it yet* group. You will likely need to continue intervention for some learners. The cycle repeats itself for these learners.

Conclusion

The best laid plans . . . . Anyone who has led a school can relate to sitting at your desk at the end of the day, staring at the wall, and wondering what happened to the day. If this is you, let's review the first five steps in school improvement: (1) master scheduling with a focus on teacher collaboration, (2) appropriate and effective teacher placement and development, (3) data-driven and data-informed tiers of intervention, (4) celebrating staff and student successes, and (5) monitoring the progress of the ten-day learning cycles. With the first five steps in mind and action, a leader will wonder what happened to the day far less often—every task or problem must first be run through the first five steps. If it will not advance the first five, delegate it or wait for another day.

Data-Analysis Protocol

1. Determine the percentage of students proficient on the assessment for each standard or target by teacher and then for all students within the team. Write the information in the following chart.

	Target 1	Target 2	Target 3	Target 4
Teacher A				
Teacher B				
Teacher C				
Teacher D				
Total Team				

2. For each standard or target, determine the number of students who are proficient, close to proficient, and far from proficient by teacher and as a team (write the number or the names of the students).

Target 1			
	Proficient	Close to Proficient	Far From Proficient	Total
Teacher A				
Teacher B				
Teacher C				
Teacher D				
Total Team				

Target 2			
	Proficient	Close to Proficient	Far From Proficient	Total
Teacher A				
Teacher B				
Teacher C				
Teacher D				
Total Team				

page 1 of 3

Target 3				
	Proficient	**Close to Proficient**	**Far From Proficient**	**Total**
Teacher A				
Teacher B				
Teacher C				
Teacher D				
Total Team				

Target 4				
	Proficient	**Close to Proficient**	**Far From Proficient**	**Total**
Teacher A				
Teacher B				
Teacher C				
Teacher D				
Total Team				

3. What skills did the proficient students demonstrate in their work that set their work apart? Which instructional strategies did teachers use that effectively produced those results?

4. In which area or areas did my students struggle? In which areas did our team's students struggle? What is the cause? How will we respond? Which strategies will we try next?

5. Which students need additional time and support to learn the standards or targets? What is our plan?

6. Which students need extension and enrichment? What is our plan?

7. Do these data show we are on track to meet our SMART goal? Why or why not?

Source: Kramer, S. V., & Schuhl, S. (2017). School improvement for all: A how-to guide for doing the right work. Bloomington, IN: Solution Tree Press.

Ten-Day Learning Cycle Checklist

The ten-day learning cycle is a plan for planning instruction, assessment, and intervention. The cycle is implemented only for essential standards.

Day	Task	Accomplished
Day one	Unpack essential standards. This process is ongoing.	[Revisit]
Day two	Create common formative assessments.	
Day three	Create a lesson plan using unpacked essential standards.	
Days four–seven	Teach a lesson plan.	
Day eight	Give a formative assessment and analyze that data; create an intervention lesson with differentiated instruction.	
Day nine	From the intervention data, develop intervention groups.	
Day ten	Reassess the *didn't get it yet* group.	

References and Resources

AllThingsPLC. (n.d.). *Big Sandy Elementary*. Accessed at https://www.allthingsplc.info/evidence /details/id,1616 on February 11, 2021.

Buffum, A., Mattos, M., & Malone, J. (2018). *Taking action: A handbook for RTI at Work.* Bloomington, IN: Solution Tree Press.

DuFour, R., DuFour, R., Eaker, R., & Many, T. (2010). *Learning by doing: A handbook for Professional Learning Communities at Work* (2nd ed.). Bloomington, IN: Solution Tree Press.

DuFour, R., DuFour, R., Eaker, R., Many, T. W., & Mattos, M. (2016). *Learning by doing: A handbook for Professional Learning Communities at Work* (3rd ed.). Bloomington, IN: Solution Tree Press.

Dweck, C. S. (2016). *Mindset: The new psychology of success* (Updated ed.). New York: Ballantine Books.

Kramer, S. V. (2015). *How to leverage PLCs for school improvement.* Bloomington, IN: Solution Tree Press.

Kramer, S. V., & Schuhl, S. (2017). *School improvement for all: A how-to guide for doing the right work.* Bloomington, IN: Solution Tree Press.

Mattos, M., & Buffum, A. (Eds.). (2015). *It's about time: Planning interventions and extensions in secondary school.* Bloomington, IN: Solution Tree Press.

Spiller, J., & Power, K. (2019). *Leading with intention: Eight areas for reflection and planning in your PLC at Work.* Bloomington, IN: Solution Tree Press.

Venables, D. R. (2018). *Facilitating teacher teams and authentic PLCs: The human side of leading people, protocols, and practices.* Alexandria, VA: Association for Supervision and Curriculum Development.

Index

Charting the Course for Collaborative Teams
Edited by Sharon V. Kramer
Develop the know-how to work collaboratively in the PLC at Work process to overcome barriers and challenges in your priority school. This anthology gathers numerous expert contributors who share strategies and tools used to successfully turn around their underperforming schools.
BKF978

School Improvement for All
Sharon V. Kramer and Sarah Schuhl
Ensure all students learn at high levels by targeting specific needs with an immediate course of action within a professional learning community. Each chapter includes space for teacher teams to determine next-action steps and questions to bring greater focus to improvement efforts.
BKF770

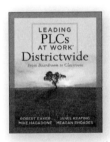

Leading PLCs at Work® Districtwide
Robert Eaker, Mike Hagadone, Janel Keating, and Meagan Rhoades
Ensure your district is doing the right work, the right way, for the right reasons. With this resource as your guide, you will learn how to align the work of every PLC team districtwide—from the boardroom to the classroom.
BKF942

Leading PLCs at Work® Districtwide Plan Book
Robert Eaker, Mike Hagadone, Janel Keating, and Meagan Rhoades
Champion continuous improvement with the support of our *Leading PLCs at Work Districtwide Plan Book*. Divided into weekly and monthly planning pages, the plan book helps guide leaders in identifying and acting on major responsibilities, tasks, and goals throughout the year.
BKG004

a division of

Solution Tree | Press
Solution Tree

Visit SolutionTree.com or call 800.733.6786 to order.

"Tremendous, tremendous, tremendous!

The speaker made me do some very deep internal reflection about the **PLC process** and the personal responsibility I have in making the school improvement process work **for ALL kids."**

—Marc Rodriguez, teacher effectiveness coach, Denver Public Schools, Colorado

 PD Services

Our experts draw from decades of research and their own experiences to bring you practical strategies for building and sustaining a high-performing PLC. You can choose from a range of customizable services, from a one-day overview to a multiyear process.

Book your PLC PD today!
888.763.9045

Solution Tree